TRAVELLERS' SCOTLAND

Katie Wood was born and educated in Edinburgh. She read Communications then English at university and worked as a freelance journalist before specializing in travel in 1981. Author of the best-selling *Europe by Train* and many other guidebooks, she has made a name for herself both in Britain and internationally for her practical, down-to-earth approach, and the quality of her research and analysis of travel. She writes freelance for numerous newspapers including the *Scotsman*, and also broadcasts regularly on BBC and ITV on travel. She holds a fellowship of the Royal Geographical Society.

Married with two children, she lives in Perth, Scotland.

Available by Katie Wood

Europe by Train
The Best of British Country House Hotels
The Cheap Sleep Guide to Europe
The 100 Greatest Holidays in the World
The 1992 Business Travel Guide
The Good Tourist – A Worldwide Guide for the
  Green Traveller
The Good Tourist in the UK
The Good Tourist in France
The Good Tourist in Turkey

TRAVELLERS' SCOTLAND

A Practical Guide

KATIE WOOD

Editorial Assistant
Louise Storie

MAINSTREAM
PUBLISHING

EDINBURGH AND LONDON

First published by Fontana 1991

This edition published in 1993 by
MAINSTREAM PUBLISHING COMPANY (EDINBURGH) LTD
7 Albany Street
Edinburgh EH1 3UG

ISBN 1 85158 519 2

A catalogue record for this book is available from the British Library

Typeset by Saxon Graphics Ltd, Derby
Printed in Great Britain by BPCC Wheatons

Contents

Part Three When You're There

Part Four The Country

Maps

Part One

BEFORE YOU GO

KEY FACTS

ENTRY REQUIREMENTS – Same as for UK for foreign nationals, no entry requirement for UK nationals.

POPULATION – 5,136,000

CAPITAL – Edinburgh

CURRENCY – Sterling

POLITICAL SYSTEM – Constitutional Monarchy

RELIGION – Protestant with significant Catholic minority, notably in west and on islands.

LANGUAGE – English. Gaelic is still spoken by some Scots, mostly in the west and the Highlands.

PUBLIC HOLIDAYS – New Year's Day, and 2 January
Good Friday, Easter Monday
1 May
Christmas and Boxing Day
and regional bank holidays

What to Expect

For centuries, Scotland has been of great fascination to people the world over – 15 million people come to visit every year, bringing with them six per cent of Scotland's total income. But the recent images spread abroad are often embarrassing stereotypes: false notions of haggis and tartan, bagpipes and kilted, whisky-drinking Scotsmen. For too many people, Scotland is regarded either as the tartan fringe of England, or else some great mountainous area of unexplored natural beauty somewhere to the north of London.

Of course it is not impossible to see a living tourist attraction striding down Edinburgh's Princes Street, busking on the bag-pipes, fully decked out in kilt, sporran and dirk, but it is a rare sight, and more often than not, done for the benefit of the tourists. Having said that, the Scots, more than any other nation of the UK, have an identifiable image and a strong culture and heritage that they are proud of. Most Scots will wear a kilt at some stage of their lives; most weddings end with a ceilidh; and most children are brought up with a wealth of songs, poems and rhymes that tell of their country's rich past and draw on the Gaelic and Highland influences.

Scotland today is one of the more lively parts of the United Kingdom, particularly in the Capital, Edinburgh, and in Glasgow where the 'Miles Better' campaign and Cultural Capital of Europe accolade turned the city into one of the most fashionable in Europe. Although the country's industrial heartland in and around the central belt of the country has greatly declined since the end of the Second World War, new industries are helping to revitalize Scotland's economy which has been in decline for much of that postwar period.

Edinburgh and Glasgow, Scotland's two main cities, together account for over a third of the country's five million population, and the proximity of two such attractive, yet contrasting cities is certainly special. Few visitors fail to be impressed when they encounter these large, bustling modern cities, diametrically opposed in terms of history, culture and reputation, but separated by only a 45-minute journey by train or car. Although Glasgow developed into a prosperous town long before Edinburgh, in appearance today, Edinburgh looks the older. In its Old Town, the narrow wynds and tenements, once the highest buildings in Europe, have remained essentially unchanged for the last 300 years, while Glasgow is an outstanding example of a Victorian metropolis.

One of the most deep-rooted cultural stereotypes attached to Scotland is the old clan system, the ancient family groupings upon which the foundations of Scotland were first built. Although clan gatherings still take place for ceremonial and social reasons, many Scotsmen, until the Victorian period with the subsequent popularity of things Scottish, were excluded from them because their family lacked any Highland clan connection. Queen Victoria, John Brown *et al*, ensured that new clans and new clan septs were added, until virtually every Scottish family had a claim to some tartan and a clan. Tartan, as we know it today, only originated in 1832. Our concept of the 'clan' is therefore a comparatively modern interpretation. Interestingly, the biggest annual clan gatherings are to be found, not in Scotland, but in Canada.

One of Scotland's great contributions has been its people who have spread all around the world. The Highland Clearances saw thousands of crofters evicted from their land in the 19th century, with many of the dispossessed emigrating to the US and Canada. Right up to the 1960s, people were leaving Scotland in order to find prosperity in far-off places, with Canada, Australia and New Zealand the destinations most emigrating Scots turned to. Opportunities there were greater than in the States, and assisted passages were offered to attract them to settle. As a result, there are few families in Scotland today without at least one branch in Canada, Australia, or New Zealand.

Scotland today is in the position of having a declining population. In the 1960s, estimates suggested that by the end of the century the country would have seven million inhabitants. With Scotland suffering particularly badly in the economic slump of the 1980s, however, many more people than before were forced to look to England and abroad for work, with the consequence that revised estimates predict that Scotland's population will drop below its present five million by the end of the century.

It would be wrong to suggest that none of the romantic images of Scotland await visitors. On the contrary, for Scotland's famous scenery is every bit as impressive as legend and reputation make out. Nowhere in Scotland is far from wild moorland, sweeping valleys, wide lochs or misty snow-capped mountains. The further north you travel, the more rugged the landscape becomes and the population more sparse.

If you are able to spend a long time touring the different regions in Scotland you will soon be struck by the famous Highland/Lowland divide. Although quite definitely part of the same country, the Lowlands of Scotland contain some striking differences to the sweeping Highlands.

One of the most obvious differences is the denser population in the Lowlands. The Highlands comprise over 40 per cent of the total landmass of Scotland, yet contain only about a fifth of the country's population. Towns in the north are thinly scattered and noticeably smaller. Rural roads tend to be much narrower and contain less traffic. On the islands in the west, the people are often bilingual, with English being spoken as a second language to Gaelic. Life goes more slowly here, particularly on a Sunday when there is strict observation of the Sabbath.

The natural landscape and scenery is, of course, not only spectacular to look at, but also offers plenty of activities for visitors to enjoy. The north-west Highlands and Cairngorms are the areas in Britain most akin to true wilderness. There are still places in Scotland where man has made little impact on the landscape, and the Green movement has a strong following. Sports and outdoor activities play a large part in Scottish life. Fishing in the scenic lochs and rivers, for example, is not only a splendid way to relax, but it is also likely to be highly productive. The country's salmon and trout are famous worldwide, and are to be found in abundance in many stretches of water, but particularly in the rivers Tweed, Tay and Spey. Scotland is the home of golf and its courses are the best in the world, not only because of their careful design, but also because the natural lie of the land presents the golfer with an irresistible challenge, at once more tempting and arduous than anything that men could contrive.

Amid all this natural beauty are landmarks and reminders of the nation's turbulent history for which Scotland is well known.

Wherever you go in Scotland, you will not be far from a ruined castle, fort or sundry other ancient monuments which have survived, at least in part, for many hundreds of years. In this respect, the Borders region of south-east Scotland is particularly well endowed with its grand ruined abbeys at Melrose, Jedburgh, Dryburgh, and Kelso. Aberdeenshire in the north-east boasts a countryside dotted with living history – the wonderful inhabited castles of Mar are so interesting for the touring visitor. With perhaps the exception of the sun worshipper, Scotland really does have something for everyone!

The Climate

Scotland has a reputation for bad weather – rain, wind, more rain, and cold, even in the height of summer. While you shouldn't be too quick to believe everything you hear about the Scottish weather, it is nevertheless sensible to make sure that you never travel far in Scotland without an umbrella and raincoat. The only honest description of the Scottish weather is 'unpredictable'.

Being so far north (Edinburgh is slightly further north than Moscow) Scotland can be colder than the rest of the UK in the summer. The average July maximum temperature is 17–18.7°C and Scotland certainly receives a fair share of rain. Most rainfall occurs in the west, where, for example, Fort William receives 1,981 mm of rainfall each year. In the east, the average rainfall is less than half that. Scotland's northerly location does have its advantages – the far north of Scotland has 20 hours of daylight in midsummer and, although never unbearably hot, a good Scottish summer will give you as good a suntan as anywhere else in Britain.

Mean temperatures, based on Edinburgh:

	JAN	FEB	MAR	APR	MAY	JUNE
°F	39	39	42	47	55	62
°C	4	4	5	9	12	15

	JULY	AUG	SEPT	OCT	NOV	DEC
°F	65	63	57	49	45	40
°C	17	16	14	10	7	4

When to Go

Deciding when to visit Scotland will be an important factor in planning your holiday. Visitors come to Scotland in spite of the weather rather than because of it, but the meteorological conditions are usually more attractive between April and September than at any other time of the year and, during this period, rainfall is lightest between April and June. A more important reason for timing your holiday for those months is that many museums, monuments and other tourist attractions are open only at this part of the year.

Despite May and June being undoubtedly the best times to come, July and August are the busiest tourist months. Edinburgh in particular is crowded to bursting point in August when it is swamped by an estimated half million visitors, doubling the city's population, who have come to the world-famous Edinburgh Festival. This cultural extravaganza has been going on since 1946 and, for three weeks every August, Edinburgh is the undisputed cultural capital of the world. More information on the Edinburgh Festival can be found in the chapter on Edinburgh. May and June are the months for the best weather and sightseeing, and have the added attraction of long light nights.

If you have more flexibility in planning your holiday, then the best time to see the country is really late May or September. The weather tends to be kind in both months, accommodation is easier to find, coaches and trains are less busy, and the spring and autumn colours give an extra appeal to the Scottish countryside.

Where to Go for What

THE LIE OF THE LAND

This northern part of Great Britain is divided into three distinct parts:

The Highlands and Islands – an upland area, largely depopulated after the infamous Clearances of the 19th century, and economically reliant on whisky, fishing, forestry, tourism, hydro-electric power, stock-rearing, and, on the north-eastern coast, oil.

The Central Lowlands – containing four-fifths of the Scottish population, based in industrial towns and commercial centres such as Glasgow, Edinburgh, Stirling, Dundee and Perth. It was here that the wealth of the Industrial Revolution was concentrated: shipbuilding on the Clyde, and the iron and coalfields gave Scotland a heavy-industry base. Since the Second World War there has been a rationalization programme and new industries such as aluminium smelting, plastics, petro-chemicals and electronic and business machinery have been introduced.

The Southern Uplands – the area bordering England, has stock-rearing and arable farming as the main occupations.

The 19 million acres of Scotland also encompass numerous islands, including Arran and Bute in the Firth of Clyde, and the Inner and Outer Hebrides off the west coast. The west coast is very broken, with several sea lochs, while the east is regular by comparison.

Major rivers are Don, Dee, Esk, Forth, Tay, Tweed and Spey, which flow into the North Sea; the Annan, Cree and Nith which flow into the Solway Firth; and the Ayr, Carron, Clyde and others which flow into the Atlantic.

If travelling around Scotland by car, look out for the National Tourist Route signs which mark ten separate routes throughout the country, taking you away from the main motorways and trunk routes and on to the more picturesque routes leading to areas of historical and natural interest. These signs are easily recognised by their white lettering on a brown background. For more information on these routes pick up the first in a series of three 'Practical Information' booklets, printed by the Scottish Tourist Board and available from any Tourist Information Centre.

So often people spend weeks deliberating which country to choose for their holiday destination, then leave the final choice of where they stay within the country to either a photograph and brief optimistic write-up in a travel brochure, or the discretion and persuasive talk of a travel agent (many of whom haven't actually visited the country). This lottery results, not surprisingly, in people having a disappointing holiday simply because they got the facts wrong on this crucial decision. If anything, the decision about which parts of the country you visit is more important than the choice of country itself for there is good and bad in every country – Scotland offers the tourist a superb holiday destination, but if the visitor were to go to the new town of East Kilbride, mistaking it for a quaint village, he would be sadly disappointed.

In order to match your needs to the most suitable destinations I have divided holidaymakers into certain stereotypes. Doubtless most of you fall into several of the categories, but the idea is to find which resorts crop up under the headings which interest you, and match your needs accordingly. The following symbols representing the various interests appear throughout this book as an easy guide to the places likely to be of interest to you:

The Sightseer

The Socialite

The Sportsperson

The Nature Lover

Away from it all

Family Holidays

The Sightseer: *sights, historical monuments and archaeological remains*

Throughout the whole of Scotland, there is an abundance of buildings, monuments, and historic sights to fascinate the visitor. How long you plan to tour will, of course, be governed by how much you can afford in terms of money and time away from home, but you would need at least a full week to really do justice to the sights and shops of EDINBURGH alone.

Although the dominant image, there is much more to the capital than its **Castle**. The **Royal Mile**, running from the city's famous fortification to the **Palace of Holyrood House**, is lined with so many places of architectural and historic interest, that visitors could easily spend a day walking the length of this cobbled thoroughfare without having enough time to visit the regal edifices at either end. Elsewhere, Edinburgh is a city of contrasts: the spacious Georgian New Town, for example, is only a stone's throw from the narrow streets and winding alleys of the 17th-century Old Town.

Edinburgh also offers an excellent touring base for the sightseer, being within a short drive from many places of historic and cultural interest. The closely grouped Borders towns of KELSO, JEDBURGH and MELROSE are each renowned for the impressive ruins of their 12th-century abbeys. In the opposite direction from Edinburgh, just over the Forth, the unique town of CULROSS has been preserved wholly intact since the 18th century, thanks to the redoubtable efforts of the National Trust for Scotland.

Here are some of the outstanding sights to be found in some of the other regions of Scotland:

PERTH
For the keen sightseer Perth is within easy reach of many historic buildings and castles such as **Scone Palace** and **Huntingtower** and **Elcho Castles** on the outskirts of the town. Slightly further afield are **Loch Leven** and **Burleigh Castles** near Kinross, and **Castle Menzies** near Aberfeldy.

INVERNESS
Culloden battlefield, on the eastern outskirts of Inverness, has monuments to the Jacobites who fell there in the course of the battle that saw the demise of Bonnie Prince Charlie's hopes. Just south of the battlefield, **Clava Cairns** are thought to be 4,000 years old, and represent one of the two most important archaeological sites on the Scottish mainland.

ORKNEY AND SHETLAND
Although they are separated by a distance of 60 or so miles, Orkney and Shetland have a great deal in common both culturally and historically, particularly due to their Scandinavian heritage. An important difference, however, is the greater concentration of archaeological material on the islands of Orkney, particularly Mainland, which is renowned as the most important location of prehistoric remains in Britain. Of the many fascinating relics, the most remarkable is the well-preserved Stone Age village of **Skara Brae** on the east Mainland coast. Seven miles north of Stromness, this is a remarkable relic, having been buried under sand for 4,000 years until uncovered by a storm in 1850. The extent to which the

minutiae of daily life have been preserved suggests that the village was still occupied when some disaster occurred and it was buried suddenly.

STIRLING
This historic town's most imposing feature is **Stirling Castle**. Most of its present buildings date from the 16th century, but it is believed that the castle rock may have been occupied by the Romans and subsequently, according to legend, by King Arthur.

ABERDEEN
There is much more to Aberdeen than North Sea oil. **Old Aberdeen**, in particular, contains buildings of great historic and architectural significance. Especially noteworthy is the edifice of **Marischal College**, the second largest granite building in the world. There are also many interesting castles and country houses within a short distance of the city, such as the National Trust's 16th-century **Castle Fraser**. Aberdeen is but a short drive from **Balmoral**, the private residence of the Royal Family, which is open from May to July, Monday to Saturday, with opening hours 10 a.m. to 5 p.m., except when in use by members of the House of Windsor. Prince Albert bought the estate in 1852 when it was called Bouchmorale and had the castle rebuilt by William Smith. Of interest inside are the works of art decorating the ballroom, while its extensive grounds and gardens offer attractive country walks and pony-trekking. The journey from Aberdeen can also take in the magnificent 16th-century **Crathes Castle**, an outstanding National Trust property, whose rooms are most notable for their painted ceilings. Its magnificent 600-acre grounds contain nature trails, a visitor centre, and formal gardens.

 The Socialite

The socialite in Scotland will be best accommodated in Glasgow or Edinburgh, though Aberdeen, Dundee, Inverness and Perth also have much to offer. Top of the list must be GLASGOW, which is rapidly turning into the most fashionable city in Britain, with more live music than anywhere outside London; a proliferating choice of wine bars, and an abundance of nightclubs and discos. Among the latter, the practice is for a club to go under different names on different nights of the week, each one having a separate identity and concentrating on a particular style of music. Up-to-date information can be found in *The List*, a fortnightly listings magazine for Glasgow and Edinburgh.

Each year, since its inception in 1981, Glasgow's arts festival, **Mayfest**, has expanded, not only in terms of its duration, but also in the number of performers and size of audience it attracts. It now runs for the first three weeks of May and is second only to the Edinburgh Festival as the most important arts event in Britain. One important difference between the two jamborees is that, in spite of its increasing international content, Mayfest retains its original sense of being a community event for the people of Glasgow, with performances and events scheduled beyond the city centre and into the outlying areas.

For nightlife, one of the chief assets of **EDINBURGH** is its liberal licensing hours, which mean that landlords don't call last orders until long after publicans in the rest of Britain have locked up and gone to bed. Most city-centre pubs serve until midnight or 1 a.m. on Friday and Saturday, although there are a few which stay open longer. The choice of nightclubs and discos is as good as that in Glasgow, and many pubs offer live music and entertainment all year round. The character of the city and its nightlife is transformed totally for three weeks in August when it plays host to the biggest arts festival in the world, involving something in the region of 500 stage groups putting on 1,000 shows, and half of the city's pubs become venues for late-night cabaret. The streets of the capital are venues for outdoor performances and one cannot escape being drawn into the jovial carnival atmosphere.

ABERDEEN is particularly lively during the summer months with the longer, lighter evenings, host to an endless variety of pubs, cafés, winebars and nightclubs. It also boasts a wide choice of restaurants and hotels offering Scottish cuisine of the very best quality. Highly recommended is the region's beef, acclaimed to be the best in the world. More notably, Aberdeen is a city of many festivals held throughout the year. The **Bon Accord Festival** in

June begins by welcoming its visitors to the city with a colourful parade. The **International Football Festival**, later in the summer, offers youngsters the opportunity to compete with teams from all over the world. The summer also welcomes the city's **International Youth Festival**. The Christmas period similarly lends itself to a flurry of festivals with the **Christmas Shopping Festival** and the **Santa Lucia Festival** celebrating Aberdeen's Scandinavian connections, as well as the **Festival of St Nicholas**.

   DUNDEE, is another festive city worth highlighting for its annual summer Festival which involves the entire community, incorporating theatre, dance, music and children's events. Dundee also promises a lively Jazz and Blues Festival, a Folk Festival, and later in the summer, a Water Festival. Throughout the year, many of the city's pubs have live acts, folk singing and cabaret, alongside a lively performing arts scene with the city's own drama repertory and dance company.

   From June to September, the city of **STIRLING** plays host to an award-winning string of **royal events**, with its nationally acclaimed Living History Programme, taking you back to the time of Mary Queen of Scots. There, you can rub shoulders with Stirling's residents past and present through the many street performances, plays, spectacular pageants and medieval markets and banquets. There is something for everyone from ceilidhs and pipe bands, to a carnival on 14th June followed by a thrilling firework finale held on the castle esplanade, mid-August.

   People in **THE BORDERS** are continually celebrating some local tradition or past event, so entertainment is certainly not thin on the ground in this part of the country. The Borders is particularly renowned for its **common riding events**, held in **SELKIRK** and **HAWICK** during the summer, which proudly mark past battles and lost heroes. Country fayres can also be enjoyed in May, at the **Borders Country Fayre** in Ayton Castle and **Traquair Fair**, Peebleshire, held in August. Civic and summer festivals are plentiful from June to August in all of the Border towns with battle re-enactments, sports, music and art festivals. For more information you can pick up a 'What's on in the Scottish Borders' guide from any local Borders tourist information centre.

   Traditional entertainment in Scotland is the ceilidh (from the Gaelic word meaning 'visit' and pronounced 'kaylay') which is still common in rural areas, particularly in the north. The occasion consists of folk music and dancing. Most of Scotland's folk music is based on the fiddle and the accordion, and ranges from long, haunting melodies through to fast-moving jigs and 'foot-tappers'. It has many similarities to traditional Irish music.

Ceilidhs are held all over Scotland and at most times of the year, but are especially abundant around the 25th of January when the Scots celebrate Rabbie Burns, with the traditional cutting of the haggis, dancing and poetry recitals. In the **Western Isles**, 'Taste of the West' evenings are organised throughout the summer at various venues on the islands, serving up a traditional menu of Gaelic singing and local music and a visual presentation of the local history by way of slides.

Highland Games are a large part of traditional entertainment in Scotland. Not only are they to be found in the **Highlands** as the name suggests, but also in many of the Border towns and lowland cities, each hosting their own tossing of the caber and 'wellie' hurling events, Highland dancing and pipe band competitions. **EDINBURGH**, between 25–28 June, presents the **Royal Highland Show** at Ingliston with livestock competitions, crafts and a flower show, whilst farther north, just south of **ABERDEEN**, there is the celebrated **Braemar Highland Gathering**, held in September, where members of the royal family can often be seen.

The Sportsperson

Whether you want to participate or spectate, Scotland is home to a wide variety of sporting pastimes. Top of the list is **football**. The professional season runs from mid-August until mid-May, and every town of any size in Scotland has a professional football team, represented in one of three divisions – premier, first and second. **GLASGOW** is one of the great footballing cities of the world, famous and infamous for the torrid local rivalry of Rangers and Celtic. It is also the home of the national stadium, Hampden Park, the venue for international matches, and also the Scottish Cup Final each May. The stadium has undergone a sorry decline since the days when it set attendance records for club and international matches which still stand today.

The **BORDERS** is the country's principal **rugby** territory, where teams like Hawick and Kelso regularly dominate the annual competitions and supply the majority of the players in Scotland's national team. The latter play their home matches at **Murrayfield** in **EDINBURGH**, and against France, Ireland, Wales and England they compete in the Five Nations Tournament with games scheduled from January to March – and, of course, in 1990 they won the competition with a glorious Grand Slam.

Fishing is one of the most popular participant sports in Scotland, and each year hundreds of visitors arrive with this end specifically in mind, such are the rewards to be had from Scottish waters. Fishing falls into three categories: game, sea and fresh-water (coarse). Game and fresh-water fishing require a licence, which is easily obtainable for a few pounds. Exact prices vary according to the type of angling and locality, but sea trout and salmon fishing rights tend to be among the most expensive, sometimes up to £200 a day in the autumn months for a fine stretch of fast-flowing river, which is the best for salmon. Salmon fishing can also cost as little as £10 to £20 on small rivers such as the North and South Esk in Angus, and trout fishing from £1 to £3 per day on the Tweed. Stocked trout waters can cost up to £6 for a bank permit and between £10 and £15 for a boat permit. Salmon and trout can only be fished during the season, which runs from February until October for trout, and January/March until October/November for salmon. There is no substitute for local advice on where to find the most rewarding stretch of water to cast a line, and there are few parts of the country where the angler will be disappointed. For very general guidance there are three outstanding rivers notable for the quality and quantity of their salmon. The foremost is the **River Tweed** – running through many of the Borders towns – closely followed by the **River Spey** – flowing south-west from the Moray Firth through Aviemore, Kingussie and Newtonmore – and finally the **River Tay**, on whose banks stands the town of Perth. A useful address for general information is the Scottish Anglers National Association, 307 West George Street, Glasgow (Tel. 041–221 7206).

For many visitors to Scotland, the **golf** clubs are the most important item on the luggage rack. Although the game was first played in the Low Countries, it was here that the rules were developed and the sport took its modern form. The obvious destination for golf enthusiasts is the Fife town of ST ANDREWS, whose name is almost synonymous with the sport. Of its four world-famous championship courses, three are open to visitors without the need for a letter of introduction, though pre-booking is absolutely essential. Also on the east coast, but further north, near Dundee, is CARNOUSTIE. Although only a small town, it is surrounded by no less than seven 18-hole courses, including a past venue for the British Open. Nowhere in Scotland is far from a fairway, but for an extensive choice and world renowned courses, the 60 miles of Ayrshire coast – said to have a course for every mile of shoreline – are without comparison, and include the famous golfing centres of TURNBERRY and TROON, as well as PREST-WICK, which staged the first ever British Open in 1872. One of the most pleasant surprises in store for English golfers is the low price of Scottish green fees. The snobbery attached to the game south of the border does not exist on the Scottish side, and virtually every town has a public course where visitors can play for a few pounds.

Hillwalking can be as gentle or arduous as you want it to be: from simple country rambling – possible anywhere in Scotland but especially recommended in GALLOWAY – to strenuous moun-taineering in the CAIRNGORMS. Long-distance footpaths cross the country, and the Scottish Tourist Board can provide the up-to-date information about which paths are currently open. They also have excellent leaflets on 'Walks and Trails' and 'Hillwalking' available at Area Tourist Board offices. Among the better known, and most scenic, are the SOUTHERN UPLAND WAY stretching over 200 miles from Portpatrick in Galloway across to Cock-burnspath in the Borders, the SPEYSIDE WAY which runs 60 miles from Tugnet and Tomintoul down to Spey Bay on the Moray Firth, and the WEST HIGHLAND WAY which stretches nearly 100 miles from the outskirts of Glasgow up to Fort William.

The **ski season** in Scotland, lasting from mid-January into April or May, is well catered for with five resorts, namely: the **Nevis range** and **Glencoe** to the west, **Cairngorm** on Speyside and **Glenshee** and **The Lecht** further east in the Grampian Mountains. Each resort has a good choice of graded runs for both the novice and the experienced skier, as well as the hire of equipment and ski instruction. The Lecht, however, is especially good for beginners, with an excellent nursery run and creche facilities. If you have your own equipment a daily ski lift pass will only set you back, on average, £12. Cross-country skiing is available at **Glenisla**, **Glenmulliach** and **Glenmore Forest**. Pick up the 'Ski Scotland' brochure, produced by the Scottish Tourist Board, from any Tourist Information Centre.

Further information on sport in Scotland, from the point of view of either a participant or spectator, is available by post from: The Scottish Sports Council, Caledonia House, South Gyle, Edinburgh EH12 9DQ (Tel. 031–317 7200).

The Nature Lover

Inland, Scotland's magnificent landscape is largely characterized by large mountain ranges, rolling hills, lochs, and lush green glens, while round the coast the variations in scenery combine the pleasant sandy shores with rugged cliffs and promontories. Of the country's varied geographical features, it is the hills and glens which have formed the dominant image of Scotland, and made it such a delight for nature lovers from all around the world.

In the **BORDERS**, the River Tweed flows through some of the most beautiful rolling countryside in Britain, and has fired the poetic imagination of the anonymous Borders balladeers as well as Sir Walter Scott and his protégé, James Hogg. Scott regarded it as 'the most precious river in the world'. Throughout the Borders, the inland scenery is dominated by undulating hills and woodland, while the coastline is rugged and often makes a dramatic sight where the sea lashes the rocks far below the cliff top. Such breathtaking views can be taken in at **ST ABB'S HEAD**, not far north of Eyemouth, where there is a nature reserve which is home to many species of seabird.

Although only a short drive from the centre of Glasgow, the **TROSSACHS** is one of the most outstanding areas of natural beauty to be found anywhere in Britain. The name is said to derive from a term meaning 'bristly country' and refers, strictly speaking, to the narrow wooded gorge running between Loch Achray and Loch Katrine, but in common parlance it spans the wider surrounding area, including Ben A'an in the north and Ben Venue in the south-west. Loch Katrine, in the middle of this splendid setting, has been widely celebrated in literature, most notably by Sir Walter Scott, who used it as the setting of his novel *Rob Roy*. The scenic beauty of the loch and its surroundings can best be enjoyed by boat, and there are regular cruises on the SS *Walter Scott* with this very aim in mind.

At 24 miles long and five miles across at its widest, LOCH LOMOND is the largest inland stretch of water in Britain. More important for the visitor, however, is that it is also one of the most attractive. The wide southern half contains almost all of the loch's 30 islands, of which **Clairinch**, **Torrinch**, and **Inchcailleoch** form part of a nature reserve teeming with many species of birds. The best way to appreciate the beauty of the loch and its islands is by boat, either on a scheduled cruise or by hiring your own. There are many operators to choose from, and full details can be found in the relevant chapter.

With the Highland Boundary Fault running through the county, visibly separating the hilly Highlands from the rolling Lowlands, PERTHSHIRE's 2,000 square miles provide the visitor with scenery as varied as it is spectacular. The south-east is an area of gently undulating farm and woodland, while further north and to the west, the land is that of blue hills and rugged peaks sheltering long wooded glens and peaceful lochs. The Scottish Wildlife Trust's **Loch of Lowes Nature Reserve** (open from April to September) is to be particularly recommended. In addition to the variety of plants and animals it shelters, it offers visitors the rare opportunity, chance permitting, of observing ospreys from a hide.

ARGYLL AND THE ISLES is an area endowed with considerable and varied natural beauty embracing magnificent woodland, mountain and coastal scenery, while the warming effect of the Gulf Stream encourages many excellent floral displays in public gardens throughout the region. The name of the island of LISMORE means 'Great Garden' and hints at the verdant countryside and abundance of flowers to be seen here. COLONSAY combined with the smaller island of ORONSAY near its shore, has a population of around 200 which is greatly exceeded by the wildlife at home there, such as seals and seabirds. Colonsay benefits from the Gulf Stream which contributes in no small measure to the island's flora of 500 different species, many of which can be seen in **Kiloran Gardens**. Within its 300 miles of coastline, MULL, the third largest of the Hebridean islands, has tremendously varied scenery, from fine sandy beaches and trout-filled lochs to volcanic cliffs and wooded hills. The best way of observing its abundant wildlife is by taking part in the **Isle of Mull Wildlife Expedition**, which is an all-day Landrover excursion in search of eagles, otters, red deer and other wildlife. From Ulva Ferry on Mull, there are regular sailings to the **Treshnish Isles** abounding in marine wildlife, and the uninhabited island of **Staffa**, famous for its spectacular rock formations and caves, the best known of which is **Fingal's Cave**.

LOCH NESS is only six miles from Inverness and one of the best ways of getting there is to take a boat cruise from the outskirts of the town, down the Caledonian Canal and along the length of the loch. Taking the car round the banks is an equally enjoyable means of exploring the natural beauty of the area.

ROSS AND CROMARTY has magnificent scenery around the southern half of **Loch Maree** and the **Beinn Eighe National Nature Reserve**. Almost adjacent is another nature reserve, **Torridon Estate**, which, in addition to its immense natural beauty, is home to a variety of wildlife such as deer, mountain goats, wildcats and eagles. The National Trust for Scotland's **Torridon Countryside Centre** (open from June to September) provides invaluable information on the area's wildlife, hillwalks and climbs, and houses a deer museum.

Both SKYE and SOUTH-WEST ROSS are impressive mountainous regions, the former possessing in the beautiful Cuillins the steepest and most rugged range in Britain. Equally dramatic is its coastline, made uneven by many sea lochs, and the magnificent scenery throughout the island is what attracts its many visitors. Here is the archetypal 'romantic Highland Scotland'. The scenery is outstanding, the pace of life slow, and the potential for a touring holiday enormous.

Away from it all

Scotland is a perfect holiday destination for anyone wanting to 'get away from it all'. The Highlands have one of the lowest population densities in Europe, and even the busy cities of Glasgow, Edinburgh, and Aberdeen are only a short drive from the tranquillity of unspoilt countryside. For general guidance, it is easier to state which parts of the country to avoid if this is the type of holiday you are looking for. Obviously the three main cities already mentioned should be bypassed, along with the central Lowland belt between Edinburgh and Glasgow (where 70 per cent of the population live), and popular tourist resorts. In general, the latter are restricted to the east coast between the Firth of Forth and Nairn, and in the west, to the Ayrshire coast, and the towns and islands of the Firth of Clyde. The rest of the country all has something to offer, within a short drive.

The **BORDERS** region is largely a farming region, rather underrated as tourist territory. The largest of the towns is Hawick, with a modest population of 6,000, but scattered throughout the picturesque landscape of Lauderdale, Teviotdale, Ettrick Forest, and along the banks of the River Tweed, are a number of villages and hamlets in idyllic settings.

In the west, the Trossachs and Loch Lomond encompass some of the most attractive scenery in Britain, but they do tend to attract tourists and daytrippers from the Glasgow conurbation in vast numbers. To escape the crowd, it is advisable to travel further west or north. Avoid the islands of Great Cumbrae and Bute as they contain the very popular resorts of Millport and Rothesay. The **ISLE OF ARRAN**, however, has only one town and very few villages scattered around its coast. Should you wish to retreat further still, then the mountains and hills, which cover almost the whole of the island, offer a splendid haven. Across the Kilbrannan Sound, the long peninsula of **KINTYRE** is equally quiet.

The islands off the west coast of Scotland probably offer the most secluded holiday spots in Britain, if not Europe. **COLONSAY** and the adjacent island of **ORONSAY** have a combined population of only around 200. With 300 miles of coastline, **MULL** has tremendously varied scenery – from fine sandy beaches and trout-filled lochs to volcanic cliffs and wooded hills – and has hardly been touched by tourists. **TOBERMORY**, the island's capital in the north-east, is a colourful and quiet town in an attractive location overlooking the bay, noted for its sea angling. **Calgary Bay** has splendid, often deserted, sandy beaches. From Ulva Ferry there are regular sailings to the uninhabited island of **STAFFA**, famous for its spectacular rock formations and caves.

For those not seeking quite as much seclusion as that offered by Staffa, the adjacent islands of **COLL** and **TIREE**, like Colonsay further south, are ideal venues for a quiet holiday, particularly if you are fond of fine sandy beaches and wildlife. All three islands can be reached by ferry from Oban, while Tiree also receives regular flights from Glasgow. The most populous of these three islands with 800 inhabitants is Tiree, whose excellent beaches and long hours of brilliant sunshine, combined with exceptional surfing conditions, have earned it the nickname of the 'Hawaii of the North', and, along with Coll, it is rich in historic sites.

Further up the west coast, both **SKYE** and **SOUTH-WEST ROSS** are impressive mountainous regions. With a steep, rugged coastline, the magnificent scenery throughout the area is what attracts many visitors.

ROSS AND CROMARTY covers an extensive area spanning the width of the country. The **Black Isle** peninsula in the east is an area of rolling farmland and woodland with good beaches and a variety of seabirds along its coast. The most notable seaside resort is **Fortrose**. In the west the scenery features spectacular hills and peaks and the adjacent nature reserves of **Beinn Eighe** and **Torridon Estate** are visits to be strongly recommended for nature lovers. Both the east and west coast are easily reached from Inverness. For those who enjoy the scenic route I would highlight the journey from Inverness cross-country to Kyle of Lochalsh, in South-west Ross. The road runs beside what British Rail calls the 'Great Scenic Railway' and whether travelling by car or train, the magnificent hills and peaks of Ross and Cromarty, which continue into South-west Ross, make it one of the most memorable journeys in Britain.

In addition to the considerable difference in size, the scenery of **SUTHERLAND** is markedly different from neighbouring Caithness, although the two are often talked about as though they formed an inevitable pair. The 2,000 square miles of Sutherland are regarded by many as the most beautiful in the country with lochs, rivers and moors, and the mountains rising in the west. In common with Caithness it has a very sparse population, scattered almost exclusively along its two stretches of coastline, and they share a Norse heritage – the name Sutherland ('south land') was coined by the Norsemen. The most northerly county of Scotland is CAITHNESS – a land of rolling barren moor and peat bog – now the much-discussed 'Flow Country'. The northern coast has a more interesting appearance than the east, although visitors will have to branch off from the main road to gain sight of the sandy beaches and striking cliff and rock formations. Unlike Sutherland this is a rolling, gentle landscape. The sparse population of the area today belies the fact that this part of Scotland was the first to be inhabited; the iniquity of the Highland Clearances in the 18th and 19th centuries was particularly felt here. Along with Orkney and Shetland, the far north of the mainland was for many centuries under Norse occupation, although little evidence of this has survived other than in place names such as Wick, meaning 'bay', and Lybster, meaning 'farmstead'. There are, however, many remains attributable to earlier settlers and the area is well endowed with prehistoric monuments. The rare wildlife at home in the area includes puffins at **Dunnet Head**, while inland there is always the possibility of catching sight of a white-tailed eagle, an osprey or a red squirrel. The area is easily reached by road or rail, but once there, communications across the region are few.

At the closest point, ORKNEY is only eight miles from the Caithness coast. Of its 67 islands less than one third are inhabited, and, like Shetland, the largest and most populous of these is called Mainland. Although they are separated by a distance of 60 or so miles, Orkney and Shetland have a great deal in common both culturally and historically, particularly due to their Scandinavian heritage. Both are ideal holiday locations for the escapist. An important difference, however, is that there is a greater concentration of archaeological material on the islands of Orkney, particularly Mainland, and it is renowned as the most important location of prehistoric remains in Britain. Of the many fascinating relics, the most remarkable is the well-preserved Stone Age village of **Skara Brae** on the east Mainland coast. SHETLAND lies 60 miles north of Orkney and consists of almost 100 islands, of which only 17 are inhabited. The most important is Mainland, containing Shetland's capital, Lerwick, and the airport at Sumburgh which receives daily flights from Glasgow, Edinburgh, Wick in Caithness, Inverness, Aberdeen, and Kirkwall in Orkney. From here there are flights to the other Shetland islands of Fair Isle, Whalsay, Fetlar, and Unst, all of which are guaranteed to distance you far from the madding crowd.

 Family Holidays

Scotland's coastline contains some marvellous stretches of unspoilt sandy beaches and seas that are safe, if usually a little cold, for swimming. The seaside towns complement these natural amenities with a variety of recreational facilities to keep visitors of all ages thoroughly amused throughout their stay. The best resorts to consider are to be found on three stretches of coastline: the Ayrshire coast in the south-west of the country; the east coast from the mouth of the Forth to Aberdeen; and the coastline of the Moray Firth.

Most of AYRSHIRE's places of interest are situated along its 60 miles of coastline, where the visitor will find sandy beaches, resorts, castles, and a bountiful selection of golf courses. The golfer will immediately recognize the names of Troon and Turnberry as hosts of the British Open Golf Championship. For family holidays, AYR has excellent amenities and beach, while being at the same time close to the tranquillity of the countryside which provided so much inspiration for Robert Burns. The picturesque fishing village of TROON provides a quieter setting for a family holiday, while the excellent beaches at GIRVAN in the south make it one of the most attractive resorts in Scotland. Nearby is Robert Adam's magnificent 18th-century **Culzean Castle and Country Park** providing a highly enjoyable day out for the entire family.

Edinburgh now enjoys the title 'The Most Child Friendly City in the UK'. This is a new vision aimed at making the capital a more fun and welcoming place for youngsters and their parents, providing not only a growing list of attractions and entertainment, but friendlier policies in the service sector to make shopping and eating out more pleasurable. See page 143 for more details.

On the northern bank of the River Forth, ABERDOUR, a few miles south-east of Dunfermline, is a small holiday resort with much to recommend it. It has pleasant beaches, a scenic golf course, and with its sheltered harbour it has become a popular sailing centre. Further north, the sandy stretch of coastline between Elie and Crail is known as the East Neuk, and contains many quaint little ports and attractive resorts. The fishing village of PITTENWEEM has been a royal burgh since 1542, and, in addition to its good beaches and pleasant appearance, it is near to a number of interesting sights such as St Fillan's Cave and Kellie Castle. Not far up the coast is ANSTRUTHER or, to give it its full title, the United Burgh of Kilrenny, Cellardyke, Anstruther Easter and Anstruther Wester. Until the 1940s it was one of the main herring fishing centres in Scotland. Today it is a bustling holiday town, with fine clean beaches and a large number of sporting facilities. East Neuk Outdoors offers a variety of activity holidays: abseiling, archery, canoeing, climbing, cycling, bird-watching and more. Equipment for wind-surfing, which is very popular in the town, can be hired locally, and there is also a riding centre and nine-hole golf course. Further up the coast, CRAIL has ceased to be a smuggling centre and is now a popular choice for the family on holiday. The natural attraction of its fine shoreline is backed up by a swimming pool, squash courts, and snooker tables at East Sands Leisure Centre. In summer, ST ANDREWS loses its students and replaces them with holidaymakers. The excellent family attractions here include a good sand-dune beach (where *Chariots of Fire* was shot), and St Andrews Sea Life Centre, which is home to a variety of marine life. Craigtoun Park, two miles south, is a 50-acre site with a wide range of attractions: boating lake, trampolines, gardens, miniature railway, and so on, which are free after the entrance charge has been paid.

On the eastern outskirts of Dundee is BROUGHTY FERRY, enjoying an attractive location, with fine sandy beaches stretching the two miles along the coast to Monifieth. Not far south of Aberdeen is the popular seaside resort of STONEHAVEN, offering various outdoor pursuits including golf, sea angling, boating, and wind-surfing. The town has two easily discernible parts: the Old Town, built around the harbour, and beyond this the 19th-century New Town. ABERDEEN is well known for its granite buildings and North Sea oil industry, but few people outside are familiar with its very extensive beach – which is amongst the best in Scotland – and the floral displays in the city's many parks and gardens which have won national awards. Aberdeen's golfers are spoilt for choice with eight courses to choose from.

Deviating from the coastline to the Central and Northern Highlands, we come to AVIEMORE and the SPEY VALLEY, set between the vast mountain ranges of the **Monadhliath** and the **Cairngorms**, and surrounded by an abundance of forest, river and loch scenery. It is the perfect location for a family holiday with something for everyone all year round. You can ski on the Cairngorms or on the many dry ski slopes in the area, or partake in the various watersport activities, as well as birdwatching on **Loch Morlich** and **Loch Insh**. There is fishing on the **River Spey**, and there are also several 18-hole golf courses to choose from. The many typical little villages and towns found along the A9, stretching through the valley, are well worth visiting. The **Clan Museum**, is situated in the small town of NEWTONMORE as well as 'Waltzing Waters' (see page 221). KINGUSSIE, a little farther north, is home to the **Highland Folk Museum**. Also well-signposted on the A9, near KINCRAIG, is the **Highland Wildlife Park** where you can spot wolves, bison and deer. **Aviemore Centre**, a lot less typical in style and content, is a complex of hotels, restaurants and cinemas as well as an ice rink and a dry ski slope. North again on the A9, between Aviemore and Inverness, lies the **Landmark Highland Heritage Centre and Adventure Park**. Situated on 30 acres of native caledonian pine woodland, you can enjoy the scenery of the park with the interpretive trails provided through the forest, or better still, the tree-top trails which promise you spectacular views 20 feet up. There is also the **Highlander Multi-Vision Show and Exhibition**, telling the story of the Highlanders from the clan period to the twentieth century, and Britain's only **Forestry Heritage Park** with its new **Mini Museum Centre** telling the story of the Scottish forestry industry. It also has the UK's only operational steam-powered sawmill operating from April to October.

On the Moray Firth there is a host of attractive seaside towns along a short stretch of sandy coastline. Most notable among these are such popular family resorts as **FINDHORN, LOSSIEMOUTH, BUCKIE**, and **CULLEN. NAIRN**, 16 miles east of Inverness, has miles of excellent beach, several golf courses (one of championship standard), and many colourful parks and gardens, all of which combine to make it a highly enjoyable resort for family holidays.

Just north of Dornoch, on the north-east coast, lies **SUTHER-LAND**. It is here that **Wildcat Adventure Holidays** provide action-packed adventure holidays for children between the ages of 8 and 16. They can learn fishing and canoeing as well as certain survival skills. Beautiful Highland lodge accommodation is included in the price along with the travel arrangements. For more details contact: **Wildlife Ventures**, Sutherland Estates, Golspie, Sutherland (Tel. 04083 3268).

Practicalities

Red Tape

Entry requirements to Scotland are identical to those for the rest of the United Kingdom. Visitors from EC countries, the United States, and Canada do not need a visa to enter the country, nor do visitors from Commonwealth and most South American countries.

Money

Due to the fact that there are three banks in Scotland issuing bank notes, compared to only one in England, visitors will find a variety of paper money in circulation. The Clydesdale Bank, Bank of Scotland and Royal Bank of Scotland issue their notes in the same colour per denomination – blue £5, brown £10 and purple £20. Another important distinction between Scotland and England is the survival of the one pound note in Scotland.

The coinage in daily use is identical to that elsewhere in the United Kingdom, although you will see far fewer pound coins because of the common preference for the pound note.

Banking

All main bank branches are open 9.15 a.m. to 4.45 p.m. Monday to Friday; smaller rural branches close for lunch 12.30 p.m. to 1.30 p.m. Most branches extend their opening hours to 5.30 p.m. on Thursdays.

Insurance

Visitors from other parts of the UK are allowed free treatment from any NHS doctor or hospital while on holiday in Scotland, and therefore have no need to take out medical insurance. Holiday insurance to cover your personal belongings, on the other hand, is strongly recommended. Package holidays usually include this as part of the overall deal. For independent travellers, many household insurance policies will automatically cover your belongings while on holiday in the UK. If not, travel agents offer holiday insurance to suit everyone's needs. Tell him what you're taking (remember such items as photographic equipment), what you envisage doing (i.e. if you plan spending a lot of time doing water sports) and how long you'll be away. This is a particularly good idea if you're planning on taking some expensive equipment with you (many package policies put a limit of around £200 per item on your valuables).

Health

Visitors are entitled to use any of the NHS services while on holiday, free of charge. For names and addresses of local doctors, dentists etc. check the Yellow Pages or any public library. If it is something minor, try a chemist first. Pharmacists are well trained and able to recommend non-prescription drugs for minor ailments.

Pre-planning and Free Information

The more you know about a country before going, the more you'll get out of your holiday once you're there. For the latest, up-to-date information write to the Scottish Tourist Board at 23 Ravelston Terrace, Edinburgh EH4 3EU (Tel. 031–332 2433); or 19 Cockspur Street, London SW1Y 5BL (Tel. 071–930 8661). They have an impressive supply of leaflets and brochures which they will send out, free of charge.

A sensible first step in planning your holiday would be to request the STB's general brochure on Scotland, giving brief details on the whole of the country, including the addresses of the head office of each Area Tourist Board. The latter produce and distribute their own brochures, containing valuable information on each area in some detail. If you have any specific interests which you want to pursue when you are on holiday (such as golfing or fishing) write to the ATB (list in the section 'Tourist Information' on page 80) for advice and to send you any leaflets that they might have. Ask Area Tourist Boards for a map and accommodation listings if you are touring independently. These are also free and save you buying maps and accommodation guides at the other end. Another source of free info on Scotland is your local library. Reams have been written about Scotland, covering just about every imaginable interest, from the Wars of Independence to Scottish folk-tales.

The National Trust for Scotland, a separate organization from the English National Trust, but it runs along the same lines, owns and manages around 100 sites in Scotland: houses, castles, islands, mountains, gardens, coastline and mansions. Over two million people visit them every year, and the chances are you'll want to be among them. Most of their buildings are open from April to October, and admission charges apply, though an annual membership can be bought. For further information, write to The National Trust for Scotland, 5 Charlotte Square, Edinburgh EH2 4DR (Tel. 031–226 5922).

A leaflet entitled 'Information about National Trust for Scotland properties for Disabled Visitors', outlines the disabled facilities available and also the difficulties which may be encountered.

Historic Scotland: Scotland's historic ruins, of which there are many, are overseen by the Historic Buildings and Monuments division of the Scottish Development Department. The directorate offers an annual membership, which gives free access to around 330 sites. For further information write to Historic Scotland, 27 Perth Street, Edinburgh EH3 5RB (Tel. 031–556 8400), or 20 Brandon Street, EII3 5RA (Tel. 031–244 3144).

The Forestry Commission is Scotland's largest landowner which, apart from providing much-needed timber to the UK, also allows free access on foot to the 1,800,000 acres under its control. In addition to the five forest parks of Glenmore, Queen Elizabeth, Argyll, Tummel, and Galloway, the Commission also provides a range of recreation facilities including eight camping and caravan sites; 185 picnic places; 246 forest walks and nature trails; eight Visitor Centres, four arboreta, two forest drives and 71 forest cabins. For further information, write to The Forestry Commission, 231 Corstorphine Road, Edinburgh EH12 7AT (Tel. 031–334 0303).

Scottish Natural Heritage is a newly independent body, established by Parliament in 1992 and responsible to the Secretary of State for Scotland. It is the outcome of the recent marriage between the Countryside Commission and the Nature Conservancy Council, taking on board the responsibilities of both along with other more sustainable approaches towards tourism. With the partnership of the Scottish people, it has been charged with overseeing nature conservation matters in Scotland. It will do this by continuing to manage National Nature Reserves and protecting Sites of Special Scientific Interest, as well as developing new Natural Heritage Areas to ensure appropriate management in those important areas in Scotland. Its role is also to foster greater awareness and understanding of Scottish Natural Heritage and to promote responsible access to it, engaging in public support and encouraging more sustainable forms of development. It will also provide grants and facilities to further appropriate recreation in the Scottish Countryside. For further information contact: Scottish Natural Heritage Headquarters, 12 Hope Street, Edinburgh, EH9 2AS (Tel. 031–447 4784).

The Scottish Wildlife Trust, 16 Cramond Glebe Road, EH4 6NS (Tel. 031–312 7765) manages more than 80 nature reserves in Scotland, and if you're travelling to stay in a specific area, the headquarters in Edinburgh will put you in touch with a local group offering detailed information on your area.

The Royal Society for the Protection of Birds, 17 Regent Terrace, Edinburgh EH7 5BN (Tel. 031–557 3136), is Scotland's main ornithological body which owns the many bird reserves in Scottish territory. With over 450 species of birds recorded in Scotland, interest in the subject is considerable. **The Scottish Ornithologist's Club** is at 21 Regent Terrace, Edinburgh EH7 5BT for enthusiasts (Tel. 031–556 6042).

Groups, large or small, travelling together may consider using the services of the **Scottish Tourist Guides Association**. The fully qualified freelance guides are available for walking tours in Aberdeen, Dundee, Edinburgh and Glasgow and for half-day, full-day and extended tours throughout Scotland. Driver guide tours and Special Interest Tours also available (Tel. 031–661 7979 or 041 776 1052).

Budgeting

Accommodation will exercise the biggest drain on your budget, but depending on how much comfort you want, this is an area where considerable savings can be made. At the most cost-conscious end of the market, Youth Hostels charge around £2.85 to £6.50 per person per night. Very simple bed-and-breakfast accommodation can be enjoyed all over Scotland from around £10 per person per night. Simple hotels will range from £12 up to about £25; middle of the range, three-star hotels cost between £25 and £45. Accommodation costing more than £45 a night comes under the luxury category. The price you will be quoted for any type of accommodation, in this book as elsewhere, will include a bed for the night and breakfast in the morning (usually a hearty affair, consisting of bacon, eggs, toast, generous quantities of tea and coffee). Evening meals are an optional extra, normally offered by even the most modest guest house, and this can work out cheaper than dining in a local restaurant.

The options for eating out in Scotland are as varied as those for accommodation. No matter what part of the country, you can always find a good value restaurant offering dinner at under £10 per person. For something more special, you can dine extremely well for £20 per person, including wine. If your budget allows more than that you can have the pick, particularly in Edinburgh, of some of the United Kingdom's finest restaurants.

As for nightlife, if you are a nightclub fan without much money, you won't have to worry about extortionate prices in the night-spots. Whilst none are cheap, with drinks costing between twice and one and a half times as much as they would in the pub, nowhere in Scotland will charge the ludicrous prices of the fashionably exclusive London venues. Cheaper and more authentic entertainment is found at a local ceilidh or listening to folk music in a local bar. Popular leisure activities such as wind-surfing or pony-trekking are not beyond the limits of most people's budgets. Scotland has some excellent municipal golf courses which are much cheaper than any in England (£3 is a typical price for a round during the week, with a slight increase at weekends) although, obviously, you will have to pay more if you want to practise your golf on one of Scotland's top-class courses.

Your mode of transport also offers room for economy. Taking the car is the cheapest option, while coach fares are usually less than half of those on the train, although there is a perplexing variety of fare schedules available on the latter which can save you a considerable amount of money. Day returns offer a substantial saving, as much as 50 per cent, on ordinary return fares, although they are subject to restrictions on times and days of travel. Significant savings can be made if you avoid rail travel on certain days, such as Fridays and bank holidays. A Young-Persons Rail Card is available to anyone between the ages of 16 and 23 or in full-time education. For an initial cost, currently £16, it will entitle the user to a 33 per cent reduction in fares, although tickets bought this way are subject to restriction, precluding travel during the busiest periods. Similar concessionary options for rail travel include: a Family RailCard for £20 with 33 per cent off all fares, and reduced entry for children into certain museums; a Senior Citizen RailCard for £16 with the same reductions on fares, and a Disabled Persons RailCard available for £14 allowing for half-price travel on cheap day returns, and first class and standard day returns. For further discounts, a Young Scot Card is available to anyone under 26. For only £6, you will be entitled to a 33 per cent discount on all Scottish City Link Coach journeys. Hiring a car can also work out much cheaper. There are 164 restaurants which welcome the Young Scot Card including Pizza Hut, Panini Express and McDonalds, and almost every theatre in Scotland, including most of the events at the Edinburgh Festival Fringe and Glasgow's Mayfest. Up to £20 will also be saved if you decide to purchase a Scottish Activity Holiday through the Sports Council. For more information, contact: Young Scot, Edinburgh, EH12 5LQ (Tel: 031–313 2488).

Getting Yourself Organized

What to Take with You

Knowing what to pack can be a big problem, especially if you are arriving in Scotland by air, which will restrict you to a single suitcase and one piece of hand luggage on your flight. Whatever time of year you choose to visit Scotland you will need to pack warm clothes. It is untrue to suggest that Scotland never gets any good weather, but the only accurate word to describe the climate is 'unpredictable'. Even in July and August the evenings can be chilly, particularly north of the central belt, so one or two warm woollen jumpers are essential, as is a rain-proof. Smart dinner dress is required in most of the major Scottish hotels (four- or five-star categories).

Another very important item for inclusion in the luggage is insect repellent. The Scottish midges – small mosquitoes – are legion in summer, particularly in some of the idyllic glens and lochsides where they can be an intolerable irritation.

If you're travelling independently you might consider taking a few extra items, such as a travelling alarm clock and, if you're planning on walking, a compass, a whistle and an empty water-bottle to fill up with drinking water when you get the chance. For those camping or hostelling, it's advisable to take a money-belt to keep your valuables in and a padlock for youth hostels. A good first-aid kit is a must for independent travellers heading off to remote parts.

Part Two
HOW TO GO

Package v. Independent

While there are some tour operators offering package holidays in Scotland, the tourist industry is mainly aimed at the independent holidaymaker. The fact that England and Scotland are part of the same island means that travel between the two is quick and easy, and accommodation arrangements are simply made. Once there, there are good internal communications in Scotland to make travel within the country relatively cheap and easy. Bed-and-breakfast accommodation can be found in even the most remote villages, and this very reasonable form of accommodation makes independent travel easy and attractive to those on a low budget.

The majority of tour operators listed in the following pages offer special interest holidays. In addition to travel and accommodation arrangements, this type of holiday package includes all the necessary arrangements for you to pursue your favourite hobby (golf, fishing, etc.) during the course of your holiday. In these specialist areas the independent traveller is also catered for – there are many centres combining accommodation with a particular recreation, so that, as well as bed and board, matters such as daily transport, equipment hire and so on are taken care of, leaving the holidaymaker with only travel arrangements to organize.

On the following pages are the names, addresses, telephone numbers, and details of British tour operators who offer holidays in Scotland. Some of these firms are relatively obscure and their brochures will not be widely available, but if in the sections following this list you find they specialize in the type of holiday you're interested in, give them a ring and request a brochure. Every effort has been made to ensure this list of operators is comprehensive and accurate, but please remember that in the fluctuating world of the travel business, tour companies come and go with regularity. Contact the Scottish Tourist Board in Edinburgh or London for the very latest information.

Package Holidays

Tour Operators Offering Packages to Scotland

ABERCROMBIE & KENT LTD
Sloane Square House, Holbein Place, London SW1W 8NS
Tel. 071–730 9600

AYRSHIRE'S GOLFING HOLIDAYS
Ayrshire Administration Centre, Suite 1005, Prestwick Airport, Prestwick, Ayrshire KA9 2PL
Tel. 0292 79000

BEST OF SCOTLAND HOLIDAYS
6a Main Street,
Upper Largo
Fife KY8 6EJ
Tel. 033 336 395

BEST WESTERN HOTELS
143 London Road, Kingston-upon-Thames, Surrey KT2 6NA
Tel. 081–546 1638

THE BIKE BUS COMPANY
The Adventure Traveller, Compston Road, Ambleside, Cumbria LA22 9DJ
Tel. 445394 33285

BLAKES HOLIDAYS LTD
Roxham, Norwich, NR12 8DH
Tel. 0603 783221

BOBSPORT (SCOTLAND)
17 Rutland Square, Edinburgh EH1 2AQ
Tel. 031–229 9999

BÖD HOLIDAYS
Shetland Islands Tourism, Market Cross, Lerwick,
Shetland ZE1 0LU
Tel. 0595 3434

BOWEN TRAVEL
101 Cotterills Lane, Alun Rock, Birmingham B8 3SA
Tel. 021–327 3543

CALEDONIAN MACBRAYNE
The Ferry Terminal, Gourock PA19 1QP
Tel. 0475 33755

CALEDONIAN WILDLIFE
19 Stretton Close, Cantley, Doncaster DN4 6UE
Tel. 0302 371050

CAMPUS HOTELS SCOTLAND
PO Box 808,
Edinburgh EH14 4PS
Tel. 031 449 4034

CARMICHAEL COUNTRY COTTAGES
Carmichael Estate, by Biggar,
M42 6PG
Tel. 08993 336

CHIEFTAIN TOURS
A8 White Crook Centre, White
Crook Street, Clydebank, Glasgow
G81 1QF
Tel. 041–951 1470

CLASSIQUE TOURS
8 Underwood Road, Paisley
PA3 1TD
Tel. 041–889 4050

C-N-DO SCOTLAND
Howlands Cottage, Sauchieburn,
Stirling FK7 9PZ
Tel. 0786 812355

COUNTRYWIDE HOLIDAYS
50 Cromwell Range, Manchester
M14 6HU
Tel. 061–225 1000

DA STUDY TOURS
Williamton House, Low
Causeway, Culross, Fife
KY12 8HL
Tel. 0383 881700

DISCOVER BRITAIN
Shore Mews, Shore Street
Worcester
Tel. 0905 613744

EDINBURGH COLLEGE OF ART
Heriot-Watt University, Lauriston
Place, Edinburgh EH3 9DF
Tel. 031 229 9311

FAIRISLE LODGE AND BIRD CONSERVATORY
Fairisle, Shetland ZE2 9JU
Tel. 035 12258

FAIRWAY TOURS
8d Rosebery Place, Gullane, East
Lothian EH31 2AN
Tel. 0620 842349

FINDHORN FOUNDATION
Cluny Hill College, Forres
IV36 0RD
Tel. 0309 672288

GARRY GUALACH COUNTRY HOLIDAYS
Invergarry, Inverness-shire
PH35 230

GHILLIE PERSONAL TRAVEL
64 Silverknowes Road East,
Edinburgh EH4 5NY
Tel. 031–336 3120

GOLF VACANCES (ST ANDREWS) LTD
3 Pilmour Links, St Andrews,
Fife KY16 9JG
Tel. 0334 72299

GRAMPIAN BIRD SAFARIS
Cliff Jones Associates, Kirkton
Cottage, Forgue, By Huntly,
Aberdeenshire
AB54 6BT
Tel. 0466 82327

GREAT BRITISH HOLIDAYS
61 Seamoor Road, Bournemouth
BH4 9AE
Tel. 0202 751700

HEATHERLEA BIRD WATCHING SERVICES
Heatherlea, Deshar Road, Boat of
Garten, Inverness PH24 3BN
Tel. 0479 83674

HEBRIDEAN ISLAND CRUISES
Bank Newton, Skipton, North
Yorkshire BD23 3NT
Tel. 0756 701338

HEBRIDEAN PURSUITS LTD
1 Grosvenor Crescent, Connel,
Oban, Argyll PA37 1PQ
Tel. Connel 063 171 317

HF HOLIDAYS LTD
117 Barkby Road,
Leicester LE4 7LG
Tel. 0533 460046

HIGHLAND ACTIVITY HOLIDAYS
Norheim, Church Street,
Dufftown, Glenfiddich AB55 4AR
Tel. 0340 20892

HIGHLAND ADVENTURES LTD
Tyndrum, Perthshire, Scotland
FK20 8RY
Tel. 08384 289

HIGHLANDS AND ISLANDS
Hi-Line House, Station Road
Dingwall, Ross-shire IV15 9JE
Tel. 0349 65000

HIGHLIFE LONDON AND UK BREAKS
PO Box 139, Leeds LS2 7TE
Tel. 0800 700400

HOLIDAY COTTAGES IN SCOTLAND LTD
Lilliesleaf, Melrose,
Roxburghshire TO6 9JD
Tel. 08357 481/485

HOSEASONS HOLIDAYS LTD
Sunway House, Lowestoft,
Suffolk NR32 3LT
Tel. 0502 500505

ISLAND HOLIDAYS
Ardross, Comrie, Perthshire
PH6 2JU
Tel. 0764 70107

JOHN RIDGWAY ADVENTURE SCHOOL
Ardmore, Rhiconich, by Lairg,
Sutherland IV27 4RB
Tel. 097182 229

JUDY McALLISTER
Park House, Corriecravie, Isle of
Arran KA27 8PD
Tel. 077087 226

LADYTREK
'Foxgloves', Leacanashie,
Lochcarron, Wester Ross
IV54 8YD
Tel. 05202 238

LOCH INSH WATER SPORTS CENTRE
Kincraig, Inverness-shire
PH21 1NU
Tel. 05402 272

LORNE LEADER
Ardfern, Lochgilphead, Argyll
PA31 8QN
Tel. 08525 212

MACKAYS AGENCY
30 Frederick Street, Edinburgh
EH2 2JR
Tel. 031–225 3539

A T MAYS LTD
21 Royal Crescent,
Glasgow G3 7SZ
Tel. 041–331 1200

MOUNTAIN CRAFT
Glenfinnan, Fort William
PH37 4LT
Tel. 039783 213

P&O FERRIES
Jamieson's Quay, Aberdeen
Tel. 0224 572615

**PGL ADVENTURE
HOLIDAYS**
Alton Court, Penyard Lane,
Ross-on-Wye, HR9 5NR
Tel. 0986 768768

**PRINCIPALITY TRAVEL
LTD**
St Brides Hill, Saundersfoot,
Dyfed, Wales SA69 9NH
Tel. 0834 812304

**RUA REIDH EXPLORATION
CENTRE**
Rua Reidh Lighthouse, Melvaig,
Gairloch IV21 2EA
Tel. 0445 85263

SAGA HOLIDAYS
Middleburg Square, Folkestone,
Kent CT20 1AZ
Tel. 0800 300500

**SALTATION YACHT
CHARTERS**
10 Lochaber Road, Kinlochleven,
by Fort William, Inverness-shire
PH40 4QW
Tel. 08554 676

SCOTIA TRAVEL
Bonnington Road Lane,
Edinburgh EH6 5BJ
Tel. 031–553 1455

**SCOTLAND'S ISLAND
EXPERIENCE**
Balfour, Shapinsay, Orkney
KW17 2DY
Tel. 0856 71252

SCOTLINE TOURS
87 High Street, Edinburgh
EH1 1SG
Tel. 031–557 0162

SCOTSELL
2d Churchill Way, Bishopbriggs,
Glasgow G64 2RH
Tel. 041–772 5920

SCOTTISH BORDER TRAILS
'Drummore', Venlaw High Road,
Peebles EH45 8RL
Tel. 0721 22934

**SCOTTISH CONSERVATION
PROJECTS**
Scotsell Ltd, 2d Churchill Way,
Bishopbriggs G64 2RH
Tel. 041 772 5928

**SCOTTISH COUNTRY
COTTAGES**
2d Churchill Way, Bishopbriggs,
Glasgow G64 2RH
Tel. 041–772 5920

SCOTTISH CYCLING HOLIDAYS
Ballintuim Post Office
Biairgowrie, PH10 7NJ
Tel. 0250 886201

SCOTTISH FARMHOUSE HOLIDAYS
Drumtenant, Ladybank, Fife
KY7 7UG
Tel. 0337 30451

SCOTTISH GOLF HOLIDAYS
6 Avon Walk, Town Centre,
Cumbernauld, Glasgow G67 1EQ
Tel. 0236 723444

SCOTTISH HIGHLAND RAILWAY COMPANY
42a Queen Street,
Edinburgh EH2 3PS
Tel. 031–220 6441 (Toll free: 0800 838539)

A SCOTTISH WELCOME BY AILEEN HAY
East Cottage, Pitmurthly,
Redgorten, Perth PH1 3HP
Tel. 0738 827224

SCOTTS CASTLE HOLIDAYS
1E Harbour Road, Musselburgh
EH21 6DL
Tel. 031–226 7615

SHEARINGS HOLIDAYS
Mirylane, Wigan, Greater
Manchester WN3 4AG
Tel. 0942 824978

TIGHNABRUAICH SAILING SCHOOL
Tighnabruaich, Argyll
Tel. 811 396

TWEED VALLEY HOLIDAYS
Tweed Valley Hotel
Walkerburn
Tel. 089 687 636

UNIVERSITY OF GLASGOW
Department of Adult and
Continuing Education
59 Oakfield Avenue,
Glasgow G12 8LW
Tel. 041 330 4394

UNIVERSITY OF STIRLING
Summer School Office, Airthrey
Castle, Stirling FK9 4LA
Tel. 0786 67944

UNIVERSITY OF STRATHCLYDE
Continuing Education Centre,
McCance Building, 16 Richmond
Street, Glasgow G1 1XQ
Tel. 041 553 4147

TRANSCOTLAND
216 Newhaven Road, Edinburgh
EH6 4QE
Tel. 031–552 8360

WALLACE ARNOLD LTD
16 Torbay Road, Paignton, Devon
Tel. 0803 521441

WILDCAT VENTURES
Sutherland Estates, Golspie,
Sutherland, KW10 6RR
Tel. 04083 3268

WINDSOR CHAUFFEUR DRIVE
Windsor House, 4 Gleneagles
Avenue, Westerwood Village,
Cumbernauld G68 0E4
Tel. 0236 458424

GENERAL TOUR OPERATORS

For visitors from the British Isles, the ease of getting to Scotland makes it mainly a destination for the independent traveller. Where package holidays are offered they tend to be very specific, catering for particular interests: golf, fishing, hiking holidays, and so on. Having said that, there are a number of general tour operators who can provide a holiday package that includes both accommodation and travel arrangements and leaves the decision of what to do once there to the visitors.

Scotsell's 'Tour Scotland by car' brochure allows holidaymakers the freedom to roam around at their own pace without worrying about accommodation at the end of the day. The package offers holidaymakers a choice of hotels in 24 locations throughout Scotland to suit various tastes and pockets, from the grandeur of castle hotels to the simple comfort of small family-run establishments. For English visitors, the proximity of Scotland makes it ideal for a long-weekend break, and there are a number of operators catering for this type of holiday. **Best Western Hotels** have 21 establishments throughout Scotland and their series of Getaway Breaks offers a wide range of accommodation, in terms of both price and location. Travel arrangements by rail, ferry, air, and car hire, can be included in the package to suit individual needs. Similarly, **Stakis Hotels** have an excellent selection of short activity and touring holidays combining the same travel arrangements. **Scotsell** operates Heritage Breaks, a short break programme of Scotland's top Heritage Hotels rich in history and architecture. **Principality Travel**'s Welcome Holidays and Countess Breaks programme, provide 'Go As You Please' selfdrive holidays throughout Scotland, with a superb choice of hotel accommodation. **AT Mays** provide an interesting range of package holidays at destinations throughout the country, while Great British Holidays specialize in offering packages to seaside destinations as well as organising City Breaks with a selection of selfcatering and hotel accommodation suited to meet all budgets. Rail travel can also be included in the package if required. **Saga** offer rail or coach travel at reduced rate as part of their holidays for the over 60s to Rothesay, Pitlochry, and Strathpeffer. At all locations, the package includes optional excursions and a courier service. If you want to explore all or any of Scotland's islands, then the Scottish Island Holidays run by **Scotsell** are well worth considering. From Shetland, far off the Caithness coast, the Isle of Skye and down to Bute in the Firth of Clyde, accommodation on almost all of Scotland's islands is on offer, with travel provided by P&O Ferries, Caledonian MacBrayne, British Airways and Loganair.

SELF-CATERING HOLIDAYS

Self-catering is an attractive and cost-conscious option for the holidaymaker, although this type of accommodation is not as widely available as the bed-and-board type. Self-catering can be an excellent idea for those seeking to get away from it all – including other holidaymakers. There are many country cottages in the small ads of national and local newspapers, particularly the *Sunday Times*, *Independent*, and *Observer*. Most of those on offer are run as small private concerns. Among the few agencies with properties in various locations throughout the country, are **Scottish Country Cottages**. They have houses situated, as the name suggests, mainly in the country, and are able to accommodate from two to eight persons. The cost varies from £140–£490 per week, depending on the time of year and the size of the property. The price includes all bed linen, towels, and a colour television in every cottage. The well-established **Hoseasons** also offer a wide range of good-quality self-catering accommodation in both town and country throughout Scotland. For reliable properties with no small-print surprises, they are good operators. Their prices are also generally much lower than competitors'. **Great British Holidays** also has a good selection of self-catering holiday properties throughout the country. **Mackay's Agency** can offer self-catering holiday houses as well as bungalows and traditional farmhouses, along with Blakes Holidays Ltd, who also specialise in country cottages. With **Discover Britain**, Holiday Cottage Guide you can find a wide choice of cottages and apartments all year round. **Campus Hotels** provide a choice of self-catering flats in most university towns including Aberdeen, Dundee, St Andrews, Stirling, Edinburgh and Glasgow. But if you are looking for the basics, why not consider a holiday in a **böd**. These traditional Shetland buildings, formerly the seasonal homes of fishermen, are set in attractive and historical locations and offer basic accommodation at bargain prices. Contact Shetland Islands Tourism, Market Cross, Lerwick (Tel. 0595 3434).

Other sources for holidaymakers looking for self-catering accommodation are the glossy brochures published by the Area Tourist Boards, which give information on all types of accommodation particular to the area covered by each board. Also available is the **Forestry Commission**'s 'Cabins and Cottages' brochure, which describes the log cabin facilities situated at Strathyre and Dalavich by Loch Awe, and holiday cottages in forest settings throughout the Scottish countryside. For further information write to Forestry Commission HQ, 231 Corstorphine Road, Edinburgh EH12 7AT (Tel. 031–334 0303). **Holiday Cottages in Scotland** produce a most helpful booklet (price 80p) detailing cottages to let all over Scotland.

The most comprehensive source, however, is the guide published by the Scottish Tourist Board entitled 'Scotland, Self-Catering 1993', available for a few pounds from bookshops or by post from the STB in Edinburgh (23 Ravelston Terrace, Edinburgh EH4 3EU) and London (19 Cockspur Street, London SW1Y 5BL).

COST-CONSCIOUS HOLIDAYS

Although it need not be expensive to visit Scotland on a package holiday, it is, more often than not, cheaper to make travel and accommodation arrangements yourself. Coach tours can represent very good value for money, especially if the itinerary takes in remote Highland and Island areas where public transport tends to be more expensive than in the more populous parts of the country. **Wallace Arnold** and **National Holidays** both offer very reasonable holidays in this category. Another inexpensive way of visiting Scotland is to take one of the Breakaway Holidays offered by the

Scottish Youth Hostels Association. Travel by train is included in the package which offers a range of activity holidays lasting from a weekend to two weeks, with accommodation at one of the many Youth Hostels in Scotland. Activities on offer range from watersports on Loch Morlich to pony trekking in the Borders. The 'Highland Wayfarer' package price includes unlimited travel by train and ferry plus a third off coach fares giving hostellers the opportunity to see as much as possible in Scotland's Highlands and Islands area. 'Explore Scotland' packages offer a great value way to see the Scottish mainland, plus the Isle of Skye, this time with Scottish Citylink Coaches. The price includes six overnight vouchers for use at any Scottish Youth Hostel, a Scot Pass Discount Card, as well as an Explorer Pass if you want to visit historic monuments on your chosen routes. Facilities naturally vary from place to place, but all offer fully equipped self-catering kitchens, small stores selling souvenirs and foodstuffs, and dormitory accommodation. Many hostels now also provide double and family rooms, continental quilts, television or games rooms, central heating, hot showers, and laundry facilities. Böd holidays should appeal to those on a very tight budget. Contact Shetland Islands Tourism Board for information (Tel. 0595 3434). Böds provide what can be described as a cross between self-catering cottages and camping, offering only the basics from £2.50 per person, per night. **Campus Hotels** also have very comfortable, attractive and economically priced accommodation for individuals, families or groups, in most university towns. Many Campus Hotels can also offer a range of activities. Camping is another cost-cutting alternative – the full list of current sites is available from the STB. The **Forestry Commission**'s brochure 'Caravan and Camping Forest Holidays' details sites in the Highlands, the Trossachs, Argyll and Galloway.

COACH TOURS

Coach tours are undoubtedly one of the cheapest ways to have a holiday, and are a good way to do a whistle-stop tour of the major sights of Scotland.

Bowen Travel offer a number of very enjoyable scenic tours around the north of Scotland. Each tour is based at one hotel in each area, lasts four to five days and involves two excursions, returning to the hotel each night. The locations on offer are Royal Deeside; Oban and the western Highlands; Callander and the Trossachs; the Road to the Isles (Fort William to Mallaig); Pitlochry and Royal Scotland; and the Highlander, a five-day holiday, based in a splendid location at Arrochar on the banks of Loch Long, and involving excursions to Fort William and Mallaig, and the Trossachs. Their prices compare very favourably with other operators'. Shearings Holidays' Scottish programme offers two tours: the seven-day Hebrides and Highlands schedule travels north through the central Highlands to Fort William, before exploring the road to the isles and boarding the ferry to the Isle of Skye. It is then on to Stornoway, capital of the Outer Hebrides, before taking the southbound return journey, via Ullapool and the outskirts of Inverness. The Enchanting Islands is a seven-day tour that ventures as far north as Lochmaddy on North Uist, taking in Fort William *en route* and the Isle of Skye. A short journey across the causeway, connecting the islands, will lead to the island of Benbecula, spending time later on South Uist, the Isle of Barra and later, on the return journey, Oban, before returning home. **Chieftain Tours, Scotia Travel, Scotline Tours and Classique Tours** all offer good choices of itineraries throughout Scotland combined with comfortable accommodation. **AT Mays** run a variety of tours in their own luxury coaches, and have a range of schedules which offer the chance to cover as wide or as specific an area of Scotland as you want, including packages to Orkney and Shetland.

Wallace Arnold have an extensive Scottish programme in their series of British Coach Holidays, with tours lasting seven, eight, or 14 days. Each of the 13 tours is based at one or two hotels, depending on location, and takes holidaymakers on day excursions through some of the most magnificent scenery in the Highlands.

DE LUXE HOLIDAYS

For holidaymakers unrestricted by financial constraints, there are several packages worth special consideration: the *Hebridean Princess*, a luxury liner cruising the islands off the west coast; and the *Queen of Scots*, offering a leisurely train journey through Scotland, arguably far more stylish and comfortable than anything experienced on board the *Orient Express*. There is also the more modern *Royal Scotsman*.

Between May and October, run by **Hebridean Island Cruises**, the *Hebridean Princess* operates three-, four-, five-, seven-, nine- and fourteen-day cruises, carrying a maximum of 46 passengers in luxuriously appointed staterooms. Cruises depart from Oban and take in most of the world-famous islands of the Inner and Outer Hebrides, among them St Kilda, Colonsay, Tiree, Stornoway, Rhum, Eigg, Harris, Mull, Jura, Skye and Arran, all of them offering a wealth of culture, history, and awe-inspiring beauty; and with garage space available on board for passengers' cars, there is the added advantage of independent exploration at various ports of call. For those with sporting interests, sailing, fishing trips and clay-pigeon shooting are included in the price of the holiday, while for those who favour more leisurely pursuits, the lounge and relaxation areas exude the atmosphere of a country house hotel, providing excellent viewing in elegant surroundings. With a new menu each day and using only fresh produce, the ship's restaurant offers the very best in food and wines, including traditional Scottish fare, *nouvelle cuisine* and barbecues on deck. The cost of a seven-night cruise ranges from £1,195 to £2,895, depending on the type of accommodation chosen and the time of year.

The two de luxe tour trains, the *Queen of Scots* and the *Royal Scotsman*, have combined their efforts through the **Scottish Highland Railway**. The *Royal Scotsman* is more modern but no less luxurious, carrying up to 32 passengers through the Scottish countryside. From May to November there are grand six-day tours from £3,300 per person and three to four day tours to the Highlands in the spring, midsummer and autumn. There are special tours at other times of the year – such as the New Year – visiting those places in Scotland not normally visited in the summer. Private charters can also be arranged from November to April including various activities such as clay pigeon shooting *en route*. You can similarly book through Abercrombie and Kent Ltd.

Ghillie Personal Travel specialize in exclusively tailored tours. Their 'Blue Blood' tours offer accommodation in privately owned castles or mansions at £99–£187 p.p. per night including dinner with fine wines and liqueurs. 'Golden Coronet' refers to the most luxurious hotels in the country and 'Silver Sword' tours use the best country house hotels, £38.50–£55 p.p. 'Purple Heather' accommodation at £24.50–£38.50 p.p. is also available. Sightseeing, golf, shooting, stalking and fishing can all be arranged. Limousine tours of Scotland with multilingual driver guides can be individually tailored. Ghillie also offer a three-day tour from Aberdeen to Skye on board their luxury private train *The Highland Prince*. The price of £1,100 p.p. includes overnight stays in top class hotels, gourmet meals and sightseeing tours.

Windsor Chauffeur Drive are much more than a luxury car company. Although tours of Scotland, from half-day city ones to tours of the Highlands or Western Isles, are provided in Rolls-Royces, Daimlers and Mercedes, the company specialize in inclusive holidays. One of their more unusual packages is a photography holiday. Itineraries are chosen to include some of the most beautiful scenery in Scotland and clients are advised of the best vantage points. Evening discussions on photographic technique may be arranged if desired. An unexpected bonus comes at the end of the holiday when guests are presented with their own photographs mounted in an album. A new luxury special occasion package is now available, arranged with Cameron House Hotel, Loch Lomond and PLM Helicopters. Clients are collected from home, transferred to the helicopter, flown to the hotel for a meal, and returned home by limousine.

Scotts Castle Holidays is a unique agency which offers both self-catering and catered holidays and all of the accommodation is in private castles or fortified homes. At the catered properties you will stay as a guest of the laird and his family and in the self-catering properties (accommodating from 4–40), you can host your own house-party-style holiday or get away from it all in a country retreat. Properties range from, for example, Manderston (see page

118) in Berwickshire; Blairquhan near Maybole in Ayrshire – the Tudor-style family mansion has magnificent public rooms and is situated in the beautiful wooded valley of the Water of Girvan; to Muckrach Castle near Grantown-on-Spey in Morayshire. Muckrach is a recently restored 16th-century castle commanding spectacular views over Strathspey and the Cairngorms. The company can also provide vehicle hire, golf, shooting, fishing and horseriding.

CRUISES

The only true cruise holiday is that provided by **Hebridean Island Cruises** aboard the *Hebridean Princess* (see the section on 'De Luxe Holidays'). **Lorne Leader**, however, is one of the only three Brixham Sailing Trawlers in the UK which are offering a variety of cruises along the Western Isles of Scotland. Packages are from three to 14 days, including a range of interests such as birdwatching, geology, history and archaeology, as well as learning the skills of sailing and navigation. If you have a particular interest, there is also a selection of theme weeks to choose from with expert guides on board to show you the ropes. Prices start at £275. **Saltation Yacht Charters** also provide cruises to the Western Isles from six to 13 days from £225 for smaller groups of six persons. **Hebridean Pursuits** offer walking, sailing and painting holidays on board a 66ft converted fishing vessel, sailing from Oban to the Outer Hebrides, and beyond to the Island of St Kilda. Prices are from £430. **Wave Yacht Charters** take cruises to the West of Scotland on board the luxurious and spacious Sealgair Charter Yacht, including such locations as St Kilda, the Outer Hebrides and the Faroe Islands, lasting seven, ten or 21 days. It is the first yacht charter company to appear in the 'Taste of Scotland' guide, offering cuisine of the highest standard. Prices can vary for each package depending on the season and the number of persons booked. They have some interesting itineraries for island-hopping cruises. **John Ridgway's Adventure School** will gladly show how it's done through its cruising courses on offer to St Kilda and the Hebrides, as well as packages to the Faroe Islands. Prices start at

£393. There are also a couple of packages which, although not exactly cruises, do provide ferry transport as part of an overall package to allow you to go island-hopping. If you want to explore all or any of Scotland's islands, then the Scottish Island Holidays run by **Scotsell** are well worth considering, with travel provided by P&O Ferries, Caledonian MacBrayne, British Airways and Loganair. The company offers no less than 21 tour schedules which can be combined for greater holiday choice. A similar programme is provided by **Classique Tours**, who offer a number of packages taking in the Highlands and Islands including their most comprehensive itinerary, the eight-day Grand Hebridean Tour. Both Classique Tours and **P&O Ferries** include cruises to Orkney and Shetland. P&O offer three days and three nights visiting both Orkney and Shetland, with an *en-suite* cabin, inclusive of meals, for around £175, or the 'island fling' package lasting one day and two nights for only £90. **Caledonian MacBrayne** also offer package island touring holidays by car or by coach including ferry travel, accommodation and certain meals.

GOLF HOLIDAYS

For many visitors to Scotland, it is the sport of golf that brings them north of the border. The map of Scotland contains many names famous throughout the world because of their links with the sport, names such as Troon, Turnberry, St Andrews, Carnoustie, and Gleneagles. The ideal way to pit your skill against some of the most challenging courses in the world is to take advantage of a golfing package holiday. It saves considerable time and trouble by making all the necessary arrangements on your behalf, from transport to and from your hotel, to booking times and payment of green fees. It can also offer the latter at reduced cost.

In addition to their five-day Royal Deeside package and seven-day Golfing Heritage tour, **Bobsport** can put together a tailor-made package to suit your individual requirements. The Golfing Heritage tour gives enthusiasts of the sport an opportunity to tread the same ground as their heroes, offering the chance to play on the world famous championship courses of Royal Troon, Turnberry,

Gleneagles, St Andrews, Gullane, and Muirfield. The starting price of £800 includes dinner, bed and breakfast, transport, and green fees. **Fairway Tours** run de luxe golf packages catering for groups of no more than 11, and provide accommodation in top quality hotels. **Scottish Golf Holidays** offer self-drive or group tours that visit top grade courses throughout Scotland. **Ghillie Personal Travel** offer de-luxe golf programmes for seven to 18 days including top class guest house accommodation and transport from either Edinburgh or Glasgow Airport. Sightseeing tours are also part of the package. **Golf Vacances** can cater for the golfer right across the board, from championship golf tours to sightseeing tours, as well as providing golf tuition during the summer, and British golf packages. For the more cost-conscious **Ayrshire's Golfing Holidays** offer ideal packages at reasonable prices starting from £70 per person for a short break package which includes bed and breakfast accommodation and day tickets for six courses, to the higher price of £300 per person for a championship course package for up to five nights, including bed and breakfast accommodation at a quality hotel with an opportunity to play on the best courses. **The Scottish Youth Hostel Association** offers the best economy packages by far, with its two-week Ayrshire packages; from £185 you can learn the basics or improve on what you know, and from £245 you can use grade 1 and 2 courses. Both packages include instruction, green fees and full board accommodation at Ayrshire Youth Hostel. From £128, the Island Golfing Package offers the chance to play all seven courses on the Isle of Arran, staying at the Whiting Bay Youth Hostel.

In addition to the above tour operators, who arrange travel as well as accommodation, green fees and so on, there are a number of agents who can make all of the necessary arrangements for visiting local courses as part of a package which includes accommodation but not travel from home. There is a plentiful choice of golf-plus-accommodation packages throughout Scotland (few towns are far from a good 18-hole course), particularly in the famous golfing regions of Fife (St Andrews and Carnoustie), the Ayrshire coast (Troon and Turnberry), and East Lothian (Muirfield and Gullane). The Scottish Tourist Board publishes a good golfing map of Scotland showing course locations throughout the country as well as the 'Activities and Special Interests Holiday Magazine', detailing all the hotels dealing with golf packages. Caithness Tourist Board provides a booklet on the 'Highland Golf Trail' featuring 20 golf courses and accommodation in the area.

ACTIVITY HOLIDAYS

Scotland's outstanding countryside is the ideal location to pursue many varied outdoor pursuits, such as shooting and fishing, and a number of tour operators specialize in a range of activity holidays. **Bobsport** allows visitors to make the most of Scotland's excellent angling by running salmon fishing holidays. The package includes accommodation, transport, fishing tackle, permits, and expert tuition, with anglers being given the opportunity to try their luck on three of Britain's best salmon rivers: the Tweed, the Tay, and the Teith. If you have only a day to spare, 'Shuttlefish' and 'Diamond Fly Fish' packages can meet you directly from the airport and within an hour you will be taken to one of Scotland's finest salmon rivers. 'Diamond Fly Fish' is more exclusive, tailor-made to suit your requirements. **Scotsell** offer Shetland trout fishing holidays, inclusive of air transport and car hire to reach the lochs and accommodation of your choice, as well as one day's company of a ghillie, and a written guide to trout fishing in Shetland's 100 lochs. A fishing permit is also included. Prices can vary from £474 to £823. Various establishments deal exclusively with fishing holidays. **Carmichael Country Cottages**, for example, deal in fly fishing for trout. Packages include equipment and tuition with luxury self-catering accommodation. Prices are between £150 and £320. From £365 **Derek Herbert of Parkburn Guest House** offer a fully inclusive one-week salmon fishing holiday on the River Spey, complete with ghillie, permit and accommodation (Tel. 0479 3116). For the field sportsperson, **Bobsport** offers shooting holidays on the vast tracts of open countryside and woodland that provide some of the finest sport in the country, encouraging visitors to take a pot at grouse, pheasant, partridge, woodcock, snipe, duck, geese, rabbits, and deer. Many establishments in Scotland can offer clay pigeon shooting plus accommodation, including **Stakis' Dunkeld House**, Perthshire (Tel. 0350 727771), **Gleneagles Hotel** (Tel. 0764 62231) and **Rothiemurchus Estate** near Aviemore. **Balnacoil Hotel**, in the heart of Royal Deeside, specializes in country pursuit breaks, clay pigeon shooting, stalking, fishing and carriage driving (Tel. 03398 86806). **Fairway Tours** offer similar programmes to cater for anglers and hunters at locations throughout Scotland.

A growing activity in Scotland is cycling, and there is an increasing number of operators offering superb cycling packages. **Bike Bus Holidays** provide a cycling tour package with coaching combined, so that you might reach the numerous cycling routes which the remoter areas of Scotland's Highlands have to offer. The package includes the hire of bikes, two leader drivers and luxury bed and breakfast or guest house accommodation. **The Scottish Youth Hostel Association** offer three fully inclusive cycling packages to the islands of Mull, Skye and Raasay, to the Border country and Northern Coast to Coast, starting from £99. They also have a cycling holidays brochure which you can pick up from any Scottish hostel or the headquarters in Stirling, which highlights certain routes opened up for cyclists.

Scottish Border Trails also comes highly recommended, offering mountain bike packages as well as half-day and day tours with the hire of high quality mountain bikes to best enjoy the wide choice of routes available in the Scottish Borders. **Scottish Cycling Holidays**, offer a wide choice of cycling holidays lasting from eight to fifteen days, including such tours as the Central Highlands, Lochs and Bens, the Grand Tour, the Fishing Heritage Trail, Over the Sea to Skye, Royal Deeside and the West Coast and Mull Tour.

With Scotland's many lochs and mountain rivers it is hardly surprising that watersports are so well catered for in Scotland. **Tighnabruaich Sailing School**, based along the north shore of the Kyles of Bute, is the ideal situation for sailing and windsurfing. There are various weekly courses on offer for either sport, for the novice to the more experienced. Accommodation can be arranged from an excellent selection of hotels and private and self-catering accommodation. **Loch Insh Watersports Centre**, situated at Kincraig, offer two-, five- and seven-day inclusive packages with dinghy sailing, windsurfing, canoeing or sport-a-day packages from £81. Accommodation, meals, hire and instruction are included in the price, or Loch Insh Chalets can be let to family groups.

For the more adventurous, **Mountain Craft** provide quality packages for the enthusiastic hill walker or experienced climber. Mountain rock climbing packages for five days instruction and full board hotel accommodation can cost from £425. The Classic Mountain Rock package, taking in the more challenging rock climbs, includes Ben Nevis, Glencoe, Skye and Applecross. It costs from £445 with full board accommodation and instruction with snow and ice climbing packages from £449 in the winter. **Rua Reidh Holidays** offer the best in exploration holidays from its unique lighthouse base, and full weekly programme including such activities as canoeing, rock sports, expeditions, art of survival, fishing, rock pool studies and even kite flying. Prices begin at around £90. **Garry Gualach Country Holidays**, is a small family-run company offering outdoor holidays in the Scottish Highlands, including: Icelandic horse riding, trout and salmon fishing, hill walking, field sports and camping expeditions. The package includes transport to and from Inverness, Fort William or Invergarry. **The John Ridgway Adventure School** offers challenging adventure holidays, where you can measure yourself against the elements. Adult courses run weekly from £393 with an entire range of activities to match your needs. The International Summer School from £430 encourages self-reliance and positive thinking with its programme of sailing, navigation, orienteering and two-day expeditions. **Wildcat Ventures**, also situated in Sutherland, offers action-packed adventure holidays to children between the ages of eight and 16. **PGL Adventure Holidays** offer family adventure holidays as well as multi-activity holidays for six to 18-year-olds, including abseiling, climbing, all watersports and more, at very agreeable prices.

To make the most of the skiing opportunities open to you in Scotland, there are various tour operators offering ski holiday packages from January to April. **Bobsport** can provide excellent skiing holidays to Aviemore and Glenshee and can also put together tailor-made packages. **Highlands and Islands** offer various packages to all five of Scotland's ski resorts with instruction, ski hire and lift pass included in the price. Accommodation and travel is not usually included in the package. Rail and air inclusive packages are also available, however. Excluding travel in their packages, the following tour operators offer excellent ski packages: **Countrywide Holidays, Best Western Hotels** and **High Life London and UK Breaks**. For less costly packages the **Scottish Youth Hostel Association** provides skiing in Glenshee for up to six days at around £94. This includes self-catering accommodation, ski instruction and hire of equipment. For more information there is a '**Ski Scotland**' brochure produced by the Scottish Tourist Board available from any Tourist Information Centre.

Perthshire is one of Scotland's prime areas for recreational and sporting pursuits. Perthshire Tourist Board has joined forces with leading activity and accommodation providers in a unique venture to offer an exciting new range of activity holidays for all ages and abilities. There is a choice of 42 different sporting or special interest breaks. **Perthshire Activity Line** offers all-inclusive packages, one-day 'tasters', tailor-made, à la carte and twin-centre holidays throughout the region. Send for a brochure to: Perthshire Activity Line, 22 Atholl Road, Pitlochry, Perthshire PH16 5BX or phone 0796 474114.

The Scottish Tourist Board produces a free brochure entitled 'Adventure and Special Interest Holidays in Scotland' which gives details of all types of activity holidays from archaeological digs to waterskiing. Activity holidays need not be physically demanding. **Judy McAllister** offers patchwork and quilting holidays on the Isle of Arran. **DA Study Tours** help you to appreciate the wonderful scenery and attractions of the Scottish Isles with special interest packages, from four to six days, each with its own specialist guide to tell the story of the island people and their history. Ferry travel is always included, as is excellent hotel or bed and breakfast accommodation with dinner and free excursions. **A Scottish Welcome by Aileen Hay** specializes in historical visits, specialist shopping trips, outings of unique interest and sporting activities, as well as providing excellent evening activities combining the best in Scottish cuisine and theatre. Packages can be organized to suit individual needs and budgets. Most Scottish universities offer a variety of courses plus accommodation during the summer. **The University of Strathclyde** in Glasgow can offer courses in Scottish fiddle playing, meditation, art in Glasgow, calligraphy and an introduction to the Gaelic language and culture. **Edinburgh College of Art** has an impressive programme for its Festival Summer School in Visual Arts, complementing the Edinburgh International Festival from mid-August to September. Figure drawing, painting, photography and sculpture are supplemented by lectures, private views and receptions with optional trips to famous country houses. **The University of Stirling** also run Scottish summer schools with a traditional Scottish menu of bagpipe playing, accordion playing and family history research. The Gaelic summer schools offer ideal courses on Gaelic culture in Scotland. Weekend courses are also available including a valuable insight into the history of Roman Scotland. **The Findhorn Foundation** is an international spiritual community situated in north-east Scotland, and a centre of education and demonstration. Anyone from any denomination is welcome to enjoy the rural setting and the activities offered, such as meditation, nature outings, group games as well as helping out in the garden and kitchens. 'Experience week' is the preliminary package, being a valuable introduction to the centre, costing between £210 and £300.

Photography is proving popular as an enjoyable holiday activity. **Best Western Hotels** offer week-long photography holidays from their selection of Getaway Breaks; **Tweed Valley Holidays** run photography courses throughout the year in the beauty of the border country and **HF Holidays** combine both photography and video filming in their packages.

WALKING/NATURAL-INTEREST HOLIDAYS

Scotland's magnificent countryside and abundant wildlife make it an excellent holiday choice for anyone interested in the great outdoors. The sparsely populated Highlands and Islands off the west coast, are a paradise for those interested in the study of fauna and flora. **Classique Tours** offer a range of package tours of these areas using coaches and top quality hotels. **Scotsell** offers a package to Shetland to observe the famous bird and seal populations on the islands. The package includes boat trips, a guide, and accommodation in an island castle. **Island Holidays** operate natural-interest holidays to Orkney and Shetland. Small groups are led by one of the partners, a well-known ornithologist. **Scotsell** also offers special three-night Natural History tours to the Western Isles, Bute and Arran for clients 'on their own'. Single rooms are available at no extra charge. **Hebridean Pursuits** offer walking, painting and sailing holidays with unique visits to the remote islands 40 miles beyond the Outer Hebrides to see rare bird and marine life. **Fair Isle Lodge and Bird Conservatory** offer special weeks for those who have specific interests or want to learn more about the island and bird life. The package includes full board accommodation, island transport, and airfare from Edinburgh. **Heatherlea Bird-watching Services** offer fully inclusive holidays from £250 in a traditional Highland guest house. The package includes six days' bird-watching in the Cairngorms and Strathspey areas, all meals, minibus transport when you are there, and expert guidance from a professional bird-watcher. Weekend breaks are also available for those with only limited time. **Grampian Bird Safaris** cater specifically for experienced or casual bird-watchers in the north–east of Scotland, with a leading naturalist and ornithologist as guide. Boat trips for seabird-watching can also be made available. Price includes accomodation. **Caledonian Wildlife** operate a number of natural history holidays in the Scottish Highlands and Islands where special species can be observed through the carefully designed itineraries. **The University of Glasgow** organize natural history holiday courses at the Marine Station on the Isle of Cumbrae. Full accommodation and all tuition is included in the package price. **Scotland's Island Experience** offers guided tours on many of the west coast islands noted for their interesting fauna. Accommodation is in first-class hotels. **Scottish Conservation projects** have a selection of conservation holidays, where you can learn with the experts how to improve Scotland's environment as well as enjoy it, set in the Aviemore area of the Cairngorms and Ballater on Deeside.

If you enjoy striding through the unspoilt countryside, far from the clamour of city life, then consider the well-respected operator **Countrywide Holidays**, which offers hillwalking and bird-watching as part of a range of activity holidays based at Kinfauns Castle, Perthshire. **HF Holidays** offer a wide range of walking holidays based at country houses throughout Scotland and **Ladytrek** aims to provide a complete 'getaway' package for those who wish to wander into the wilder regions of Scotland's mountains. **C-'n-do Scotland** have a varied programme of fixed-centre walking holidays throughout the country and lasting from six to 16 days, as well as short break holidays which can include a variety of other activities such as climbing and mountain biking. **Transcotland** can provide walking, cycling and canoeing holidays for all ages and abilities. **Scottish Farmhouse Holidays** offer holidays on working farms, giving the opportunity to see farm activities close at hand. **Highland Activity Holidays** arrange a variety of five-, seven-, or eight-day walking holidays in the Grampians and the Glenfiddich Whisky region, with a choice of half board hotel accommodation and bed and breakfast accommodation. **Mountain Craft** offer various levels of walking holidays from east to west Scotland, on the Isle of Skye, as well as hotel-based hill walking holidays from Glenfinnan and mountaineering holidays in the winter. **The Scottish Youth Hostel Association** has an interesting selection of walking holidays which are very reasonably priced, complete with full board youth hostel accommodation, tour leader and transport where necessary. Packages include the Isle of Skye, the West Highland Way, the Isle of Arran, the north-west, Scotland's top three mountains and the classic hills of the Northern Highlands. **Highland Adventures** organize walking holidays on the West Highland Way complete with accommodation and transport. **The John Ridgway Adventure School** cater well for the walker, offering special week-long hill walking courses in Sutherland, for men and women aged between 30 and 70, the object being to increase fitness and well-being, with evening activities and accommodation included in the package price of around £370.

Walk Scotland is a free magazine from the publishers of *Country Walking* magazine and associated with the Scottish Tourist Board, giving a general introduction to walking in Scotland with 15 specified walks highlighted. It is available from any tourist information centre in Scotland.

Independent Travel

By Air

Scotland has extensive air services which connect not only to most of Britain's regional airports, but also to major European business capitals and an increasing number of long-haul destinations.

By far the most competitive routes are those from Glasgow and Edinburgh to London Heathrow, with both British Airways and British Midland vying for important business. Both airlines operate frequent services seven days a week, throughout the year, and offer a variety of fares to match: from a £102 'two-week advance purchase return' fare to the 'standard' fare of £212 return.

British Midland, with their superb 'Diamond Service' available on all flights, operate a 15 minutes-before-departure late check-in facility and have a range of fares to suit both the businessman and the budget-conscious traveller, with the added flexibility of being able to change even the cheapest of fares.

British Airways, who operate more flights than British Midland, recently relaunched their 'Super Shuttle' service, and in doing so lost a little of that 'turn up and take off' flexibility. Now all fares, with the exception of the standard full fare, must be pre-booked, with no change of reservation permitted thereafter. The concept of British Airways operating an aircraft 'just for you' now only applies to full fare passengers.

Air UK have been operating the Glasgow and Edinburgh to London Gatwick routes since taking over from British Airways in October 1988. Using the new range of economical BAE 146 aircraft, they have made significant gains in passenger numbers in the short space of time they have been operating their 'Sterling Service' on the routes. As with British Airways and British Midland, Air UK offer a range of fares to suit from a two-week advance purchase return fare of £102 to a standard return of £212, and recently, a new £83 one-way Sterling Saver fare. Although non-refundable, changes to the initial booking are permitted.

British Airways also operate services between Aberdeen and Heathrow. Inverness to Gatwick is operated by DanAir.

Scotland's best domestic airline is Loganair, which has its

origins in a small air-taxi company formed in 1962. Based in Glasgow, this British Midland subsidiary operates routes connecting Glasgow and Edinburgh to Manchester and Belfast. It also operates life-line services in the Highlands and Islands of Scotland and seasonal services to the Channel Islands.

Air 2000, also based at Glasgow, operates charter flights to many of the Mediterranean holiday destinations, and now, direct from Glasgow to Orlando, using twin-engine Boeing 757 aircraft. Of the many charter airlines in Britain, Air 2000 has a reputation for offering some of the best in-flight catering, served by friendly and willing cabin staff.

By Rail

Travelling to Scotland by rail is undoubtedly one of the most relaxing ways to enter the country and definitely the best for enjoying the scenery. Scotland is well connected with the rail network of England. The two main transport hubs for Scotland are, of course, Edinburgh and Glasgow, taking now only 4 hours from Edinburgh to London eight times a day, thanks to the new 225 service. The slightly slower 125 InterCity service ($4^1/_2$ hours) also has several daily runs between the two capitals. Glasgow is equally well served with 16 daily services operating each way at just under 5 hours. From Edinburgh and Glasgow you can connect to anywhere else in Scotland.

Trains between Scotland and England tend to be very crowded in the summer months, so seat reservations for an extra £1, or on some services free, are advisable. The standard return ticket, valid for one month, costs around £114 to Edinburgh or Glasgow from London, with off-peak saver tickets costing about two-thirds of that. If you have time, a 'seven-day advance purchase' ticket will cost you around £44 return, with free seat reservations on both journeys. Stagecoach, formerly a coach company, has now introduced 'Stagecoach Rail', offering the same fares between Scotland and London as British Rail. However, a standard return ticket is valid for up to three months and two meals are also included in the price as well as free coach connections to and from the rail station. But there are fewer services and they tend to take that little while

longer. You can purchase your Stagecoach Rail tickets from any
British Rail station in London and Southern England and in
Scotland.

Several British Rail InterCity Sleeper services leave London
Euston between 8 p.m. and midnight bound for Edinburgh,
Glasgow, Inverness and Aberdeen. For a charge of £25 standard
class and £30 first class, on top of the ticket price, you can reserve a
sleeping berth which includes a cup of tea or coffee first thing in the
morning. There are various other InterCity Sleeper options newly
introduced by British Rail. These include the new 'solo package',
where by paying a little extra you can enjoy the exclusive use of a
standard cabin for £99 from London to Glasgow return, with
sleeper one way, and £134 for both ways. If there are two of you,
the 'duo package' is probably a better deal, where from London to
Edinburgh return, it will cost £149 for a sleeper one way and £174
both ways. There is also ordinary seating accommodation on some
of these services, and whereas there is no extra charge, the
disadvantage is that the journey is less comfortable. Prices,
especially with the introduction of other fares, can vary considerably depending on when and where you decide to travel. For more
details you can pick up the 'InterCity Sleeper' leaflet from any
station and rail appointed travel agents.

By Car

The cheapest way to travel to Scotland from England is by road.
The journey north from London to Edinburgh or Glasgow on good
motorways takes about seven or eight hours. The quickest route to
Edinburgh from London follows the M1, A1 and A68, and to
Glasgow via the M1, M6 and A74. Both trunk routes are well
signposted, although a good road map is a sensible investment if
you have not made the journey before. Membership of the AA or
RAC is also a wise precaution, especially for travellers to remote
areas.

By Coach

Until recently, a growing number of bus companies operated

overnight services from most English cities to Scotland. With the recent acquisition of Stagecoach by National Express, this is now the main bus company running cross-border services between England and Scotland. The old Stagecoach services will continue to be operated by National Express, with the return fare to Glasgow and Edinburgh from London costing no more than £36 if you travel on a Friday (or any Saturday during July and August) and £34 any other day, with some services having the added bonus of hostess service throughout the journey. More details are available from Caledonian Express Ltd, Walnut Grove, Perth (Tel. 071 730 0202 or 031 452 8777). Knightrider is the very latest coach company operating between Edinburgh/Glasgow and London, Kings Cross, where a return fare will only set you back £15. You can book from either Transpak, 71 Pancras Road, London (Tel. 071 833 4472) or SMT, St Andrew Square Bus Station, Edinburgh (Tel. 031 556 8464).

Accommodation for the Independent Traveller

Visitors to Scotland are spoiled not only by the choice of where to stay during their visit but also by the range of accommodation available to all budgets. By far the majority of hotel classifications in Scotland are awarded by the Automobile Association network, recognizable by a rectangular yellow sign displayed near the main door. It should be stressed that AA signs, and the less common but equally reliable Royal Automobile Club (RAC) blue and white star signs, refer to facilities available rather than simply how 'good' a particular place might be. All starred hotels have meal facilities for residents.

One-star hotels are generally small-scale establishments offering simple, clean accommodation with shared bathroom facilities. Two-star hotels offer a higher standard of accommodation, with at least a fifth of bedrooms having private bathroom facilities and all rooms having their own washbasins. Three-star hotels tend to be the most popular with package tour operators who come to Scotland. These are well-appointed hotels with very good dining facilities and *en-suite* bathrooms in most bedrooms. Some Edinburgh and Glasgow three-star establishments offer a much higher than average service because of fierce city competition. Four-star hotels offer high international standards, very good service and luxury accommodation. Private facilities and all the trimmings (probably a swimming pool, health club and so on, depending on the individual hotel) are standard. Five-star hotels offer the ultimate in luxury. There are only three AA five-star hotels in Scotland: the Caledonian Hotel and the Balmoral Hotel in Edinburgh and the famous Gleneagles Hotel near Auchterarder. These offer 24-hour room service, all *en-suite* facilities, a choice of restaurant, and service and amenities of the very highest standard.

The Scottish Tourist Board also operate a grading and classification system, applicable to all types of accommodation, from the most humble to the most luxurious. The classification is indicated by the number of crown symbols attached to an establishment – from 'Listed' (with no crowns) to five crowns – and gives you an idea of the range of facilities on offer (from the bare minimum to *en-suite* bathrooms, solarium and jacuzzi). The grading, on the other hand, is designed to indicate the quality of an establishment, and is assessed on a variety of factors, ranging from the tidiness of the gardens to the quality of the furnishings. There are three levels of grading: 'Approved', 'Commended', and 'Highly Commended'.

As far as price is concerned, AA one-star bedrooms begin at under £15 per night, while a five-star hotel will charge approximately 10 times that for a double room. A number of the larger hotel chains have hotels in Scotland, chiefly in Edinburgh and Glasgow. The **Forum** group has one hotel in both Edinburgh and Glasgow. The **Sheraton** has one in Edinburgh, and there is one **Holiday Inn**, which is in Glasgow, with another Holiday Inn due to open in Edinburgh soon. The **Crest** group has hotels in Edinburgh, Glasgow and near Erskine Bridge, by Glasgow airport. The **Stakis** chain operates a number of similarly well-appointed hotels, the most notable ones being in Edinburgh, Glasgow, Aberdeen and Aviemore, and **Forte** and **Thistle** Hotels also have hotels in the major towns and cities. The **Hilton** Group also have hotels in Glasgow and Edinburgh.

All hotel recommendations in this book give an indication of the nightly charge for bed-and-breakfast accommodation per person.

Some of the most prestigious, and luxurious, places to stay are Scotland's country house hotels. These are old and distinguished buildings, formerly private mansions or castles in the heart of Scotland's magnificent countryside, but within easy reach of mainline road and rail links. A number have been featured on the appropriate pages of Part Four of this book.

There is, of course, a wealth of accommodation available to visitors whose budget will not stretch to a fortnight's stay in a hotel. Very reasonable bed-and-breakfast accommodation can be enjoyed in Scotland's guest houses. For around £10 a night, occasionally even a few pounds less and seldom much more, you can find a comfortable, clean single or double room in a private home. The price usually includes a traditional Scottish breakfast of porridge or cereal, bacon, eggs and as much tea and toast as you like. If you're lucky, you may be offered a traditional Scottish kipper as well. A very useful buy, for £3.75, is the Scottish Tourist Board's 'Scotland, Bed and Breakfast' guide. All Area Tourist Boards can suggest local accommodation in hotels and guest houses, and most run a Book-a-Bed-Ahead service, offering to arrange your accommodation in advance of your arrival.

For people young at heart, or very budget conscious, there are about 80 Youth Hostels all over Scotland offering cheap, clean and basic accommodation for short stays of usually no more than three nights. They are graded A, B, and C depending on facilities available and marked by a triangle on most maps. Overnight stays cost between £2.85 and £6.50 depending on the grade of hostel and your age – although anyone over five can stay in a Scottish Youth Hostel provided they have paid their membership fee (between £2 and £5) in advance. Full details of Scottish youth hostelling facilities are available from: **The Scottish Youth Hostelling Association**, 7 Glebe Crescent, Stirling FK8 2JA (Tel. 0786 51181).

Camping facilities are available all over Scotland, whether you prefer to take a tent and hitch (seldom more than £3 a night on an official site) or hire a camper van or caravan and just drive. Caravan hire is possible from most larger towns from around £50 a week depending on the size of van you want. For more details on camping in Scotland, the 'Scotland, Camping and Caravan Parks' guide, produced by the Scottish Tourist Board, is well worth buying for £3.25. All sites in the guide have been inspected and hold thistle awards from the British Graded Holiday Parks Scheme. Also usefully highlighted in the guide are those parks which have won 'Calor Green' awards, having embraced the environmental aspects of park design and management.

Part Three
WHEN YOU'RE THERE

Tourist Information

Even the smallest towns in Scotland have a Tourist Information office open during the summer months, usually from April until October. The larger offices in the bigger towns and cities remain open all year round, usually from 9 a.m. until 6 p.m.

The main office of the Scottish Tourist Board is at 23 Ravelston Terrace, Edinburgh EH4 3EU (Tel. 031–332 2433). Here, you can pick up free glossy brochures giving information about accommodation and tourist attractions throughout Scotland. The Scottish Tourist Board also has a London office at 19 Cockspur Street, London SW1Y 5BL (Tel. 071–930 8661). For specific information on certain areas, write to the relevant Area Tourist Board from the following list of addresses. For information on a specific town, write to the relevant Information Office, the list of which is printed in full below the ATBs.

Area Tourist Boards

CITY OF ABERDEEN TOURIST BOARD
St Nicholas House, Broad Street,
Aberdeen AB9 1DE
Tel. Aberdeen (0224) 632727

AVIEMORE AND SPEY VALLEY TOURIST ORGANIZATION
Grampian Road, Aviemore,
Inverness-shire PH22 1PP
Tel. Aviemore (0479) 810363

AYRSHIRE AND BURNS COUNTRY TOURIST BOARD
39 Sandgate, Ayr KA7 1BG
Tel. Ayr (0292) 284196

AYRSHIRE TOURIST BOARD
Prestwick Airport, Administration
Centre, Suite 1005
Tel. (0292) 79000

BANFF AND BUCHAN TOURIST BOARD
Collie Lodge, Banff AB4 1AU
Tel. Banff (0261) 812419

CAITHNESS TOURIST BOARD
Whitechapel Road, Wick,
Caithness KW1 4EA
Tel. Wick (0955) 2596

CLYDE VALLEY TOURIST BOARD
Horsemarket, Ladyacre Road,
Lanark
Tel. Lanark (0555) 61661

DUMFRIES AND GALLOWAY TOURIST BOARD
Campbell House, Bankend Road,
Dumfries, DG1 4TH
Tel. Dumfries (0387) 50434

CITY OF DUNDEE TOURIST BOARD
4 City Square, Dundee, DD1 3BA
Tel. Dundee (0382) 27723

DUNOON AND COWAL TOURIST BOARD
Information Centre, 7 Alexandra Parade, Dunoon, Argyll PA23 8AB
Tel. Dunoon (0369) 3785

EAST LOTHIAN TOURIST BOARD
Brunton Hall, Musselburgh
EH21 6AF
Tel. 031–665 6597

EDINBURGH AND SCOTLAND INFORMATION CENTRE
3 Princes Street, Edinburgh
EH2 2QP
Tel. 031–557 1700

FORT WILLIAM AND LOCHABER TOURIST BOARD
Cameron Centre, Cameron Square, Fort William, Inverness-shire PH33 6AJ
Tel. Fort William (0397) 703781

FORTH VALLEY TOURIST BOARD
Burgh Halls, The Cross, Linlithgow, West Lothian
EH49 7AH
Tel. Linlithgow (0506) 844600

GORDON DISTRICT TOURIST BOARD
St Nicholas House, Broad Street, Aberdeen (0224) 632727

GREATER GLASGOW TOURIST BOARD
35 St Vincent Place, Glasgow
G1 2ER
Tel. 041–204 4400

INVERNESS, LOCH NESS AND NAIRN TOURIST BOARD
23 Church Street, Inverness
IV1 1EZ
Tel. Inverness (0463) 234353

ISLE OF ARRAN TOURIST BOARD
Information Centre, The Pier, Brodick, Isle of Arran KA27 8AU
Tel. Brodick (0770) 2140/2401

KINCARDINE AND DEESIDE TOURIST BOARD
45 Station Road, Banchory
AB3 3XX
Tel. Banchory (03302) 2066

KIRKCALDY DISTRICT COUNCIL
Information Centre, South Street, Leven, Fife KY8 4PF
Tel. Leven (0333) 429464

LOCH LOMOND, STIRLING AND TROSSACHS TOURIST BOARD
41 Dumbarton Road, Stirling
FK8 2QQ
Tel. Stirling (0786) 75019

MID ARGYLL, KINTYRE AND ISLAY TOURIST BOARD
The Pier, Campbeltown, Argyll
PA28 6EF
Tel. Campbeltown (0586) 52056

MORAY DISTRICT COUNCIL
Chief Tourist Officer, 17 High
Street, Elgin, Morayshire
IV30 1EG
Tel. Elgin (0343) 543388

**OBAN, MULL AND
DISTRICT TOURIST BOARD**
Boswell House, Argyll Square,
Oban, Argyll PA34 4AN
Tel. Oban (0631) 63122/63557

ORKNEY TOURIST BOARD
Information Centre, Broad Street,
Kirkwall, Orkney KW15 1NX
Tel. Kirkwall (0856) 2856

**PERTHSHIRE TOURIST
BOARD**
45 High Street, Perth PH1 5TJ.
Tel. Perth (0738) 38353.

**ROSS AND CROMARTY
TOURIST BOARD**
Information Centre, North
Kessock, Black Isle, Ross-shire
IV1 1XB
Tel. Kessock (0463) 73505

**ROTHESAY AND ISLE OF
BUTE TOURIST BOARD**
15 Victoria Street, Rothesay, Isle
of Bute PA20 0AJ
Tel. Rothesay (0700) 502151

**ST ANDREWS AND NORTH-
EAST FIFE TOURIST BOARD**
78 South Street, St Andrews, Fife
KY16 9JX
Tel. St Andrews (0334) 72021

**SCOTTISH BORDERS
TOURIST BOARD**
70, High Street, Selkirk TD7 4DD
Tel. Selkirk (0750) 20555

**SHETLAND TOURIST
ORGANIZATION**
Information Centre, Market Cross,
Lerwick, Shetland ZE1 0LU
Tel. Lerwick (0595) 3434

**SOUTH-WEST ROSS AND
THE ISLE OF SKYE
TOURIST BOARD**
Tourist Information Centre,
Portree, Isle of Skye IV51 9BZ
Tel. Portree (0478) 2137

**SUTHERLAND TOURIST
BOARD**
The Square, Dornoch, Sutherland
IV25 3SD
Tel. Dornoch (0862) 810400

**WESTERN ISLES TOURIST
BOARD**
4 South Beach Street, Stornoway,
Isle of Lewis PA87 2XY
Tel. Stornoway (0851) 703088

Information Offices

CITY OF ABERDEEN
St Nicholas House, Broad Street,
Aberdeen AB9 1DE
Tel. Aberdeen (0224) 632727

ABERFELDY
Aberfeldy and District Tourist
Association, The Square,
Aberfeldy PH15 2DA
Tel. Aberfeldy (0887) 320276

ABERFOYLE
Information Centre, Main Street
Tel. Aberfoyle (08772) 352

ABINGTON
'Little Chef' (A74 Northbound)
Tel. Crawford (08642) 436

ABOYNE
Information Caravan, Ballater
Road Car Park
Tel. Aboyne (0339) 86060

ALFORD
Information Centre, Railway
Museum, Station Yard
Tel. Alford (09755) 62052

ANGUS
Tourist Information Centre,
Market Place, Arbroath DD11
1HR
Tel. Arbroath (0241) 72609

ANSTRUTHER
East Neuk Information Centre,
Scottish Fisheries Museum
Tel. Anstruther (0333) 311073

AUCHTERARDER
Auchterarder and District Tourist
Association, 90 High Street,
Auchterarder PH3 1BJ
Tel. Auchterarder (0764) 63450

AVIEMORE AND SPEY VALLEY
Grampian Road, Aviemore
Tel. Aviemore (0479) 810363
(24-hour service)

AYRSHIRE & BURNS COUNTRY
Tourist Information Centre, 39
Sandgate, Ayr KA7 1BG
Tel. Ayr (0292) 284196

AYRSHIRE VALLEYS
62 Bank Street, Kilmarnock,
Ayrshire KA1 1ER
Tel. Kilmarnock (0563) 39090

BALLACHULISH
Tourist Office.
Tel. Ballachulish (08552) 296

BALLATER
Information Centre, Station
Square
Tel. Ballater (03397) 55306

BALLOCH
Information Centre, Balloch Road
Tel. Alexandria (0389) 53533

BANCHORY
Information Centre, Dee Street
Car Park
Tel. Banchory (03302) 2000

BANFF & BUCHAN
Collie Lodge, Banff AB4 1AU
Tel. Banff (0261) 812419

BANNOCKBURN
Motorway Services Area, by
Stirling
Tel. Bannockburn (0786) 814111

BETTYHILL
Information Centre
Tel. Bettyhill (06412) 342

BIGGAR
Biggar TIC, High Street, Biggar
Tel. (0899) 21066

BLAIRGOWRIE
Blairgowrie and District Tourist
Association, Wellmeadow
Tel. Blairgowrie (0250) 2960

BOAT OF GARTEN
Boat Hotel Car Park
Tel. Boat of Garten (047983) 307

BONAR BRIDGE
Information Centre
Tel. Sutherland (08632) 333

BOTHWELL
Bothwell TIC, Road Chef Service
Area, M74 Southbound, Bothwell
Tel. (0698) 854538

BOWMORE, ISLE OF ISLAY
Information Centre
Tel. (049681) 254

BRAEMAR
Information Centre, The Mews,
Mar Road
Tel. Braemar (03397) 41600

BRECHIN
Angus Tourist Board, Information
Centre, St Ninian's Place
Tel. Brechin (0356) 623050

BROADFORD, ISLE OF SKYE
The Isle of Skye and South-west
Ross Tourist Board
Tel. Broadford (04712) 361/463

BUCKIE
Cluny Square
Tel. (0542) 34853

BURNTISLAND
4 Kirkgate
Tel. Burntisland (0592) 872667

CAITHNESS
Tourist Office, Whitechapel Road,
Wick, Caithness
Tel. Wick (0955) 2596

CALLANDER
Rob Roy and Trossachs Visitor
Centre, Ancaster Square
Tel. Callander (0877) 30342

CARNOUSTIE
Angus Tourist Board, Information
Centre, 24 High Street
Tel. Carnoustie (0241) 52258

CARRBRIDGE
Information Centre, Main Street
Inverness-shire
Tel. (0479) 84630

**CASTLEBAY, ISLE OF
BARRA**
Information Centre
Tel. Castlebay (08714) 336

CASTLE DOUGLAS
Information Centre, Markethill
Car Park
Tel. Castle Douglas (0556) 2611

CLYDE VALLEY
Horsemarket, Ladyacre Road,
Lanark ML11 7JT
Tel. Lanark (0555) 61661

COLDSTREAM
Henderson Park
Tel. Coldstream (0890) 2607

CRIEFF
Town Hall, High Street
Tel. Crieff (0764) 2578

CULLEN
Information Centre, 20 Seafield
Street
Tel. Cullen (0542) 40757

CULZEAN CASTLE
Tel. Kirkoswald (06556) 293

CUMNOCK
Tourist Information Centre,
Glaisnock Street
Tel. Cumnock (0290) 23058

CUNNINGHAME
Tourist Information Centre, The
Promenade, Largs KA30 8BG
Tel. Largs (0475) 673765

CUPAR
Information Centre, Fluthers Car
Park
Tel. Cupar (0334) 52874

DALBEATTIE
Information Centre, Town Hall
Tel. Dalbeattie (0556) 610117

DALMELLINGTON
Tourist Information Centre
Tel. Dalmellington (0292) 550115

DAVIOT WOOD
Daviot Wood Information Centre
A9 by Inverness
Tel. Daviot (0463) 772203

DUFFTOWN
Information Centre, The Clock
Tower, The Square
Tel. Dufftown (0340) 20501

DUNBLANE
Tourist Information Centre,
Stirling Road
Tel. Dunblane (0786) 824428

CITY OF DUNDEE
4 City Square, Dundee, DD1 3BA
Tel. Dundee (0382) 23141

DUNFERMLINE
Abbot House, Maygate
Tel. (0383) 720999

DUNKELD
Dunkeld and Birnam Tourist
Association, The Cross
Tel. Dunkeld (0350) 2688

DUNOON
Tourist Information Centre,
7 Alexandra Parade,
Argyll
Tel. Dunoon (0369) 3785
(24-hour service)

DURNESS
Information Centre, Sango,
Sutherland
Tel. (0971) 511259

EAST LOTHIAN
Tourist Information Centre, Town
House, Dunbar
Tel. Dunbar (0368) 63353

EDINBURGH
Edinburgh and Scotland
Information Centre, 3 Princes St
Tel. Edinburgh (031) 557 1700

EDINBURGH AIRPORT
City of Edinburgh Tourist
Information and Accommodation
Service
Tel. Edinburgh (031) 333 2167

ELLON
Information Caravan, Market
Street Car Park
Tel. Ellon (0358) 20730

EYEMOUTH
Auld Kirk
Tel. Eyemouth (08907) 50678

FALKIRK
Information Centre, The Steeple,
High Street
Tel. Falkirk (0324) 20244

FORFAR
The Library, West High Street
Tel. Forfar (0307) 67876

FORRES
Information Centre, Falconer
Museum, Tolbooth Street
Tel. Forres (0309) 72938

FORT AUGUSTUS
Information Centre, Car Park
Tel. Fort Augustus (0320) 6367

**FORT WILLIAM &
LOCHABER**
Cameron Centre, Cameron
Square, Fort William PH33 6AJ
Tel. Fort William (0397) 703781
(24-hour service)

FORTH ROAD BRIDGE
Forth Road Bridge TIC,
St. Margaret's Head, North
Queensferry
Tel. (0383) 417759

FORTH VALLEY
Burgh Halls, The Cross,
Linlithgow, West Lothian
EH49 7AH
Tel. Linlithgow (0506) 844600

FRASERBURGH
Information Centre, Saltoun
Square
Tel. Fraserburgh (0346) 28315

GALASHIELS
Bank Street
Tel. Galashiels (0896) 55551

GATEHOUSE OF FLEET
Information Centre, Car Park
Tel. Gatehouse of Fleet (0557)
814212

GIRVAN
Information Centre, Bridge Street
Tel. Girvan (0465) 4950

GLASGOW AIRPORT
Inchinnan Road, Paisley
Tel. 041 848 4440

GLENROTHES
Tourist Information Centre, Lyon
Square, Kingdom Centre
Tel. Glenrothes (0592) 754954

GLENSHEE
Information Officer, Glenshee
Tourist Association,
Corsehill, Upper Allan Street,
Blairgowrie
Tel. Blairgowrie (0250) 5509

GOUROCK
Information Centre, Pierhead
Tel. Gourock (0475) 39467

GRANTOWN-ON-SPEY
Information Centre, 54 High
Street
Tel. Grantown-on-Spey (0479)
2773

GREATER GLASGOW
35–39 St Vincent Place, Glasgow
G1
Tel. Glasgow (041) 204 4400

GREENOCK
Information Centre, Municipal
Buildings, 23 Clyde Street
Tel. Greenock (0475) 24400

GRETNA GREEN
Information Centre, Old
Blacksmith's Shop
Tel. Gretna (0461) 37834

HAMILTON
Hamilton TIC, Road Chef Service
Area, M74 Northbound,
Hamilton
Tel. (0698) 285590

HAWICK
Common Haugh
Tel. Hawick (0450) 72547

HELENSBURGH
Tourist Information Centre, The
Clock Tower, The Pier
Tel. Helensburgh (0436) 72642

HELMSDALE
Information Centre
Tel. Helmsdale (04312) 640

HUNTLY
Information Centre, The Square
Tel. Huntly (0466) 792255

INVERARAY
Information Centre
Tel. Inveraray (0499) 2063

**INVERNESS, LOCH NESS &
NAIRN**
23 Church Street, Inverness IV1
1EZ
Tel. Inverness (0463) 234353 (24-
hour service)

INVERURIE
Information Centre, Town Hall,
Market Place
Tel. Inverurie (0467) 20600

ISLE OF ARRAN
Tourist Information Centre,
Brodick Pier, Brodick, Isle of
Arran
Tel. Brodick (0770) 2140/2401

**ISLE OF SKYE & SOUTH-
WEST ROSS**
Tourist Information Centre,
Portree, Isle of Skye IV51 9BZ
Tel. Portree (0478) 2137

JEDBURGH
Information Centre, Murray's
Green
Tel. Jedburgh (0835) 63435/63688

JOHN O' GROATS
Information Centre
Tel. John o' Groats (095581) 373

KEITH
Information Centre, Church Road
Tel. (05422) 2634

KELSO
Turret House
Tel. Kelso (0573) 23464

KILLIN
Tourist Information Centre, Main
Street
Tel. Killin (05672) 254

KINCARDINE & DEESIDE
45 Station Road, Banchory AB3
3XX
Tel. Banchory (03302) 2066

KINCARDINE BRIDGE
Kincardine Bridge TIC,
Pine 'n' Oak,
Kincardine Bridge Road, Airth,
by Falkirk, Stirlingshire
Tel. (032483) 422

KINGUSSIE
Information Centre, King Street
Tel. Kingussie (0540) 661297

KINROSS
Kinross-shire Tourist Association,
Information Centre,
Kinross Service Area, off Junction
6, M90
Tel. Kinross (0577) 63680 (62585
when closed)

KIRKCALDY
Information Centre,
Whytecauseway
Tel. Kirkcaldy (0592) 267775

KIRKCALDY
Tourist Information Centre, South
Street, Leven KY8 4PF
Tel. Leven (0333) 29464

KIRKCUDBRIGHT
Information Centre, Harbour
Square
Tel. Kirkcudbright (0557) 30494

KIRRIEMUIR
Angus Tourist Board, Information
Centre, 17 High Street
Tel. Kirriemuir (0575) 74097

KYLE OF LOCHALSH
The Isle of Skye and South-west
Ross Tourist Board
Tel. Kyle (0599) 4276

LANARK
Lanark TIC, Horsemarket,
Ladyacre Road, Lanark
Tel. (0555) 61661

LANGHOLM
High Street
Tel. Langholm (03873) 80976

LARGS
Information Centre, Promenade
KA30 8BG
Tel. Largs (0475) 673765

LESMAHAGOW
Lesmahagow TIC, Resource
Centre, New Tows Road,
Lesmahagow
Tel. (0555) 894449

**LOCHBOISDALE, ISLE OF
SOUTH UIST**
Information Centre
Tel. Lochboisdale (08784) 286

LOCHGILPHEAD
Information Centre, Lochnell
Street, Argyll
Tel. (0546) 602344

LOCHINVER
Information Centre
Tel. Lochinver (05714) 330

LOCH LOMOND, STIRLING & TROSSACHS
PO Box 30, Stirling
Tel. Stirling (0786) 75019 (24-hour service)

LOCHMADDY, ISLE OF NORTH UIST
Information Centre
Tel. Lochmaddy (08763) 321

MALLAIG
Information Centre
Tel. Mallaig (0687) 2170

MAUCHLINE
Information/Interpretive Centre, National Burns Memorial Tower, Kilmarnock Road
Tel. Mauchline (0290) 51916

MELROSE
Priorwood Gardens, near Abbey
Tel. Melrose (089682) 2555

MID ARGYLL, KINTYRE & ISLAY
Area Tourist Office, The Pier, Campbeltown, Argyll PA28 6EF
Tel. Campbeltown (0586) 52056

MILLPORT
Information Centre, Stuart Street
Tel. Millport (0475) 530753

MOFFAT
Information Centre, Church Gate
Tel. Moffat (0683) 20620

MONTROSE
Angus Tourist Board, Information Centre, 212 High Street
Tel. Montrose (0674) 72000

MORAY
17A High Street, Elgin, Moray
IV30 1EG
Tel. Elgin (0343) 542666/543388

MOTHERWELL
Motherwell TIC, Motherwell Library, Hamilton Road, Motherwell
Tel. (0698) 51311

MUSSELBURGH
Brunton Hall, East Lothian
Tel. 031–655 6597

NAIRN
Information Centre, 62 King Street
Tel. Nairn (0667) 52753

NEWTON STEWART
Information Centre, Dashwood Square
Tel. Newton Stewart (0671) 2431

NEWTONMORE
Information Centre, Main Street
Tel. Newtonmore (05403) 274

NORTH BERWICK
Information Centre, Quality Street
Tel. North Berwick (0620) 2197

NORTH KESSOCK
Ross & Cromarty Tourist Board, Tourist Office, North Kessock
IV1 1XB
Tel. Kessock (0463) 73505

OBAN, MULL & DISTRICT
Boswell House, Argyll Square, Oban, Argyll
Tel. Oban (0631) 63122

ORKNEY
Information Centre, Broad Street,
Kirkwall, Orkney KW15 1DH
Tel. Kirkwall (0856) 2856

OUTER HEBRIDES
4 South Beach Street, Stornoway,
Isle of Lewis PA87 2XY
Tel. Stornoway (0851) 703088

PAISLEY
Town Hall, Abbey Close
Tel. 041–889 0711

PEEBLES
Chambers Institute, High Street
Tel. Peebles (0721) 20138

PENCRAIG
A1, East Linton
Tel. Pencraig (0620) 860063

PENICUIK
The Library, 3 Bellman's Road
Tel. (0968) 613286

PERTH
Perth Tourist Association,
45 High Street
Tel. Perth (0738) 38353

PETERHEAD
Information Centre, 54 Broad
Street
Tel. Peterhead (0779) 71904

PITLOCHRY
Pitlochry and District Tourist
Association, 22 Atholl Road
Tel. Pitlochry (0796)
422215/472751

PRESTWICK
Information Centre, Boydfield
Gardens
Tel. Prestwick (0292) 79946

PRESTWICK AIRPORT
British Airports Authority,
Information Desk
Tel. Prestwick (0292) 79822

RALIA
Near Newtonmore
Tel. Newtonmore (0540) 673253

ROSS & CROMARTY
Tourist Information Centre,
Gairloch, Ross-shire IV21 2DN
Tel. Gairloch (0445) 2130
(24-hour service)

**ROTHESAY AND ISLE OF
BUTE**
15 Victoria Street, Isle of Bute
Tel. Rothesay (0700) 502151
(24-hour service)

ST ANDREWS & N.E. FIFE
Information Centre, South Street,
St Andrews, Fife KY16 9JX
Tel. St Andrews (0334) 72021

SCOTTISH BORDERS
70, High Street, Selkirk
TD7 4DD
Tel. Selkirk (0750) 20555

SELKIRK
Halliwell's House
Tel. Selkirk (0750) 20054

SHETLAND
Market Cross, Lerwick, Shetland
Tel. Lerwick (0595) 3434, Telex:
75119

SHIEL BRIDGE
Information Caravan
Tel. Glenshiel (0599) 81264

SPEAN BRIDGE
Tourist Office
Tel. Spean Bridge (039781) 576.
Letters to Fort William

STIRLING
Tourist Information Centre,
Dumbarton Road
Tel. Stirling (0786) 75019

STONEHAVEN
Information Centre, 66 Allardice
Street
Tel. Stonehaven (0569) 62806

STRANRAER
Information Bureau, Port Rodie
Tel. Stranraer (0776) 2595

STRATHCATHRO
Service Area
Tel. (067484) 474

STRATHPEFFER
Ross & Cromarty Tourist Board,
Information Centre, The Square
Tel. Strathpeffer (0997) 421415

STROMNESS, ORKNEY
Information Centre, Ferry
Terminal Building, The Pier Head
Tel. Stromness (0856) 850 716

STRONTIAN
Tourist Office
Tel. Strontian (0967) 2131

SUTHERLAND
Area Tourist Office, The Square,
Dornoch IV25 3SD
Tel. Dornoch (0862) 810400

TARBERT, ISLE OF HARRIS
Information Centre
Tel. Harris (0859) 502011

TARBERT, LOCH FYNE
Information Centre
Tel. Tarbert (0880) 820429

TARBET, LOCH LOMOND
Main Street, Tarbet, Loch
Lomond
Tel. Arrochar (03012) 260

THURSO
Information Centre, Car Park,
Riverside
Tel. Thurso (0847) 62371

TILLICOULTRY
Information Centre, Clock Mill,
Upper Mill Street
Tel. Tillicoultry (0259) 52176

**TOBERMORY, ISLE OF
MULL**
Information Centre, 48 Main
Street
Tel. Tobermory (0688) 2182

TOMINTOUL
Information Centre, The Square
Tel. Tomintoul (08074) 285

TROON
Information Centre, Municipal
Buildings, South Beach
Tel. Troon (0292) 317696

TYNDRUM
Information Centre, Main Street
Tel. Tyndrum (08384) 246

ULLAPOOL
Ross & Cromarty Tourist Board,
Information Centre
Tel. Ullapool (0854) 612135

Sightseeing

There are some wonderful sights waiting to be discovered by visitors to Scotland. Historic cities such as Edinburgh or Glasgow provide plenty in the way of famous buildings and galleries to visit, while the countryside offers some beautiful, and occasionally spectacular, scenery. The bother of organizing special day trips can be avoided through one of the plenty of companies running special outings to the most popular sightseeing destinations. All-inclusive coach tours are another option which is open to holidaymakers. Usually lasting a day or a half day, these are whistle-stop trips which give you a flavour of the history and scenery of your area. Details of tours are usually prominently displayed in travel agents' windows and hotel notice boards. Car hire is another possibility for those keen to see a lot of the country. Having your own transport certainly dispenses with the problem of having to stick to the times and locations of a bus tour, and there are many enchanting villages to be discovered off the tourist track.

Museums, galleries and other places of interest are generally open from 9.30 a.m. to 5 p.m. Monday to Saturday and from 2 p.m. to 5 p.m. on Sundays. This is only a general guideline, however, and it is advisable to check these details, particularly in rural areas where there are significant seasonal variations, with many places closing down altogether during the winter months.

Shopping

Scotland has a fine range of shopping specialities. Whisky immediately springs to mind, and Scotland's off-licences have a larger selection than those in England. The bigger towns and cities usually have speciality shops selling rare and aged malts. A more lasting souvenir of your stay would be a fine tweed or woollen garment. This is a speciality of the Highlands and Islands, the central Hillfoots area, and also the Borders, where many of the mills have visitor facilities, usually including a shop selling items manufactured on the site. It is of course easy to find tweed and woollen shops all over Scotland and in all the major tourist centres you'll be spoiled for choice. A number of large general department stores, like Frasers or Edinburgh's Jenners (the Scottish equivalent to London's Harrods) have extensive tweed and woollen departments. Cashmeres, lambswools and Shetlands, in order of price, are the most sought after. Edinburgh Woollen Mill's products are well priced and have outlets throughout the country; Scotch House is a higher quality alternative. Scottish glasswear is famous the world over, particularly that which is produced by Penicuik-based Edinburgh Crystal, and Caithness Glass which has factories in Perth, Oban and Wick. Tours on site, with factory shops for purchases, make these popular tourist attractions. The range of Caithness Glass available here is more comprehensive than that found elsewhere in the UK. Scottish smoked salmon is a famed delicacy throughout the world. For music lovers, general and specialist record shops stock wide ranges of cassettes and LPs of folk and traditional Scots music. As for Celtic jewellery – including clan crest badges and buckles, traditional luckenbooths, beautifully designed bracelets, necklets and brooches – can be found in most gift shops. Art Pewter Silver is the main company producing these – Edinburgh Woollen Mill shops, among others, are stockists.

Food and Drink

A very good reason for coming to Scotland is the food. You can eat out as well in Scotland as you can anywhere else in the world and, particularly in the cities, you will find a large selection of international restaurants.

Scotland's most famous national dish is probably haggis, consisting of oatmeal, onion and suet mixed in with sheep liver, lungs and heart before being cooked in the animal's stomach (or more likely nowadays a plastic bag). The dish sounds off-putting but is, in fact, delicious. It is generally served with 'tatties and neeps' – mashed potatoes and turnip – and downed, of course, with a glass of fine Scotch whisky.

Other fine national dishes include some of Europe's finest salmon, fresh river trout, locally caught game (especially venison and pheasant) and beef. A well-cooked Aberdeen Angus fillet steak, served with a good selection of vegetables and roast potatoes, takes some beating on a dull winter's evening. Kippers (smoked herring) or Arbroath smokies (dry salted and smoked haddock) are popular, and chicken is something which you will always find on a Scottish menu.

Scotland produces a wide range of cheeses: from the Galloway cheddar in the south, to the rich orange Orkney of the north, most regions produce some variety, almost all of which are available throughout the country. They are best sampled on a Scottish oatcake. Oatcakes and cheese are a favourite embellishment to a good haggis dinner.

At breakfast, Scots porridge is worth trying, if only for the experience, but ignore the myth that it is best eaten with salt. Sugar and cream complement it far more. You may be offered black pudding with a cooked breakfast. This unusual offering is popular in the north of England; indeed, northerners frequently claim it is as much 'theirs' as it is Scottish! The big difference lies in the way it is cooked. In Scotland it is always fried, a practice most northerners consider sacrilegious since they prefer boiling it. Either way, it's a taste worth experiencing.

One of the best value ways of eating out in Scotland is to take a traditional high tea offered by tea rooms and any of the better hotels. For only a few pounds you will be served a cooked meal followed by a choice of cakes, bread and butter, jam, and traditional Scottish scones, accompanied by a generous quantity of tea. Most hotels serve afternoon tea from mid-afternoon until around 5 p.m. and high tea from 5 p.m. to 7 p.m.

A number of restaurants offer special Taste of Scotland menus consisting of traditional Scottish fare, such as salmon, trout, sea food, venison, and beef. Taste of Scotland Ltd produces an annual guide to these establishments and this is available free of charge at most Tourist Information offices, or directly from Taste of Scotland Ltd, 331 Melville Street, Edinburgh EH3 7JF (Tel. 031-220 1900).

When it comes to drinking, there is much to recommend to Scotland's visitors. Everyone is familiar with the country's most famous export, whisky, but it is not until you come to Scotland that you begin to discover the huge variety that exists within this one type of drink. Pubs and off-licences offer a far greater selection than their counterparts in England, and it is not uncommon to see more than 30 different whiskies behind the bar of Scotland's more traditional pubs. Of the two types of whisky, blended and malt, the latter is the connoisseurs' choice. Malts are usually 'single': that is, they come from the one still and, in addition to being much smoother than blended whiskies, each single malt has a character and flavour that is distinct from all others. The country's beer is no less unique than its whisky, the Scots pint of 'heavy' tending to have a sweeter taste and more body than the English bitter.

Licensing laws in Scotland are much more flexible than those in England, although the rest of the United Kingdom is now falling in line with Scotland. Public houses – pubs – have standard opening hours of 12 hours a day, but they frequently stay open longer. With very few exceptions (mainly away from Edinburgh and Glasgow) pubs will be open from 11 a.m. until 11 p.m. Those which choose shorter hours will close between 2.30 p.m. and 5 p.m., opening in time for the evening trade. Licensing hours on a Sunday tend to be shorter than during the rest of the week.

Most Scottish city pubs have some sort of extension to their permitted hours during the summer. This is particularly the case for the Edinburgh pubs during the hectic Festival period when some pubs open as early as 7 a.m. and others close as late as 4 a.m. next morning. Residents in licensed hotels can generally buy drinks at any time.

Nightlife

The nightlife scene in Scotland is lively and varied in the cities. As is to be expected from such a popular holiday destination, there is entertainment to suit everyone: for the young ones there are assorted styles of nightclubs and live bands playing the latest sounds; for older couples, large hotels often host cabaret and old-time dance nights. Other entertainments on offer include ceilidhs (see The Socialite on pages 25 and 26), live folk music, and jazz in bars and restaurants. Obviously the larger the town, the better the range of nightclubs and eating places to choose from. However, it is not impossible to combine the quiet pleasures of a small resort with the night-time buzz of a larger place.

Moving Around the Country

There are a number of ways to move about the country. Train, local bus services, coach tours and car hire are all possible modes of travel for those who want to see a bit more of Scotland. Visit a travel agent for details of coach tours, or, as an alternative, local buses are a good way to travel. Go to the town's bus station for information.

The train network covers the central belt, the east coast, and the south-west of the country extensively. In other places the network is thin to non-existent and services are infrequent.

Car hire is another option. Roads in the Highlands are often narrow and winding, but the restrictions they impose on the speed at which you can travel are more than compensated for by the magnificent scenery.

CAR HIRE

There are many local and national car hire firms in Scotland, and this method of transport allows you the greatest freedom to see the country. Scottish roads are generally in good repair, but are known to narrow or twist alarmingly in rural areas. Car hire facilities are available at all airports and main railway stations and for any number of days. A basic requirement for all car hirers is that you are over 21 years of age and have held a valid full driving licence for at least a year. There is a good choice of car rental companies. All of the major ones have offices throughout Scotland and can usually offer a deal whereby you collect the car in one town and leave it in another. Otherwise it is a good idea to consult the car hire section of the Yellow Pages for local firms, who often offer more competitive rates. Obviously the rates and services available differ from firm to firm, but usually you should expect to get unlimited mileage, third-party insurance and an emergency breakdown service.

TRAINS

There is a special charm about rail travel in Scotland, and as a mode of transport it is definitely the most relaxing. All the main towns and cities are connected by rail until you reach the sparsely populated central Highlands. Edinburgh and Glasgow are the main InterCity hubs for Scotland and the rest of the UK.

Some journeys are worth making for their scenic value alone. Oban-Glasgow, Edinburgh-Aberdeen and the Kyle Line, which crosses Scotland from Inverness to the Kyle of Lochalsh, all provide passengers with fascinating and breathtaking views. Perhaps the most famous, and the most beautiful, journey of all is the five-hour West Highland Line from Glasgow up to Mallaig which passes some of the most stunning mountains, glens and lochs in Scotland, also passing within sight of the country's highest peak, Ben Nevis near Fort William. For the rail enthusiast Scotrail regularly operate a special steam service on this line during the summer months (for which the timetable is available from all main British Rail stations).

If you plan to see a great deal of Scotland by rail it is worth investing in a Freedom of Scotland pass. For around £64 you are allowed unlimited rail travel anywhere in Scotland for seven days. For another £33 you can extend your period of unlimited travel by a further seven days. Also available are rover tickets, which follow more specific routes for a variety of prices. For example, you can travel with the West Highland Rover from £32 for a period of seven days, or a Festival Cities Rover from £16.50 for three days, a Heart of Scotland Rover from £37 and a North Highland Rover from £35, both tickets allowing for seven days of travel. With a Scotrail ticket you are also entitled to many discounts for various attractions throughout the country. More details can be found in Scotrail's free tourist magazine, *Scene 93*, from most British Rail stations.

InterCity trains tend to get very crowded during the summer months, and it is advisable to book a seat in advance.

BUSES

Although understandably less frequent in rural areas, even the smallest village has a bus service or at least a post bus connecting it to the nearest town. Prices and frequency of services vary wildly according to which part of the country you are in, but the cities invariably fare better on both counts than the rural areas. On the islands, the post buses are the mainstay for transport, alternatives can be frustratingly infrequent, and nothing runs on Sundays. On Sundays and bank holidays, even in the cities, there is a restricted service. Details about the bus service for each area may be obtained from local bus stations or tourist offices.

Luxury coach services operate between the main cities – Edinburgh, Glasgow, Aberdeen, Perth, Dundee and Inverness – several times daily. Scottish Citylink is one of the best national bus services and their main enquiry number is 041–332 9644 for all Scottish services. Another alternative is the Caledonian/National Express network, which offers connections through all the major cities, with onward connections to major English towns. They can be contacted on (0738) 33481.

All major towns offer half-day and full-day coach tours; Edinburgh has some of the best day trips available via a number of companies, including Lothian Regional Transport (Tel. 031–554 4494) and Scotline Tours (Tel. 031–667 7512 or 557 0162).

TAXIS

Taxis in Scotland are no different from the rest of Britain. Extras are charged for large amounts of luggage, for trips out of town (especially to airports) and for late-night journeys. In the larger towns and cities there are fleets of black, metered cabs (as in London) which can be hailed in the street. Elsewhere, taxis take the form of ordinary saloon cars which have to be booked over the phone or hired from a taxi rank.

FERRIES

Scotland's many islands are easily accessible thanks to the frequent ferry services linking them to the mainland and to each other. By far the most widespread ferry operator is Caledonian MacBrayne (head office: The Ferry Terminal, Gourock, Tel. 0475 33755) which runs services connecting all of the Western Isles with each other and the mainland. Additional services in the Firth of Clyde are provided by Western Ferries (16 Woodside Crescent, Glasgow G3 7UT, Tel. 041–332 9766).

There is a choice of companies plying different routes between Orkney and Caithness. Thomas and Bews Ferries run a car-ferry service, making the 45-minute crossing several times a day from Gills Bay, near John o' Groats, to Burwick on the island of South Ronaldsay (Thomas and Bews Ferries, Tel. 095581 342/353). For foot passengers there is a connecting bus service to the Orcadian capital of Kirkwall on Mainland. P&O Ferries run a car ferry once a day between Scrabster, near Thurso, and Stromness on the Orkney Mainland. The crossing takes about two hours. There is also a twice-weekly car ferry between Aberdeen and Stromness, which takes about eight hours (P&O Ferries: Stromness: Tel. 0856 850655; Aberdeen: Tel. 0224 572615). Travel between the different Orcadian islands is provided by the Orkney Islands Shipping Company, Kirkwall (Tel. 0856 2044). The only car-ferry operator to Shetland is P&O Ferries, sailing from Stromness (an eight-hour journey, made once a week) and Aberdeen (14 hours, daily Monday to Friday) to Lerwick on the Shetland Mainland.

Communications

POST OFFICES

Post offices are open from 9 a.m. to 5.30 p.m. Monday to Friday, and from 9 a.m. to 1 p.m. on Saturday. Sub post offices close for lunch, usually 1 p.m. to 2 p.m., and on Wednesday afternoons. Even the smallest village in Scotland has a post office, often no more than a counter at the back of a small general store in the more rural areas. From any post office, mail can be sent all over the world. Airmail letters generally take up to a week to reach their destination – postcards slightly longer.

TELEPHONES

Telephoning almost anywhere in the world is possible by International Direct Dialling from most telephones and call boxes. The traditional red phone boxes are gradually being replaced by the less attractive, but more functional, smoked-glass units. The minimum call charge is 10p. The old dial-telephones have been almost completely replaced now with smart push-button machines which take all UK coins except 1p pieces. There are also a large number of Telecom Phonecard telephone boxes which take, not coins, but prepaid cards. The Mercury System of blue and silver telephones are now appearing in most cities and towns around Scotland and work on the same principle with phone cards. Both types are available from post offices, in denominations from £2 to £20. Less common, though found in the larger cities, are phones which take ordinary credit cards.

All calls to the operator are free of charge. Dial 100 for operator-assisted dialling; 192 for UK directory enquiries; 153 for international directory enquiries; and 155 for the international operator. For emergency fire, police or ambulance services dial 999.

Problems and Emergencies

MEDICAL

If it is a minor problem, head for a chemist. Most towns have at least one late-night chemist. If it is more serious, you are entitled to visit an NHS doctor free of charge if you are a UK citizen or an EC resident holding an E111 form. For names and addresses of local doctors check the Yellow Pages or ask in your hotel.

POLICE

The police must be contacted if any of your belongings have been stolen. Insist on a copy of your statement – insurance companies often require this as proof of theft before they will reimburse you. Telephone 999 in emergencies.

A Potted History of Scotland

The history of Scotland is one of the most colourful, bloody and fascinating of any country in the world. Scotland is an old country. Indeed, some of the rocks found in the north-west Highlands are among the oldest in the world, dating back well in excess of 1,200 million years. Despite being a small nation on the edge of Europe, the Scots have contributed a disproportionately large amount to the world through a distinctive culture, and in the fields of engineering, science, philosophy and medicine. With the great emigrations of the 18th, 19th and 20th centuries, Scots have scattered themselves throughout the world. Who are these people, and what is their history and background?

The first permanent settlers in Scotland were nomadic Celts from central Europe and western Asia, who arrived towards the end of the Stone Age in 5–6,000 BC. Evidence of these early prehistoric settlers abounds in Scotland, notably at the archaeological site of Skara Brae in Orkney.

The first written mention of Scotland's history dates from Roman times. In AD 79 the Roman historian Tacitus recalls Agricola making the first push north into the Southern Uplands, from England, in an attempt to extend the Roman Empire to the westernmost shores of Europe. Agricola was largely successful in southern Scotland, but met with fierce resistance further north from natives whom he termed '*picti*', meaning 'painted ones', whence comes the term 'Pict'.

The Picts proved strong adversaries for the Romans, who were forced to retreat south after heavy losses. In AD 121 the Emperor Hadrian built his famous wall from the Solway Firth across to the Tyne, in order to prevent the Picts from advancing south. By the fifth century AD the Romans were retreating from England, and the Picts found themselves overrun by a new invader, the Irish Celts calling themselves Scots, who were eventually to dominate the small nation, known as Alba at this time.

The most significant event in Scotland during the Dark Ages was the coming of Christianity in AD 397. St Ninian founded the first

Christian Church at Whithorn, in Galloway. During this time he lived in a small cave which can still be seen today and in which excavation work is currently being carried out. In 563 Columba, an Irish prince, founded a Christian community on the island of Iona, from where he wandered throughout Scotland, spreading the message of Christianity. So effective was he in disseminating his message, such was his indefatigable faith and eloquence in transmitting the word of God, that by the end of the following century the country was converted.

In the ninth century, Scotland, in common with the rest of western Europe, was frequently pillaged by Viking invaders. However, Kenneth MacAlpine forged a union between the Scots and Picts in 843 to establish the first recognizable Scottish kingdom, uniting its people in a common culture and purpose. What minor dissent he met with from small bands of recalcitrant Picts was quickly and ruthlessly dealt with. Consolidation of this national identity was the chief characteristic of the 10th century. Almost inevitably, however, this spirit of co-operation gave way to instability and squabbling in the 11th century as claims and counter claims over the right of succession to the throne came to the fore. One of the successful challengers, Mac Beathad mac Finnlaich from Moray, ruled successfully from 1040 to 1057. Better known under the anglicized form of his name, Macbeth's reign and character were more stable than Shakespeare would have us believe.

The anglification of the Celtic Church during the reign of Malcolm Canmore (1057–93) was chiefly instigated by his second wife, the English Queen Margaret. She brought in an English clergy and court, and 'civilized' Scotland, turning it into a kingdom akin to that in Norman England.

With the accession of David I (1124–53), the monarchy gained direct control over the whole of the country more or less as we know it, with the exception of the Western Isles, Orkney and Shetland. The system of central government was strengthened when David established the feudal system, introduced a Scottish currency, and simplified the system of succession whereby the crown was passed down from father to son. By the time of his death, David I had extended his rule to include Northumbria and

Cumbria, but these territorial gains in northern England were later squandered by his grandson and heir, Malcolm IV (1153–65). Malcolm's brother and successor, William the Lion (1165–1214) spent most of his reign trying to regain Northumberland. He not only failed to do so but was captured in the process, and, as a condition of his release, was forced by Henry II of England to acknowledge the kingdom of Scotland as a heritable grant from England. Although William was able to buy back his submission on Henry's death in 1189, the idea that the English monarch was the natural overlord of Scotland took root in English minds. However, no one attempted to act on this belief as vigorously as Edward I.

It was during the reign of England's Edward I, 'Hammer of the Scots', which began in 1272, that Scotland's history entered its most turbulent period. The Plantagenet King was determined to extend his sovereignty throughout the whole of Britain. Edward I's initial successes in subjugating southern Scotland almost led to total English victory, but the heroic efforts of two men in particular ensured the preservation of Scotland's independence. William Wallace led the Scottish army in a rout of Edward's troops at the Battle of Stirling Bridge in 1297, but it was Robert the Bruce, crowned King of Scotland in 1306, who conclusively saw off the English threat in Scotland's most famous victory at Bannockburn in 1314. For the next two centuries there continued to be an uneasy co-existence between Scotland and England. The romantic, though ultimately tragic, Stuart family came to the throne in 1371 in the person of Robert II. From this point (until the abdication of Mary Queen of Scots) Scotland's history was characterized by war with England and frequent opposition to the monarchy from the country's nobles.

The next four kings were all ill-fated and Scotland underwent a very black period: Robert II was succeeded by Robert III, a sickly man who abdicated in 1399 leaving the country in the hands of scheming regents for 25 years. James I took the throne in 1424. A clever and skilful king, he took steps to curtail the powers of the plotting nobles (the execution *en masse* of the Albany family was his first act of power), and he likewise subdued the Highland chiefs and Lowland earls. Killed by enemies in 1437, his six-year-old son,

James II, was next in line. He took the throne in 1449, aged 19. During his 11-year reign he quashed the powerful Douglas family, but his good work stopped when he was killed in 1460 by a cannon which exploded at the siege of Roxburgh. James III, then nine years old, had to wait a decade to take the crown. He married the King of Denmark's daughter Margaret, and by her dowry Scotland gained the territories of Orkney and Shetland. The intellectual James III was not liked by his nobles, who in retaliation proclaimed his son James IV king in his place. James III tried to regain power in the Battle of Sauchieburn in 1488, but was killed there.

James IV, the most popular of the Stuarts, was a fervent supporter of the alliance with France, and aided that country in its war with England. The Scottish forces, however, were ill-prepared, and the fighting culminated in their disastrous defeat at Flodden in 1513. The French alliance proved to be the downfall of the next king of Scotland, James V. His nobles resented the French influence and failed to support him when Scotland was invaded by Henry VIII. He fell in battle at Solway Moss in 1542 and subsequently died of his wounds, leaving as an heir his six-day-old daughter Mary.

The Scots' refusal to ratify the marriage between the infant Mary and Henry VIII's son, Edward, engendered the attacks of 1544–5 on southern Scotland known as the 'Rough Wooing'. When the English won the Battle of Pinkie in 1547, Mary was sent to France, where she married the French heir, the Dauphin.

Following the death of her French husband, Mary returned to Scotland after 13 years in France and married her cousin Lord Darnley, in 1565. The marriage lasted for only two troubled years, in which time Darnley arranged the murder of Mary's secretary, the Italian Rizzio, on suspicion that the two were lovers. Darnley himself was murdered 12 months later in 1567.

Mary was publicly humiliated, forced to abdicate in favour of her infant son, James VI, and eventually fled to England fearful of her own life. Her English cousin, the Protestant Elizabeth I, immediately imprisoned her and, 20 years later, had her beheaded upon the suspicion that Mary was plotting against the English queen's life. The two queens, despite the many myths which have grown up since, never met.

Ironically, when Elizabeth died childless in 1603 her heir was Mary's son James VI of Scotland, who became the first monarch to unite the crowns of England and Scotland. England, however, was clearly the dominant partner, and the decline of Scotland as a sovereign state can be traced to the move by James and his courtiers from the Royal Court in Edinburgh in favour of that in London. James VI's grandson, Charles II, tried to force Episcopacy upon the Presbyterian Scots and met with fierce resistance. His brother, James VII of Scotland and II of England, was deposed for his Catholic faith after just three years.

The Highland clans had never acquiesced to any monarch, and many were decidedly reluctant to take the oath of allegiance to James's successor, William of Orange. William was brutally insistent in enforcing his authority. Although he later denied any knowledge of the slaughter, William was behind the decision in February 1692 to proceed with the exemplary show of strength that became known as the Glencoe massacre. It was a particularly ruthless deed, involving the wanton and indiscriminate slaughter of the men, women, and children of the MacDonald clan by the neighbouring Campbells, who were acting for the king. Furthermore it was 'murder under trust' which broke the Highland code.

Although William was warmly welcomed in England, support in Scotland for the deposed Stuart cause persisted, even after the formal union of England and Scotland in 1707 by an Act of Parliament. Following the 1689 Battle of Killiecrankie and a failed rebellion in 1715, the Jacobite Rebellion of 1745–6 led by Charles Edward Stuart (popularly known as Bonnie Prince Charlie) to install his father on the throne enjoyed moments of heady success but ended in the national tragedy of the Battle of Culloden, where the Jacobite forces were slaughtered by the Government's armies.

Defeat at Culloden brought to an end, not only the hopes of the House of Stuart, but also the very way of life of the Highland communities. The English found many allies among the Lowland Scots who were hostile to their Highland countrymen, and together they enforced George II's Act of Proscription in 1747. The Act formally banned the wearing of the kilt, or any other show of old clan colours, and outlawed the bearing of arms and playing the bagpipes. The remaining Jacobites who had survived the Culloden massacre were rounded up and imprisoned. Most were either transported or executed. On the heels of this came the more odious and destructive Highland Clearances, involving the wholesale eviction of Highlanders from their crofts in order that the landowners could let the land more profitably to Lowland sheepfarmers.

In Edinburgh the 18th century was a Golden Age – an exciting time when the arts and sciences flourished. From 1752 the city expanded northward with the construction of the Georgian New Town, turning Edinburgh into one of the most elegant cities in Europe. The presence in Scotland's capital of intellectual luminaries such as David Hume, Adam Smith, Tobias Smollett and Oliver Goldsmith, made Edinburgh an important centre in the period known as the 'Scottish Enlightenment', when an enthusiasm for learning swept through Europe. They were followed in the 19th century by distinguished literary figures such as Sir Walter Scott and Robert Louis Stevenson, and medical pioneers Lister (who performed groundbreaking research into antiseptics) and Simpson (whose work on anaesthetics led him to the discovery of chloroform). The work of these men, and others, established the reputation that Edinburgh still enjoys of being at the forefront of medical science. Certain practitioners, however, also encouraged the less salubrious activities of grave robbers Burke and Hare. They received a modest reward for the supply of corpses to Doctor Knox for medical research and, to make it easier to meet demand, they resorted to murder in order to maintain the supply!

In Glasgow, the 18th and 19th centuries were a time of dramatic change. The town which had gained prosperity through its seafaring trade with America and Europe was gripped by the industrial revolution. The shipyards, engineering works, and other heavy industries, brought hundreds of thousands of people to the city in search of work, attracting impoverished workers from rural Ireland and the Highlands of Scotland. The city's population increased in size at an alarming rate. Through the shipyards, railway works, and steelworks, Glasgow's reputation for industry earned it the nickname the 'Workshop of the World' and it became the established 'Second City of the Empire'. This period of prosperity made a mark on the city that endures to the present day:

in the grand Victorian architecture, for example, and in the industrial reputation that survives even though the industries have gone. The city is also famous for its socialist politics, a tradition that began as a result of the appalling poverty of the Victorian workers and found its voice in the early 20th century, through great orators and champions of the working people such as John McLean and James Maxton. These were the Red Clydesiders who threatened to overturn the social order in Scotland. McLean was the leading figure in the Glasgow rent strike of 1915, a protest against the increase in already exploitative housing costs, at a time when family incomes were suffering because the breadwinners were fighting on foreign soil in the First World War. The campaign was a popular one which produced mass rallies that filled the city centre.

The relationship between Scotland and England has always been an uneasy one. The concentration of power in London – as home of the Parliament and the UK broadcasting media – can tend to impose an anglocentric view on the rest of the UK, and in turn transmits this view of the UK to the rest of the world. Throughout the 20th century there have been efforts to rescind the union and re-establish Scotland as an independent nation, although it was not until 1967, when the Scottish National Party won a by-election in Hamilton, that campaigns for outright independence, and the distantly related notion of devolution within the UK, gained widespread electoral appeal. The demand for greater political autonomy reached its height in the mid-1970s, bolstered by the discovery of oil off Scotland's shores, but by the end of the decade it had receded and attention turned elsewhere. In recent years, an interest in the politics of independence has been rekindled by the growing differences in political affiliation between voters in southern England and Scotland. The policies put into force at Westminster are often perceived as being geared only to London and the south-east, and are often neither suitable nor popular in Scotland. Yet the 1992 General Election did not provide the Scottish National Party with the expected major breakthrough. In fact, the Conservative Party staged a minor recovery in terms of parliamentary seats, demonstrating that although many Scots want to retain their distinctive identity and have more say over their own affairs, they are not yet sure that independence is the way forward. The prospect of closer economic co-operation in the EC has led some to argue that the United Kingdom will become a hindrance to Scotland as the EC moves towards the semblance of a federal European union. Maintaining and strengthening identity through Europe seems a positive and challenging way for Scotland to enter the 21st century.

Be a 'Good Tourist'

Tourism is the world's largest industry and while most of us think of travel as a good thing because it gives people enjoyment, encourages understanding between races and brings in needed foreign exchange, inevitably it has its negative side too – if uncontrolled it can change the face of the natural environment and break down traditional ways of life. Although Scotland still experiences less tourism pressure than the rest of the UK, it has not escaped some of the destructive environmental impacts associated with increased tourism development, and there are areas of concern which require attention. These include:

- People pressure, specifically in the countryside, damaging footpaths and making them dangerous and inconvenient to walkers. This is especially evident around Ben Nevis and other popular mountain routes, the Cairngorm areas and parts of the West Highland Way, particularly on the east shore of Loch Lomond. Wildlife is also being disturbed and there is damage to the flora and fauna. Too many people on the same paths take away the perceptions of peace and quiet.

- Traffic congestion is a growing problem, both in Scotland's urban and rural areas, particularly in high season on specific stretches of road, and on Scotland's often narrow country roads. Pollution and noise can ruin the appeal of an area for the host as well as the visitor.

- Visual intrusion from discarded litter can not only harm the wildlife but can, again, effect the overall appeal of the area. Unofficial camping, picnics and barbecues are often the culprits.

- With so many activities prevailing in the Scottish countryside, there naturally will exist a conflict of interests between them and a considerable pressure on the resources. These include: watersports, especially jet skiing and power boating, creating noise and pollution, disturbing not only the water wildlife but walkers, anglers and sightseers in the area. Motor sports as well as the popular addition of mountain biking can do serious damage to paths and vegetation, and create a conflict of interests with other activities. There is a problem in the Pentland Hills near Edinburgh from this kind of constant pressure.

Many of the problems created by tourism have resulted from the desire to benefit from economies of scale: quite simply, we are now paying the environmental price of holidays that were sold too cheaply to too many people. Now tourists are recognizing the damage done by this industry and, as the Costas lose their appeal, a new breed of 'traveller' is emerging – one who does not leave his conscience at home but who travels with an enlightened approach and an open mind.

So how can you be a 'good tourist in Scotland'? This brief checklist should provide a few pointers:

- Avoid the problem areas like Glencoe in high season, when footpaths are being constantly eroded by walkers. Why not explore the more hidden parts of Scotland during this time?
- With congestion such a major problem, consider travelling out of season. Even if you have to plan around school holidays, it is possible to travel in the Easter or autumn breaks.
- When arranging transport, look at what the locals do. To soak up the atmosphere without polluting it, use buses, bikes and your feet!
- Use the picnic and barbecue facilities provided in the country-side and do not leave litter behind, take it with you.
- If you buy souvenirs, support the local arts and crafts market. Be careful not to buy goods made from endangered species.
- Be sensitive with your camera. Always ask someone before you take their picture, and don't click away in places of worship. Use your camera constructively – to photograph rather than pick wild flowers, for instance.

Being a good tourist is all about leaving as little negative impact as possible and where you can, making a positive contribution to the environment and people of the place you're visiting. If you would like more information, look at my book, *The Good Tourist*.

Part Four

THE COUNTRY

The Borders

INTRODUCTION

The River Tweed dominates the Border country. On its banks stand many of the towns manufacturing the cloth of the same name. Curiously enough, Tweed cloth does not derive its name from the river, but from a misreading in London of the word 'tweel', a local variant of 'twill', which is what the cloth was called by those who wove it.

The river flows through some of the best farmland and most beautiful countryside in Britain. It has fired the poetic imagination of the anonymous Borders balladeers, and Sir Walter Scott regarded it as the most 'precious' river in the world. Anglers know it as one of the top three salmon rivers in Scotland. In the sport of rugby union, Borders teams like Gala and Melrose continue to dominate club competition year after year and consistently provide the players who form the nucleus of the national team.

This is a fascinating region where the traditional way of life has survived: ancient traditions such as the Riding of the Marches – a ritual to mark the boundaries – date back to the Middle Ages when Anglo-Scottish feuding was at its height.

HISTORY

The Borders have a battle-scarred history, dominated by relations with England. This is hardly surprising, as England features prominently in the history of Scotland as a whole, and the Borders towns have always been the first in the firing line. Many of the numerous abbeys and castles in the area owe their present state of ruin to English assault. One curious exception is (or rather was, for it leaves not even a trace today) the original Jedburgh castle which was actually destroyed by the town's own authorities. It was done, however, as a desperate means of bringing to an end its sporadic occupation by the English.

As if international relations were not producing enough strife, internal feuding added to these violent times. The Borders Reivers were local families whose pillaging terrorized the area. Their infamy has been romanticized in umpteen ballads and folk tales, but the truth is that they were ruthless, mercenary villains who would raze a village in order to steal a few sheep.

COMMUNICATIONS

The Borders are easily reached by road as several major routes between Edinburgh and the south pass through the region. From England, the A1 edges up the east coast, passing through Berwick-upon-Tweed and close to Eyemouth. The A697 and A68 are more central, while the A7 comes across from Carlisle in the west, through Teviotdale and up by the banks of the Gala Water to Edinburgh, passing on its way the towns of Hawick, Selkirk and Galashiels. At the latter it is joined by the A72 from Glasgow, which passes through Peebles on its way. There is also a good road network running laterally across the region, which all goes to make the Borders an ideal area to tour by car. If you hope to travel by train, however, you could have problems. This part of the country has been almost totally left out of the present-day rail network; the only line runs parallel with the A1 on the east coast and the only convenient station is at Berwick-upon-Tweed. There are, however, bus links to both Carlisle and Berwick.

WHERE TO GO FOR WHAT

With the Tweed acknowledged as one of the best, if not the best, salmon river in the world, anglers will obviously be attracted to the many towns and villages, like Coldstream and Kelso, scattered along its banks. Hillwalking is another excellent pastime in this unspoilt and sparsely populated region. For a serious trek, take the Southern Upland Way, or part of it, which begins on the west coast of Scotland at Portpatrick, near Stranraer, and runs north-east to Cockburnspath, mid-way between Eyemouth and Dunbar on the east coast. The coastline belonging to this region is short and mainly rugged, but there is a beach suitable for swimming at Eyemouth. A little further up the coast at St Abb's Head there is a national nature reserve of particular interest to ornithologists. The St Abb's Head sea colonies are one of Scotland's most spectacular – and most accessible – wildlife spectacles. When it comes to sport, it is rugby rather than golf which makes the region famous, although there are 17 varied golf courses in the Borders (not all of them have 18 holes, however). The dominant motif of this region is history. In addition to the ruined abbeys of Dryburgh, Jedburgh, Kelso and Melrose, the countryside is dotted with fortifications and castles, some ruined, some inhabited, which testify to the region's august and turbulent past. Follow the Scottish Borders Woollen trail. The drive through the Border countryside visits many Borders towns following the process from dyed wool to finished product. You can join the trail at any point or just visit one or two centres. An ideal place to begin is Tweedsmuir on the A701. Here you will find the **Border Collie and Shepherd Centre**, where you can view a photographic exhibition of shepherds, sheep and dogs as well as watch sheepdog handling demonstrations at certain times of the day and by arrangement. There is a tearoom and craft shop situated in an old shepherd's bothy.

Eight miles north of Berwick the A1, via the A1107 and the B6355, leads to **EYEMOUTH**. This has been a fishing village since the 12th century. In 1597 James VI declared it a free port which led to its development as a smuggling centre. This illicit business was at its peak in the 18th century and as a result many of the houses (a good example being Gunsgreen House, to the east of the harbour) from this period surmount a network of underground passages and storage chambers. In the market place is **Eyemouth Museum**, opened 100 years after the Great East Coast Fishing Disaster of 1881. On the 14th of October a storm at sea sank 23 out of the 29 boats which left the harbour with the loss of 129 lives. The central attraction of the museum is an illustrated tapestry containing the names of the men and boats which went down. There are also displays on local history, the fishing industry, and the marine wildlife of the area. The beach at Eyemouth is sandy and the town hosts angling festivals and competitions. There is a fairly good choice of accomodation, with several private houses all offering bed and breakfast at around £15 per night. Prices are not much higher at **Glenerne Hotel**, Albert Road (Tel. 08907 50401 or 50505), and **Ship Hotel**, Harbour Road (Tel. 08907 50224). **Northburn Holiday Home Park**, Fort Road (Tel. 08907 51050) is a family site overlooking Eyemouth Bay. Prices range from £6 per night for caravans and motor caravans. There are no tent facilities.

Tourist information is available at Auld Kirk, Eyemouth (Tel. 08907 50678) from April to October.

A few miles up the coast is the popular holiday resort of St Abb's with its magnificent coastline. The cliffs, 300 feet high, are an awesome sight at **ST ABB'S HEAD**, now a National Nature Reserve, very popular with walkers and birdwatchers alike. St Abb's and **Eyemouth Voluntary Marine Reserve** is also close by with guided walks through both reserves during the summer. Three miles further up the road are the ruins of **Fast Castle**, a former fortress standing half-way up the cliff. The approach road is off the A1107, just north of the village of **COLDINGHAM**, site of a ruined 11th-century priory.

If you seek accommodation in a scenic location you could try hotels at Coldingham Bay: **St Abb's Haven Hotel** (Tel. 08907–71491) and **Smugglers Hotel** (Tel. 08907 71273). Prices start at around £15 at each.

From Eyemouth it is a straight run south-west through Ayton (passing within sight of the castle of the same name, an extravaganza of Victorian architecture; open on summer Sundays and by appointment) then Chirnside, before arriving at **DUNS**. This is a market town in the Merse, the farming area of Berwickshire. The name comes from the Celtic word 'dun', meaning hill fort, although there are no remains of this structure which once stood at Duns Law. The **Jim Clark Room** on Newton Street is a memorial to the former Grand Prix racing driver who was born in the nearby village of Chirnside. He won the World Championship twice (in 1963 and 1965) and the display comprises an extensive collection of the trophies won in a career which ended due to his untimely death in 1968. Another famous son of the locality is the philosopher and historian David Hume, who was born at Ninewells, south-west of Chirnside, in 1711. In 1266, Duns was the birthplace of the philosopher and theologian Duns Scotus whose statue stands in the public park.

Admirers of fine Edwardian architecture will appreciate **Manderston**, an outstanding country house two miles east of the town. The interior is remarkable for its unique silver staircase while the extensive gardens are noted for their rhododendrons. It is open mid-May to September, Thursday, bank holiday Mondays and Sunday only, 2 p.m. – 5.30 p.m. Four miles to the north is **Edinshall Broch**, an example of the unusual Iron Age defensive towers (brochs) unique to Scotland.

There are a few small hotels in Duns. **Barniken House Hotel**, 18 High Street (Tel. 0361 82466), has four bedrooms at around £18 a head and the **Black Bull Hotel**, Black Bull Street (Tel. 0361 83379) starts at around £15 a head. Slightly cheaper is the six-bedroom **White Swan Hotel**, Market Square (Tel. 0361 83338) and the four bedroom **Rome's Hotel/Winebar**, 2 South Street (Tel. 0361 82085).

The A6112 south from Duns leads to **COLDSTREAM**. Its position right on the border made it popular, like Gretna, with couples eloping from England who came to marry in Scotland because of the lower age of consent; anglers will be more interested in its position on the banks of the River Tweed. The museum in the Market Square includes an exhibition on the Coldstream Guards. They were not raised here, but made the town their HQ in 1659. In 1660 they marched from here to London, helped in the restoration of Charles II, and were nicknamed after the town from where they had come.

The only trace of the Cistercian priory which once stood here (destroyed by the English in 1545) is in the town's place names: Abbey Road, Nun's Walk, and Penitent's Walk. Just outside Coldstream is **Hirsel Estate**, seat of the Douglas-Home family. The 14th Earl renounced his title in 1963 to become prime minister and is better known as Sir Alec Douglas-Home. The house is closed to the public, but the grounds are open for a variety of walks through Dundock Wood, along the river bank, or to visit the **folk museum** and working craft units in the converted stable yard.

For accommodation, in the High Street, there is the **Newcastle Arms** (Tel. 0890 2376), a small family run hotel, charging £16 per person. In the Market Square, the **Crown Hotel** (Tel. 0890 2558) charges from £15 per person. **Tilmouth Park Hotel**, just outside Coldstream at Cornhill-on-Tweed (Tel. 0890 2255), is a majestic, listed building standing in 1,000 acres. Prices are accordingly high, starting at £25 per person. The **Collingwood Arms**, also situated at Cornhill-on-Tweed, starts at £30 per person. For bed and breakfast accommodation, Mrs J. Bowie (Tel. 0890 2084) offers four elegant rooms, in her detached Victorian home, from £15 per person, as does Mrs Carol Boswell in her Scots baronial-style house (Tel. 0890 84 324). Mrs Alison Minter (Tel. 0890 2452) on the High Street starts at £10 a head. Camping facilities can be found at **Coldstream Caravan Park**, Tweed Green (Tel. 0890 2333) ideally situated by the River Tweed and not far from the town centre: £3 for tents, £5 for motor caravans and £6 for caravans.

Tourist Information is available from April to October at Henderson Park (Tel. 0890 2607).

Nine miles on from Coldstream the A698 reaches the busy market town of **KELSO**, situated near the confluence of the River Tweed and the River Teviot. **Kelso Abbey** was founded by David I in 1128, though subsequently destroyed in a series of attacks by the English in the 16th century. The town's museum, at Turret House in Abbey Court, is situated opposite the Abbey. The **Town Square** is an elegant example of Georgian architecture. **John Rennie's five arch bridge** over the Tweed was completed after three years' work in 1803 and served as the model for the former Waterloo Bridge in London.

Rennie's bridge commands a fine view of **Floors Castle**. The largest private residence in Scotland – home to the Duke of Roxburghe – lies two miles north-west of Kelso and is open to the public. Here you can see the work of two of Scotland's most famous architects; William Adam's design, completed in 1725, was augmented in 1849 by William Playfair. Inside is a magnificent collection of antiques, tapestries and paintings, while in the grounds a tree marks the spot where James II was killed by an exploding cannon in 1460 (closed on Saturday and Friday in May, June and September). Another example of Adam's work is open to the public eight miles north-west of Kelso at **Mellerstain House**, which he began in 1725 and his son Robert completed some 50 years later. This is a magnificent house – one of Scotland's finest Georgian mansions, noted for the fine Adam plasterwork and the attractive Italian terraced gardens (closed on Saturday). Seven miles to the west, just off the B6404, is the 16th-century **Smailholm Tower**. This well-preserved structure stands by the edge of a loch and boasts magnificent panoramic views. It houses a display of dolls and tapestries as part of an exhibition on Scott's 'Minstrelsy of the Scottish Borders'. Notable outdoor pursuits in Kelso are fishing and golfing.

The town has a good selection of accommodation. Prices start at around £20 at the **Black Swan Inn**, Horsemarket (Tel. 0573 224563). From £22 per person, there is the **Queen's Head Hotel**, 24 Bridge Street (Tel. 0573 224636) and **Bellevue Hotel**, Bowmont Street (Tel. 0573 224588) offering fine traditional cooking. **Cross Keys Hotel**, overlooking The Square (Tel. 0573 223303) offers rooms from around £20 per person. For a much cheaper alternative there is **Springwood Caravan Park** just off the the A699, (Tel. 0573 224396) catering for caravan and motor caravans from £6 a night. **Ednam House Hotel**, Bridge Street (Tel. 0573 24168/9), is a Georgian mansion in three acres of garden overlooking the Tweed. Prices start just under £30. Three miles south-west of Kelso is **Sunlaws Country House Hotel** owned by the Duke of Roxburghe (Tel. 0573 25331), where dinner, bed and breakfast for two costs in excess of £180.

Tourist Information is available, April to October, at The Town House in The Square from Easter 1993 (Tel. 0573 223464).

The A698 runs south-west from Kelso for 10 miles before joining the A68, and from here it is a short drive south to reach **JEDBURGH** in the valley of the Jed Water. Visitors to the town follow in august footsteps. Lying on one of the main roads connecting Scotland and England, Jedburgh has been the sojourn of personages of no less stature than Bonnie Prince Charlie (in

1745); Robert Burns (when made a freeman of the burgh in 1787); and Walter Scott (when in 1793 he made his courtroom début as a lawyer) **Mary Queen of Scots House** in Queen Street accommodated perhaps the most famous visitor of them all, Mary Queen of Scots, in 1566. It was a fortified mansion when she stayed there, but is now a museum. At the top of Castlegate is Jedburgh Castle, although this is a misnomer. No castle has stood there since the 15th century; the present building was opened in the 1820s as a prison but currently houses the **Castle Jail Museum**. The castle which did once stand here was demolished in 1409 at the behest of the local authorities who saw this as the only means of guaranteeing an end to its sporadic occupation by the English. The 12th-century **Abbey**, like those of Dryburgh, Kelso and Melrose, has a beleaguered history. It suffered frequently at the hands of the English before finally succumbing to Henry VIII, although his depredations still left much of the structure to admire. **Jedburgh Abbey Visitor Centre** is well worth a visit to understand the role of the Border abbeys in Scottish history. Ferniehirst Castle, open Wednesday only May–Oct, has been recently restored (Tel. 0835 62201). This 16th-century Border castle incorporates an information centre giving details on Border history.

A few miles north of Jedburgh lies **Harestanes Countryside Visitor Centre**, offering a complete countryside experience with organised walks, play areas, a tea room and a craft shop. Five miles south on the A68, you can observe rare breeds of farmed animals and the resident deer population at **Jedforest Deer and Farm Park**. There are also sign posted walks to enjoy around the farm as well as an interpretive centre and outdoor adventureland.

There is a good selection of guest houses in the town and the surrounding area providing bed and breakfast for around £13 per head. For hotel accommodation there is the **Royal Hotel**, Canongate (Tel. 0835 63152) with prices beginning at £15 per person. **Kenmore Bank Guest House**, Oxnam Rd (Tel. 0835 62369), offers a view across the river and reasonable prices from £17 a head. Rooms in **Glenbank Country House Hotel**, Castlegate (Tel. 0835 62258), a Georgian house with its own grounds. Prices start at around £25. Just outside the town at Camptown is **Jedforest Country House Hotel** (Tel. 08354 274/285), set in 50 acres of parkland, with prices starting around £20.

The **Tourist Information** centre at Murray's Green (Tel. 0835 63435/63688) is open all year round.

The B6358 runs west from Jedburgh around Dunion Hill before joining the A698. From here it is a short journey along the south bank of the Teviot to **HAWICK**, the largest town of the Borders. It has a thriving woollen industry, but for many, the town's fame is due to its abiding passion for, and success in, the sport of rugby union football.

Most of Hawick was built in the latter half of the 19th century, the most notable exceptions being the **mote**, a high mound near the town centre which formed the base of Norman fortifications, and the 16th-century **tower** in the High Street. To the west of the town is **Wilton Lodge Museum** which has displays on the knitwear industry, Borders history, and natural history. **Peter Scott** in Buccleuch Street, is an internationally famous manufacturer of ladies' and men's fully fashioned knitwear, providing fascinating tours of the factory, six days of the week. Visitors can also observe the process of manufacturing tweed cloth at **Trow Mill**, two miles east. **The Museum of Border Arms and Armour** at Teviothead, nine miles south of Hawick, is well worth a visit, open most days. Also to the south is **Hermitage Castle** by Newcastleton. The original was built in the 13th century but most of the remains date from the 14th century. It was to here that Mary Queen of Scots made the dangerous and exhausting ride from Jedburgh to meet Bothwell in 1566 – the journey almost cost her her life.

As one would expect from a town as large and thriving as Hawick, there is a broad range of accommodation. **Elm House Hotel**, 17 North Bridge Street (Tel. 0450 72866), has 15 rooms with prices starting at around £17.50. Prices are similar a few doors away at number 23 in the smaller **Roxburgh Inn** (Tel. 0450 75934). From around £13 there is **Oakwood Guest House**, Buccleuch Road (Tel. 0450 72896/72814), **Bridge House Guest House**, Sandbed (Tel. 0450 73351), and **Station Hotel**, 1 Dovemont Place (Tel. 0450 72340/76073).

The **Tourist Information** centre is open from April to October at Common Haugh (Tel. 0450 72547).

Twelve miles north on the A7 is **SELKIRK**, situated on a hillside looking down over the valleys of the Ettrick and the

Yarrow. Once famous for shoemaking, its reputation today is as a wool and tweed centre. The town's association with Sir Walter Scott is commemorated in the statue of him in front of the Town Hall in the market place. It sits on the site of the former tolbooth, where Scott would have presided over criminal hearings in his capacity as Sheriff of Selkirkshire. In 1803 these legal proceedings transferred to the nearby **Courtroom** in the Town Hall which now displays mementoes of the man. Just off the market place, down Halliwell's Close is **Halliwell's House Museum and Gallery**. In addition to the re-creation of a 19th-century ironmonger's shop there is an exhibition of items typically belonging to the Victorian and Edwardian home. It was one of Selkirk's townsmen who captured the English standard at the Battle of Flodden in 1513 – the only one to return from the battle. This trophy is now housed in the public library and the feat is commemorated each year during the Common Riding Festival in June when a local lad ceremoniously waves this captured standard, in remembrance of those who fell. In the High Street, there also stands the **Flodden monument**, the statue of a standard bearer. Near this is the statue of Mungo Park, the 18th-century explorer who was born four miles away in Foulshiels and drowned in the River Niger in flight from hostile natives. On the A7 just north of Selkirk is the **Selkirk Glass Visitor Centre** which is open to the public seven days a week. You will have the chance to watch the glass blowers at work and to buy the glass products later in the adjoining craft shop and tea-room.

A few miles west of Selkirk, just off the A708 is the sumptuous home of the Duke of Buccleuch, **Bowhill**, famous for its extensive art collection which includes works by Leonardo da Vinci, Gainsborough, Reynolds, Canaletto, and Raeburn. It also houses some exquisite porcelain and antique furniture, while the extensive grounds contain an adventure woodland play area, riding centre, and nature trails. **Bowhill House** is limited to viewing only in July. The park, however, is open every day except Friday. Selkirk is also a good base from which to enjoy the splendid scenery of the **Ettrick** and **Yarrow Valleys**.

Accommodation can be found from around £18.50 at the **Glen Hotel**, Yarrow Terrace (Tel. 0750 20259), and at **Heatherlie**

House Hotel (Tel. 0750 21200). The award-winning **Philipburn House Hotel** (Tel. 0750 20747) has been consistently voted the best restaurant and hotel in the Scottish Borders. Prices begin at £55 per person. Just outside Selkirk, at Ettrick bridge, is The **Cross Keys Inn** (Tel. 0750 52224). Formerly a coaching inn, it comes highly recommended for its good hospitality and home cooking. Prices start at £17.50. Additionally, weekly accommodation can be provided in its attractive courtyard cottages to the rear of the inn. Five cottages come complete with self-catering facilities, TV and shower. Prices range from £153 to £305. There is also a good choice of boarding houses charging from around £13. Caravan and camping facilities can be found at **Victoria Park**, Buccleuch Road (Tel. 0750 20897), where pitches cost around £6 per night.

    Tourist Information is available from April to October at Halliwell's House, Halliwell's Close, just off the market place (Tel. 0750 20054).

A few miles north-east of Selkirk is the town of **MELROSE**, edged on the north by the River Tweed and overlooked from the south by the trio of Eildon Hills.

    The outstanding feature of Melrose is its **Abbey**. Founded in the middle of the 12th century by Cistercian monks, it is reputedly the site where the heart of Robert the Bruce lies buried. Beside the abbey is **Priorwood Gardens** where strains of apple trees which date back to Roman times still flourish. Nearby, an impressive collection of automobiles is on display at the **Melrose Motor Museum**. Off Market Square is the old **station**. No longer in use with British Rail, it now serves as a restaurant. At the **Ormiston Institute of Melrose**, the Trimontium Exhibition can be viewed providing an educational insight into the Romans in Scotland. **Teddy Melrose**, a new teddy bear museum, can be easily found on the High Street where bear lovers are promised an enjoyable day out. There are also tea rooms selling honey tea. Melrose is the home of seven-a-side rugby, founded by a local butcher Ned Haig in the 1880s. Held annually in the month of April, the tournament in Melrose is an international event attracting spectators and teams from all over the world.

In addition to the attractions of Melrose itself, there are, in either direction, places of interest well worth a short journey along the A6091. A few miles to the south-east is the 12th-century **Dryburgh Abbey**, just over the Tweed from the town of St Boswells. Like the other Border abbeys it was the victim of frequent attacks from the south between the 14th and 16th centuries, finally being left in ruins in 1544. Here is the burial ground of Sir Walter Scott's family, and the author himself lies in the north transept. Another famous person who lies in this vicinity is Earl Haig of Bemersyde, the First World War commander.

A few miles from Melrose in the opposite direction, the A6091 leads to **Abbotsford**, the home of Sir Walter Scott. He purchased the estate in 1812 and promptly changed its name from Cartleyhole. The new name derived from a combination of history and geography: from the house Scott could see the part of the Tweed where the monks from Melrose Abbey once crossed by means of a ford. The house was completed in 1824 and has been the family home ever since. Much of it, however, is open to the public, including his 9,000-volume library and his collection of paraphernalia from some of the most famous people in history: Robert Burns's drinking mug, a lock of Prince Charlie's hair, Napoleon's cloak-clasp, Rob Roy's purse, to name but a few.

Hotels in Melrose are concentrated in Market Square and the High Street. The latter is the location of the elegant 34-bedroom **George and Abbotsford Hotel** (Tel. 089682 2308), with prices from around £30, along with **Burts Hotel** (Tel. 089682 2285) and the **Bon Accord Hotel** (Tel. 089682 2645). The more modest **Kings Arms Hotel** with seven bedrooms starts at £18 (Tel. 089682 2143). There is room for tents at **Gibson Park Caravan Club**, High Street (Tel. 089682 2969). **Melrose Youth Hostel**, a magnificent red sandstone building, overlooks the Abbey and offers excellent accommodation and comfortable family rooms (Tel. 089682 2521).

The **Tourist Information** centre at Priorwood Gardens (Tel. 089682 2555) is open from April to October.

Melrose is only three miles south-east of **GALASHIELS**, a very important textile centre and home of the internationally renowned

Scottish College of Textiles. Production has declined since the heyday in the late 19th century, but the town can still boast that the 700 patterns produced at Nether Mill make it the world's most prodigious manufacturer of tartan cloth. The **Peter Anderson Cashmere Woollen Mill** has displays on the history of the textile industry and the manufacturing process as well as exhibitions on local history. The **Borders Wool Centre**, Wheatlands Road (Tel. 0896 4293), gives a vivid insight into the industry, where live sheep provide the means for hand spinning and weaving demonstrations. **Old Gala House** dates from 1583. It is the former home of the lairds of Galashiels, boasting an original hand-painted ceiling from 1635. Its Christopher Boyd Gallery houses permanent and temporary art exhibitions throughout the year.

There are also some options for the sports-person. In addition to the usual swimming pool, tennis court and bowling greens, there is Ladhope 18-hole golf course (Tel. 0896 3431).

An alternative route from Melrose is the B6359 east and then the A68 north by the banks of the Leader Water to **LAUDER**. This is a quiet village and good angling spot. Its principal distinction is the **church**, built in 1673 in the unusual plan of a Greek cross and with an octagonal steeple. The 17th-century **Town Hall** was, until 1840, the tolbooth. The dominant tourist attraction is **Thirlestane Castle**, built late in the 16th century for Baron Maitland, private secretary to Mary Queen of Scots. The present structure, home of the Maitland family but open to the public, is composed largely of extensions to the original, built between the 16th and 19th centuries. Its outstanding feature is its decorated plasterwork ceilings. An extensive chronicle of Borders history will be found in the grounds in the **Border Country Life Museum**. Lauder's location makes it an ideal point from which to explore the magnificent Lauderdale countryside, or to rest when walking the Southern Upland Way, which passes through the castle grounds.

Accommodation is scarce. The **Black Bull Hotel** in Market Place (Tel. 05782 208) offers bed and breakfast from £15. Prices are similar at the six-bedroom **Eagle Hotel** (Tel. 05782 426). The **Lauderdale Hotel**, 1 Edinburgh Road (Tel. 05782 231), charges from just over £25.

Tourist Information is at Bank Street in Galashiels (Tel. 0896 55551), open from April to October.

Ten miles west of Galashiels on the A72 is the small town of Walkerburn and the **Scottish Museum of Wool Textiles**.

It is then a short distance to Innerleithen and then south on the B709 to **Traquair House** (open to the public from Easter to mid-October). Claimed to be the oldest residence in Scotland in continuous use, its history goes back as far as 1107, when it was a royal hunting lodge. It was the favourite residence of William the Lion and in total 27 monarchs visited the house. It makes for a fascinating visit – look out for the 'Bear Gates', the main entry gates that were closed in 1746 by the 5th Earl, a Jacobite laird, and have not been opened since, nor will be until a Stuart rules over Scotland again. Also here is an 18th-century brewhouse, a maze, and plenty of walks through the grounds. A few miles from Traquair in Innerleithen is Robert Smail's **Printing Works**. This restored Victorian printing works contains many historic items and visitors may view the printer at work.

Back on the A72 and seven miles west of Innerleithen is **PEEBLES**. The town has an ancient history having received a charter from David I to become a royal burgh in the 12th century. The town's oldest site, the ruin of the **Cross Kirk** in Cross Road, dates back to 1261, while the 12-foot-high column, the **Mercat Cross**, dates from 1320. **Tweeddale Museum**, in the Chambers Institute in the High Street, has exhibitions on local history. It occupies the former home of the Queensberry family. Other famous sons of Peebles include the publishers William and Robert Chambers, born here in 1800 and 1802. At 31 High Street is the **Cornice Museum**, where you can watch decorative plaster being made daily, from November to March. Eight miles from Peebles on the B712 lies Dawyck Botanic Garden. Open daily from mid-March to end of October, this outstation of the Royal Botanic Garden boasts a collection of rare trees, including many conifers, shrubs and rhododendrons. In the woods is Dawyck Chapel. **Kailzie Gardens**, two miles east of Peebles on B7062, is also well worth a visit.

The magnificent countryside around the town can be explored, by the suitably energetic, astride a mountain bike from **Glentress Mountain Bike Centre**, Venlaw High Road, Peebles (Tel. 0721 720336/722934). Easier and more traditional outdoor sport, with an equally scenic backdrop, can be had at the municipal **golf course** (Tel. 0721 20197), which overlooks the Tweed Valley.

One mile west of Peebles on the A72 is **Neidpath Castle** (open Easter to mid-October). It was originally built as a fortress between the 13th and 15th centuries. Subsequent work transformed it into a comfortable home and in 1886 it was purchased by the 1st Duke of Queensberry.

There are several hotels in Peebles offering special activity holidays. **Park Hotel**, Innerleithen Road (Tel. 0721 720451), specializes in angling holidays at around £30 per day. **Peebles Angling School**, 10 Dean Park (Tel. 0721 20331), provides accommodation and tuition in fly fishing for beginners and the more experienced.

Peebles Hotel Hydro runs 'drive away' golfing holidays, walking holidays, and a special Edinburgh Festival or Tattoo Package. **Peebles Hydro Stables** on Innerleithen Road (Tel. 0721 21325), also offer pony trekking and trail riding courses for novices as well as for the more experienced rider. Riding lessons are available from qualified instructors at £7 per hour. Mountain biking is the special provision of **Scottish Border Trails**, Drummore, Venlaw High Road (Tel. 0721 20336), at a price of £15 to £50 upward per day including accommodation with special family concessions. The **Tweed Valley Hotel** at nearby Walkerburn (Tel. 089687 636), offers guests a range of activities: fishing, walking, art courses, golf, and bird-watching and wildlife holidays. There is, of course, a wide range of accommodation for those seeking a more relaxed time. The **Barony Castle Hotel** is one such place, offering the best in Scottish hospitality, situated four miles from Peebles (Tel. 07213 395). The staff are also able to recommend the best places in the area to fish, shoot, ride and hill walk. The **County Hotel** on Peebles High Street (Tel. 0721 20595), has eight rooms at around £18 a night. The **Green Tree Hotel**, Eastgate (Tel. 0721 20582), is slightly more expensive at £20 a night. For highly recommended bed and breakfast accommodation with good home cooking and warm hospitality, find **Mrs Teasdale** at 4 Langside Drive (Tel. 0721 21931). For camping in Peebles there is a choice of two sites: the **Crossburn Caravan Park**, Edinburgh Road (Tel. 0721 20501), and **Rosetta Caravan Park**, Rosetta Road (Tel. 0721 20720). Both are first-class parks and are reasonably priced at between £6.50 and £7 per night.

Edinburgh

INTRODUCTION

Edinburgh is a striking city which is both elegant and dramatic. Visitors are enchanted by the fairy-tale castle dominating the city, and the hills and sea all around. This is the artistic, commercial, academic and legal centre of Scotland – a fact clearly evident in every street of its historic centre. Visitors who come during the Festival month of August will have the additional advantage of being able to see what is, without doubt, the world's largest and most extravagant festival of the performing arts.

HISTORY

Not much is known for certain about Edinburgh's origins, but in the Dark Ages it was the most northerly outpost of Anglo-Saxon England, having been overrun, along with the rest of Lothian, by the Angles of Northumbria. The great rock upon which the present castle stands was captured by the Northumbrian King Edwin, and it is from him that the city derives its name: the village founded by him around the castle rock, 'Edwin's burgh', becoming in due course 'Edinburgh'.

Successive Scottish kings kept their treasures in the castle but the fortress took on a new importance after 1329 when Robert the Bruce granted Edinburgh a Royal Charter. The town expanded rapidly, spreading down from the Castle Hill to where the present Holyrood Palace now stands. King David I built an abbey near the foot of the volcano Arthur's Seat, which was used for royal ceremonies, and the thoroughfare which emerged between the abbey and the castle stretched for a mile. The sovereign often travelled between the abbey and the castle, and the stretch soon became known as the Royal Mile. You can still walk that same 'mile' along Edinburgh's High Street today, although the actual distance is slightly over that measure. Edinburgh finally became the capital of Scotland in the mid-15th century.

The castle ceased to be the main royal residence after the Scottish defeat at Flodden Field in 1513, although it remained a national armoury, holding out during a siege which involved Mary Queen of Scots in 1563. The last shots fired in battle from Edinburgh Castle were aimed at Bonnie Prince Charlie's forces in 1745 – archaeologists uncovered a previously unknown grave site from this encounter in 1988. Princes Street still resounds to the sound of cannon fire from the battlements every lunchtime when the one o'clock gun is fired.

The Act of Union with England in 1707 brought an assured peace which allowed the city to expand northwards. In 1752 the city's Lord Provost George Drummond embarked on his ambitious plans for the 'New Town' on the north side of Princes Street. One of the New Town's first residents was a central figure in the Scottish Enlightenment, David Hume. A fitting commemoration of this philosopher is to be found in the street plan of the New Town. Hume was never an avowed atheist, but his undoubted agnosticism was enough to make him notorious among his contemporaries and, the story goes, it was this formidable reputation which inspired one wag to dub the place where Hume had newly taken up residence with the ironic title 'St David's Street'. The name not only stuck, but became official.

To this day, Edinburgh remains Scotland's financial heart, the Georgian New Town acting as home to the largest financial sector in Europe after London. In addition, Edinburgh was, and many feel still is, the undisputed cultural heart of Scotland, but recent initiatives in Glasgow, such as 'Mayfest' and the 'City of Culture' accolade, have intensified the old rivalry between these two cities, with Glasgow now usurping Edinburgh's traditional claim to be the artistic centre and premier tourist destination in Scotland. One pre-eminent industry, which is outside the service sector, and forms the bedrock of Edinburgh's economy, is brewing. Scottish & Newcastle have their headquarters here, and it is in the city's pubs that the locally produced McEwan's 80/- is at its best.

EDINBURGH

NEW TOWN

MORAY PLACE
← DEAN VILLAGE

QUEEN STREET
QUEEN STREET

CHARLOTTE SQUARE

GARDENS STREET
THISTLE STREET
GEORGE STREET

PRINCES STREET

WEST PRINCES ST. GARDENS

CASTLE HILL
EDINBURGH CASTLE

THE MOUND
MARKET
WAVERLEY BRIDGE
WAVE
STAT
STR
COO

CASTLE HILL — LAWN MARKET
HIGH
7

KING'S JOHNSTON TERRACE
STABLES ROAD
GRASSMARKET

GEORGE IV COWG
CANDLEMAKER ROW
MERCHANT STREET
BRIDGE

LOTHIAN ROAD

WEST PORT

OLD TOWN

LAURISTON PLACE

EARL GREY STREET

1 Edinburgh Castle, including
  St Margaret's Chapel,
  Scottish National War Memorial,
  Scottish United Services Museum,
  and Jewel House
2 Camera Obscura
3 Scot's Whisky Heritage Centre
4 Gladstone's Land
5 Lady Stair's House
6 Brodie's Close
7 High Kirk of St Giles
8 Parliament House

9 Mercat Cross
10 Royal Exchange (Civic Offices)
11 Tron Church
12 Richard Demarco Galley
13 369 Gallery
14 Stills Gallery
15 Museum of Childhood
16 John Knox's House
17 Canongate Tolbooth
18 Canongate Kirk
19 Huntly House
20 Acheson House, Scottish Craft Centre

COMMUNICATIONS

Edinburgh is well connected by air, rail and road to the rest of the United Kingdom. Both British Midland and British Airways operate several flights daily from London Heathrow. Air UK fly from Gatwick and Stansted and offer the cheapest available standby tickets. Whichever airline you fly with, the journey takes approximately one hour and you can reach the centre of Edinburgh by the regular Lothian Region bus (number 100) which costs about £2.80, or by taxi which will cost about £10. A useful service for visitors, and a far cheaper alternative to the airport's NCP, is provided at the airport by Secure Airparks (Tel. 0506 857085) who provide a guarded car parking service. The daily rate is around £2.60, £20.80 for a week, or £39.00 for a fortnight. A complimentary courtesy coach takes you to its Broxburn location within 10 minutes.

There are hourly train services, from early morning until early evening, between London King's Cross and Edinburgh Waverley. The express journey now takes less than four and a half hours and a Standard Class return ticket will cost about the same as an off-peak APEX air fare. The car journey takes about eight hours from London, via M1, A1 and A68. Travel by coach can take anything up to 12 hours.

Getting around Edinburgh should present few problems. The compactness of the city centre means that it can easily be covered on foot. Lothian Region Transport (with their maroon and white double-decker buses) are the main bus company operating routes to all parts of the city and suburbs, and that service is complemented by Eastern Scottish, with their distinctive green buses. Both offer one-day and weekly travel passes and these are available from their respective offices: Lothian Region Transport, Waverley Bridge Ticket Centre; Eastern Scottish, St Andrew Square bus station.

TOURIST INFORMATION

Edinburgh's City Tourist Information Office is at the east end of Princes Street in Waverley Market (Tel. 031–557 1700), and is open from November to March, Monday to Saturday, 9 a.m. to 6 p.m. (closed Sundays); April and October, Monday to Saturday, 9 a.m. to 6 p.m. (11 a.m. to 6 p.m. on Sundays); May, June and September, Monday to Saturday, 9 a.m. to 7 p.m. (Sundays from 11 a.m. to 7 p.m.); and in July and August, Monday to Saturday, from 9 a.m. till 8 p.m. (Sundays 11 a.m. to 8 p.m.).

The Scottish Tourist Board provides information on all parts of Scotland rather than just Edinburgh, and is located within the Scottish Travel Centre, 23 Ravelston Terrace (Tel. 031–332 2433). It is open from 8.30 a.m. to 10 p.m. from Monday to Saturday, and 10 a.m. to 6 p.m. on Sunday in the summer; and 9 a.m. to 6 p.m. from Monday to Friday, and 9 a.m. to 1 p.m. on Saturday between October and May.

ACCOMMODATION

Edinburgh's importance and popularity are reflected in the extensive choice of accommodation on offer in all categories, and this section aims to give no more than a very brief selection of the options available. It is of paramount importance to book well in advance of coming to Edinburgh, particularly if you plan to visit during the month of August when the city's visitors, in town to coincide with the Festival, are at their most numerous.

FIRST CLASS/DE LUXE
The Caledonian, Princes Street (Tel. 031–225 2433), fashioned in red sandstone, is a prominent sight at the west end of Princes Street and, apart from Gleneagles and Edinburgh's Balmoral, is the only Scottish hotel to receive the coveted five-star grading from the AA. With 237 well-appointed rooms and an excellent restaurant, the Pompadour Room, the Caledonian provides a truly sumptuous standard of accommodation at a price upward of £95 per person.

Scandic Crown Hotel, 80 High Street (Tel. 031–557 9797), is the city's newest luxury hotel. The four-star Scandic combines Scandinavian efficiency and style with Scottish vernacular architecture, and a central Old Town setting. Prices from £67 per person. Adopting a child-friendly approach, there are free swimming lessons available at the leisure centre whilst parents dine, or go shopping.

The Balmoral Hotel (Tel. 031–556 2414), formerly the North British, reopened in 1991 after a £23 million refurbishment. This grand edifice, with its distinctive clock tower, is one of Princes Street's most famous landmarks. It has a great deal of character, and is always popular with overseas visitors.

The **Howard Hotel**, 32–6 Great King Street (Tel. 031–557 3500), was created from three elegant 19th-century terraced houses in the New Town. This fabulous Georgian town-house hotel is one of the city's best, with 16 individually designed en-suite bedrooms, an excellent restaurant (No. 36) and with traditional British charm.

BUSINESS CLASS
Royal Terrace Hotel, Royal Terrace (Tel. 031–557 3222), formerly three four-storey Georgian houses, is one of the city's newest first class hotels. It has 97 elegant rooms and an exceptional glass-enclosed patio restaurant. Located in the east end of the New Town, this is an excellent addition to the capital's hotel options.

The **Roxburghe Hotel**, Charlotte Square (Tel. 031–225 3921), has 75 bedrooms, and its sedate charm assures visitors of a relaxing stay, overlooking the attractive gardens of the New Town's Charlotte Square. It has recently been completely refurbished and brought up to a five crown standard.

The **King James Thistle Hotel**, St James Centre (Tel. 031–556 0111), is an impressive 147-bedroom hotel in the heart of Edinburgh, providing a central location and high standards of comfort for the business executive and tourist alike.

The George, George Street (Tel. 031–225 1251), is a fine four-star hotel, with 195 bedrooms, each with private facilities. The George has an elegant appearance, and is particularly suited to the gourmet, having two excellent restaurants.

Mount Royal, Princes Street (Tel. 031–225 7161), is conveniently situated, and has comfortable rooms and a fine restaurant. The **Hilton National Hotel**, Belford Road (Tel. 031–332 2545), is highly commended with spacious bedrooms and friendly service, complemented by a good *à la carte* dinner menu available to both residents and non-residents.

Channings, Learmonth Gardens (Tel. 031 315 22726), is Edinburgh's newest and most individual town house hotel.

Recently refurbished for £750,000, it aims to attract business and leisure travellers alike, offering luxury accommodation at a reasonable cost. There are suites available for small conferences and presentations, as well as cocktail parties, private lunches and dinners. The brasserie and bar offer Scottish and international cuisine.

The **Ellersly House Hotel**, Ellersly Road (Tel. 031–337 6888), is a lovely Edwardian country house with 60 rooms and a fine restaurant. Their Silver Service package is well worth asking for – an all-inclusive deal with lots of nice little extras.

ECONOMY CLASS

In the New Town, the **Arden Hotel** (Tel. 031-556 8688), Royal Terrace, the **Halcyon** (Tel. 031-556 1033) also in Royal Terrace, and the **Osbourne** (Tel. 031-556 5746) in York Place are excellent value for money.

The **Iona Hotel**, Strathearn Place (Tel. 031-447 6264), is a pleasant two-star hotel with two attractive bars and good restaurant.

The **Buchan Hotel** (Tel. 031-337 1045) 3 Coates Gardens, near Haymarket, is a friendly family-run hotel.

The **Dickie Guest House**, East Claremont Street (Tel. 031 556 4032), is a two crown establishment offering bed and breakfast accommodation and *en suite* or shared bathroom facilities. Prices are from £17 per person with reduced prices for children.

Edinburgh University offers comfortable economy class accommodation near to the city. At **Pollock Halls of Residence**, 181 Holyrood Park Road (Tel. 031 667 1971), bed and breakfast accommodation per person starts at £14.55, ideal for groups as well as individuals and set against Arthur's Seat.

Edinburgh is certainly not short of youth hostels with the **High Street Hostel**, 8 Blackfriars Street (Tel. 031 557 3984) at £5.50 a night and the **Cowgate Tourist Hostel**, below the Royal Mile (Tel. 031 226 2153) at £10 per person and both ideally situated in the city centre; at the west end of the city there is **Bruntsfield Youth Hostel** charging £6.50 per person with a youth hostel membership card, and **Belford Youth Hostel**, 68 Douglas Gardens (Tel. 031 225 6209), starting from £6.50 per person.

If you are looking for somewhere 'on spec' then you would do well to try the Dalkeith Road/Minto Street/Newington Road area of south Edinburgh where there is a very high concentration of small hotels and guest houses.

EATING OUT AND NIGHTLIFE

For its size, Edinburgh presents its visitors with an excellent choice of entertainment in the evening. This brief account recommends some of the more interesting of the myriad pubs in town and places a selection of the capital's restaurants in three general categories: First Class (over £20 per person), Business Class (£10–15) and Economy Class (under £10). These represent the approximate cost of a good dinner per person, accompanied by a bottle of house wine.

FIRST CLASS

Pompadour, Caledonian Hotel, Princes Street (Tel. 031-225 2433): Edinburgh's premier hotel contains one of the city's finest restaurants, where the award-winning menu combines the taste of France and Scotland.

L'Auberge, 56–58 St Mary's Street (Tel. 031-556 5888): an exquisite French restaurant just off the Royal Mile, with classic cuisine. It is advisable to book ahead.

The Howtowdie, Stafford Street (Tel. 031-225 6291): not far from the west end of Princes Street, serves traditional Scottish fare in exemplary style.

Number 10, 10 Melville Place (Tel. 031-447 0256): an excellent *haute cuisine* restaurant with a tempting *à la carte* menu.

The Witchery by the Castle, 352 Castle Hill, Royal Mile (Tel. 031-225 5613): excellent Scottish/French menu, featuring beef and seafood served in a warm, friendly atmosphere.

BUSINESS CLASS

L'Alliance Brasserie, 7 Merchant Street (Tel. 031-225 2002): good French menu, and atmosphere to match.

Jackson's, Jackson's Close, just off the Royal Mile (Tel. 031-225 1793): offers a high standard of Scottish culinary expertise and service, in a central location.

Handsel's, 22 Stafford Street (Tel. 031-225 3500): an excellent Danish restaurant with an imaginative menu and good service.

ECONOMY CLASS

The Imperial, 105/109 Lothian Road (Tel. 031-229 7575): among the best of Edinburgh's many Chinese restaurants.

Lazios, 95 Lothian Road (Tel. 031-229 7788): offers a fine and imaginative selection of Italian fare.

Henderson's Salad Table, 94 Hanover Street (Tel. 031-225 2131): attracts a fairly young clientele, and serves good vegetarian and health food (open Monday to Saturday, 8 a.m. to 10 p.m., and, during the festival, on Sunday, 9 a.m. to 9 p.m.).

When it comes to pubs, Edinburgh's visitors are spoilt for choice and have the liberty of being able to carry on drinking long after publicans elsewhere in Britain have called last orders. Few streets have the high concentration of ale houses of Rose Street, just north of, and parallel to, Princes Street, although quantity, in this instance, is at odds with quality. In better days, Hugh McDiarmid and his friends spent enough time in certain establishments along here to earn the nickname 'the Rose Street Poets'. **Milne's Bar**, at the corner of Rose Street and Hanover Street, has commemorated their custom by adopting the monicker 'Poets' Pub', and hanging framed photographs of members of the Edinburgh Parnassus, which flourished in the fifties, on the walls alongside some of their verse. Another of their haunts, the **Café Royal** in West Register Street, off South St Andrew Street, has retained plenty of character, in addition to its colourful stained-glass windows. The **Acanthus Café Bar**, 17 Waverley Bridge (Tel. 031 556 2358), is very handy for the railway station, as well as the airport bus, which leaves directly from out front, attracting a very young and cosmopolitan clientele. There is an adjoining restaurant offering a varied and inexpensive menu. There are a large number of pubs in the Grassmarket, although, with the exception of the **Fiddler's Arms**, little can be said in favour of their atmosphere or beer. **Bannerman's** in the Cowgate has an unusual ambience generated by the pub's bare stone floor, vaulted ceiling, and pews. The **Pelican**, almost directly opposite, opened recently, but quickly established itself as a haunt of Edinburgh's young dandies, who also congregate at the **City Café**, nearby in Blair Street; **Harry's Bar**, 7b Randolph Place, and **Biancos**, 9 Hope Street. The City Café invariably packs out as the evening wears on, but it is open from before lunch until after midnight, and is worth visiting at a quieter period to appreciate its immaculate art deco design. It also serves a choice of coffee, and has an interesting, inexpensive lunch and dinner menu which is good on pasta dishes. Opposite is the **Ceilidh House**, 9 Hunter Square (Tel. 031 220 1550), serving lunches until 3 p.m. every day except at weekends with live music every night, including lively 'sessions' where anyone can bring along an instrument and join in. There is a very mixed and relaxed crowd. At the top of Candelmaker Row, **Greyfriars Bobby**, serving food throughout the day and open after many of the capital's publicans have gone to bed, is well suited to tourists. On the other side of the city, Lothian Road's many pubs are best ignored in favour of continuing beyond Tollcross to **Bennet's Bar**, next to the King's Theatre. This is a fine, traditional pub with elegant stained-glass windows and much of the same character as the Café Royal.

For nightclubs Edinburgh has its fair share for a city its size. One of the more popular clubs with all age groups is **Century 2000**, situated at 31 Lothian Road (031 229 6669), offering good dance music and a lively atmosphere. **Buster Browns**, situated just off Waverley Bridge at 25–27 Market Street (Tel. 031 226 4224), caters for various musical tastes.

Edinburgh has a range of cinemas far in excess of what might be expected of a city of its size. The **Filmhouse**, near the bottom of Lothian Road (Tel. 031-228 2688), shows a variety of films, old and new, for the discerning audience. The **Cannon**, 120 Lothian Road (Tel. 031 229 3030), is a triple-screen complex showing the latest commercial releases. The three-screen **Cameo**, 28 Home Street (Tel. 031-228 4141), caters for the same audience as the Filmhouse. All three can be found within the space of a few hundred yards on the same stretch of road. Elsewhere, the five-screen **Odeon**, 7 Clerk Street (Tel. 031-667 7332), shows the latest major releases, while in Morningside, the **Dominion**, Newbattle Terrace (Tel. 031-447 2660), tends to favour family films and films which have recently completed their general release on the commercial circuit.

The **Usher Hall**, opposite the Filmhouse in Lothian Road (Tel. 031-228 1155), hosts concerts each Friday evening by the Scottish National Orchestra, and is next door to the **Royal Lyceum Theatre**, Grindlay Street (Tel. 031-229 9697). The performances here are of revived works. New, often experimental, work for the stage is put on by the **Traverse Theatre** at its new venue in Cambridge Street, next to the city's Usher Hall (Tel. 031-228 1404). The **King's Theatre**, Leven Street (Tel. 031-229 1201), puts on productions ranging from Brecht to stand-up comedy. With 3,000 seats, the **Playhouse**, 18–22 Greenside Place (Tel. 031-557 2590), is Edinburgh's largest venue, and also the most varied, regularly staging pop concerts in addition to ballet and opera. Weekly jazz concerts combine with performances by the Scottish Chamber Orchestra and visiting pop bands to make up the programme at the **Queen's Hall**, 89 Clerk Street (Tel. 031-668 2019). **Ross Open Air Theatre** in Princes Street Gardens (Tel. 031-220 4351), offers a worldwide programme of music and dance from June to August.

THE EDINBURGH FESTIVAL

From small beginnings in 1947, the Edinburgh International Festival is now the largest arts festival in the world. It lasts three weeks, usually starting on the second Sunday in August, and has six constituent parts.

The Official Festival: the showpiece for major international drama, dance and music which expands in quality and reputation each year. Ticket information: 21 Market Street (Tel. 031-226 4001).

The Edinburgh Military Tattoo: a military and musical pageant which draws tens of thousands of visitors every year; it has lasted more than 40 years and not a single performance has been cancelled due to weather or any other circumstance. Information: Tattoo Office, Waverley Bridge (Tel. 031-225 1188).

The Fringe: for many people this is *the* Edinburgh Festival. More than 500 theatre companies from all over the world descend on the city and turn every tiny church hall, school yard and club room into a venue. The programme is published in June each year and, together with tickets and other information, it is available from: Festival Fringe Society, 180 High Street (Tel. 031-226 5259).

The Book Festival: a biennial event, first held in 1983, which attracts many distinguished guest speakers from the literary world. Information: Scottish Book Centre, 137 Dundee Street (Tel. 031-228 5444).

The Film Festival: running since 1946, this is the second oldest film festival in the world, and a prestigious annual showcase for new releases receiving their British première. Information: Filmhouse, 88 Lothian Road (Tel. 031-228 2688).

The Jazz Festival: one of Europe's busiest jazz events attracting some of the biggest names in contemporary jazz music. Information: 116 Canongate (Tel. 031-557 1642).

Finding accommodation for the festival is a nightmare. If you want a week or more in the city, an interesting company to contact is **Flatfinder Festival Flats**, 29–31 George IV Bridge (Tel. 031-220 6009). For less than hotel prices they can organize everything from a New Town penthouse to a student pad! Contact them well in advance and read all the conditions, so that there are no surprises, such as the deposits which have to be paid.

One final topic concerning the festival, for parents of young children: it can be frustrating not to be able to get to the shows because of the children. A useful place to deposit them while you go to soak up some culture is **Little Marco's** at 51 Grove Street, near the West End. This large indoor play area of bouncing castles, slides, mazes, and so on, keeps the little ones occupied for up to three hours for £6, and half the price for under three year olds.

The **International Science Festival** is the only one of its kind in the world. It takes place around Easter each year, this year from 4–8 April. On offer is a wide range of events from serious debate to fun hands-on exhibitions, demonstrations and workshops, while exhibitions of paintings, photographs and sculptures illustrate some of the many different ways art, science and engineering interact. Information: 20 Torphichen Street (Tel. 031-228 4756).

Traditionally, there has always been the castle and the zoo, but Edinburgh now hosts the world's only **International Children's Festival**, taking place each year for a week in May at Inverleith Park. This week of festivities offers a variety of amusements including children's theatre, music, puppet shows and clowns from all over the world. For more information: 22 Laurie Street (Tel. 031 554 6297).

Edinburgh does now in fact hold the prestigious title of 'The Most Child Friendly City in the UK', offering not only the best in family entertainment but services sensitive to children and parents' needs. Many of the city's pubs and restaurants which have been nominated as child friendly by the children and parents of the city are highlighted in Edinburgh's 'Child Friendly Guide'. These pubs welcome children until 8 p.m., with a selection of reasonably priced 'kiddies' menus and snack-sized meals available. Highchairs are provided and there is adaquate space for buggies. Some pubs offer excellent plays areas, for example the **Ratho Park**, Dalmahoy Road, and the **Bridge Inn**, Ratho. Restaurants such as **Fat Sam's Amazin' Pizza Pie Factory**, Fountainbridge, offer continual entertainment for children with their huge singing puppets and menus disguised as 'gangster and moll' masks. At **Richard's Pizzarama**, Seafield Road, children are invited to watch their pizzas being made, whilst at **Kavio's Restaurant** in Leith, they can even make their own. Shops in the guide are equally sensitive to children's needs. **John Lewis**, St James' Centre, was one of the first child and parent stores with its spacious restaurant, highchairs and easy access to it and around the store. There is a mother's room and a father's room with plenty of space for changing. Bottle warmers and baby wipes are provided. For more information, pick up a 'Child Friendly Edinburgh Guide' at the Tourist Information Centre, Waverley Market. Princes Street (Tel. 031 557 2727).

SIGHTS

Running through the heart of Edinburgh's OLD TOWN is the Royal Mile, linking the castle and the Palace of Holyroodhouse. **Edinburgh Castle** surmounts a volcanic plug which has supported a fortress since the seventh century. The present structure was built between the 14th and 16th centuries, but incorporates some of the earlier towers and walls. It was in this castle that Mary Queen of Scots gave birth to James VI, who, in 1603, became the first monarch to reign over Scotland and England together.

The castle contains Edinburgh's oldest building, **St Margaret's Chapel** – which dates from the 12th century – the **Scottish National War Memorial**, the **Scottish United Services Museum**, the **Jewel House** containing the Scottish crown jewels, and a number of palatial chambers, dating from the 15th century and still in use for state banquets hosted by Scottish Office government ministers. You can now enjoy the new visitor restaurant, situated in a converted 18th-century building next to the one o'clock gun, with the most magnificent views of the city. The castle is open from 9.30 a.m. to 4.55 p.m. Monday to Saturday from October to March, and from 12.30 p.m. to 4.55 p.m. on Sunday. During the summer it opens from 9.30 a.m. to 5.45 p.m., and from 11 a.m. to 5.45 p.m. on Sundays.

From the Castle Esplanade it is a short distance down the Royal Mile to the **Camera Obscura** where, on a clear day, the 17th century Outlook Tower offers a fascinating view of the whole city and over the Forth into Fife (open from 9.30 a.m. to 6 p.m. Monday to Saturday, and 10 a.m. to 6 p.m. on Sunday). Also on Castlehill, number 358 houses the **Scotch Whisky Heritage Centre**, providing a unique experience for visitors. There is an exhibition area, audio-visual show and a fabulous journey in a whisky barrel car depicting important landmarks in the industry's history. Tours are offered in seven languages. Further along, on the left, is **Gladstone's Land**, one of the few Royal Mile buildings to retain its original 17th-century façade. Now in the care of the National Trust for Scotland, it is open to the public for visitors to admire its period furnishings and decor. So too is **Lady Stair's**

House, situated at the end of the close of the same name. The former owner gave her name to what is now a museum devoted to Robert Burns, Sir Walter Scott and Robert Louis Stevenson, which houses memorabilia of these literary men which she avidly collected throughout her life (open Monday to Saturday throughout the year, admission free).

On the opposite side of the street is **Brodie's Close**, formerly the address of William Brodie, an 18th-century citizen of Edinburgh notorious for the double life he led. A popular city figure by day, he was a brutal thief by night until he was trapped and subsequently hanged in 1788. His double life is believed to have been the inspiration for Robert Louis Stevenson's *Doctor Jekyll and Mr Hyde*. At the south-east corner of George IV Bridge and High Street are four brass studs which mark the site of the last public execution in Scotland which took place in 1864.

The presbyterian **High Kirk of St Giles** is the third church on this site since the ninth century, the first two having been burnt down by English invaders. Most of the present building dates from the 15th century and features in Scott's *The Heart of Midlothian*. Just behind the cathedral, **Parliament House**, now home to the Scottish Law Courts, housed the Scottish parliament from 1639 until the union with England in 1707. In Parliament Square stands the **Mercat Cross**, the meeting place of the medieval city, and venue for executions, proclamations and celebrations, the present day structure being 19th-century and built on to the 16th-century original. The **Royal Exchange**, over the road from the Mercat Cross, was the mid-18th-century replacement for it as a meeting place. It is now the administrative offices of Edinburgh District Council.

It is not an act of disrespect, but a gesture believed to bestow good luck, that causes some superstitious citizens of Edinburgh to spit on the heart-shaped pattern set in the cobble stones outside St Giles, known as the **Heart of Midlothian**. The tradition stems from the time when the spot was occupied by a grid covering the cell of prisoners awaiting execution next morning, for it was considered lucky to spit through the grid and on to the doomed man's head. Royal proclamations are still read from the ornamental platform near Parliament House and St Giles Cathedral on major state occasions such as the dissolution of parliament prior to a general election.

The 17th-century **Tron Church**, just past St Giles, has long been the meeting place where Edinburgh's revellers gather to welcome in the New Year. Similar celebrations take place at the Tron in Glasgow, and elsewhere in Scotland.

Beyond the junction of High Street and South Bridge, Blackfriars Street leads off the Royal Mile to the **Richard Demarco Gallery** before reaching Cowgate and the **369 Gallery**. Back on the High Street, **Stills Gallery**, at number 105, on the left, hosts visiting exhibitions of photography. On the opposite side of the street, the **Museum of Childhood**, at number 42, claims to be the first of its type in the world. It has an extensive collection of toys through the ages, with the Victorian period particularly well represented.

John Knox's House, almost directly opposite, dates from the 15th century and contains a collection of memorabilia associated with the arch figure of the Reformation in Scotland. It is open from 10 a.m. to 4.30 p.m. Monday to Saturday.

Across from John Knox's House is the **Royal Mile Living Craft Centre**, where you can see a tartan weaver, a kiltmaker, a silversmith and a bagpipe-maker at work. You can also trace any Scottish ancestry you may have with the help of a computer, or taste traditional Scottish fare in the adjoining coffee shop. It is open seven days a week from 10 a.m.–6 p.m. and on a Sunday 10 a.m.–5.30 p.m. At 14 High Street, the **Scottish Poetry Library** is situated, with a fine selection of works from all periods.

Towards the end of the Royal Mile the High Street gives way to Canongate, so named because it was the route taken by the canons in the Middle Ages as they walked from the abbey at Holyrood up to the walled town around the castle. The **Canongate Tolbooth**, dating from 1591, once housed a jail and courtroom, but it now accommodates the 'People's Story' exhibition. Nearby **Canongate Church**, dating from 1688, had its interior restored in 1950. Its graveyard is the resting place of Adam Smith, Robert Ferguson, and New Town founder George Drummond. Opposite is **Huntly House**, three 16th-century mansions now housing the city's local history collection.

The 17th-century Acheson House, a little further down from the Canongate, houses the **Scottish Craft Centre**, which has a variety of traditional craftwork on display and for sale. Next door, the **Scottish Stone and Brass Rubbing Centre** allows absolute beginners to make rubbings of rare Scottish brasses and stone crosses. Across the road is one of Scotland's best museums: the **People's Story**, where the life of everyday Scots through the ages is explored in sound, sight and smell.

The Royal Mile comes to an end at the **Palace of Holyroodhouse**, the official residence of the Royal Family in Scotland (in contrast to Balmoral in Deeside, which is their private property) and the Royal Standard is flown when the Queen is in residence. At other times, there is public admission under guided tour, from Monday to Saturday (times and dates vary – Tel. 031–556 7371 for details). The Palace, excluding the private apartments, was built around 1500 by James IV.

The interior is notable for its spectacular plaster ceilings and a number of state rooms which have been used regularly by successive monarchs from Mary Queen of Scots through to the present day. Many fine paintings hang on the walls, and among the relics and historical memorabilia is a letter written by Mary just six hours before she was beheaded in February 1587. Addressed to her cousin, the king of France, it states that she has only just learned how 'promptly' her sentence is to be carried out. A plaque marks the spot where Mary saw her alleged lover Rizzio stabbed to death in 1566. A secret staircase which was used to connect their apartments is also displayed.

Admission to this most interesting historic building combines entrance to the adjoining **Holyrood Abbey** which now stands deprived of its roof. Founded by David I in 1128, it is the resting place for a number of royal figures, including David II, who reigned from the death of Robert the Bruce in 1329 until his own death in 1371; James II, who reigned from 1437 until his death in 1460; and James V, father of Mary Queen of Scots and successor to James IV after the Scots defeat at Flodden Field in 1513. He reigned until his own death at another Scots defeat in

1542 at Solway Moss. Lord Darnley, the ill-fated husband of Mary Queen of Scots, was murdered in 1567, just two years after his marriage, and is also buried here.

Mary Queen of Scots used to hunt boar in nearby Holyrood Park, when part of it was wild forest. Overlooking the park is Arthur's Seat. From the top of this 823 foot (251 m) high volcanic plug there is an excellent panoramic view of the city, and one which was recommended by no less a sightseer than Sir Walter Scott in *The Heart of Midlothian*. Comparable views are available via the more leisurely walk along **Salisbury Crags** which run almost perpendicular from Arthur's Seat.

South of the Royal Mile

Within easy walking distance of the Royal Mile are a number of historic sights and attractions. On George IV Bridge, the **National Library of Scotland** not only houses the largest collection of books in Scotland, but has an exhibition room open during office hours on weekdays. Admission is free.

The winding road opposite the National Library, Victoria Street, leads to the **Grassmarket**. Now characterized by its pubs and antique shops, its salient feature used to be the gallows which stood on a site marked at the east end of the market. Scott's readers will be familiar with the fate of Captain Porteous, who featured in *The Heart of Midlothian* and was lynched here by a mob in 1732.

At the south-east corner of the Grassmarket, Candlemaker Row leads to the statue of **Greyfriars Bobby**, the famous dog who guarded his master's grave for 14 years in the 19th century. The dog's grave can be seen in the nearby **Greyfriars Church**. Chambers Street, directly opposite, is the location of the **Royal Museum of Scotland**, the premier museum in the country. Exhibitions on science, art and history can all be found under the roof of this stout Victorian building. The natural history section includes the preserved remains of a number of whales washed ashore at various times on Scotland's east coast and, among these, pride of place goes to the assembled skeleton of a blue whale, measuring 100 feet from tip to tail. Elsewhere there is an informative exhibition tracing the complete history of life on earth, and displays embracing a range of topics from steam trains to anthropology. Admission to the Royal Museum is free and it is open all year, from 10 a.m. to 5 p.m. Monday to Saturday, and 2 p.m. to 5 p.m. on Sunday.

Around the corner, in Nicolson Street, Edinburgh University's Old College – of sufficient architectural merit to be an attraction in itself – is the location of the university's **Talbot Rice Gallery**. The gallery has a small permanent collection of art, in addition to hosting a variety of visiting exhibitions. It is open from 10 a.m. to 5 p.m. Tuesday to Saturday.

North of the Royal Mile

Market Street has two art galleries standing opposite each other near the south entrance to Waverley Station. The **City Arts Centre** has a small permanent collection in addition to frequent and very varied temporary exhibitions. The **Fruitmarket Gallery** hosts visiting exhibitions of modern works.

Princes Street is one of Europe's most famous thoroughfares, although its elegance and reputation have declined in recent years, and nowadays its plethora of High Street names and gaudy burger bars, gives it the appearance and character of most run-of-the-mill provincial High Streets. What makes Princes Street unique though and gives it a place among the sights of Europe is the juxtaposition of **Princes Street Gardens**, a perfect retreat from the clamour of the traffic, shoppers, and tourists. The gardens were formerly a loch but nowadays they contain colourful flower displays and the Ross Bandstand from where there are daily concerts. The slope up to the castle is very dramatic and is the site of the Glenlivet firework display which takes place every year in the second week of the Edinburgh Festival. The **Scott Monument**, an essential aspect of the Edinburgh skyline, is located on the other side of the gardens on Princes Street, near Waverley Station. It stands 200 feet tall, and was built in 1840 in honour of the lawyer, novelist and poet, Sir Walter Scott, whose likeness in stone sits at the base of the tapering tower. Inside, it has 287 steps, which, for an admission charge, make a long, narrow and steep climb to the top.

Scotland's foremost collection of art is housed in the **National Gallery of Scotland** (admission free) on Playfair Steps and the Mound. Most noteworthy artists and schools are represented in an extensive permanent display, which includes a significant collection of Turner's watercolours. The delicate nature of the latter, however, means that they are displayed only in January, to protect them from the light. The adjacent building, at the foot of the Mound, half-way along Princes Street, is the **Royal Scottish Academy**, which hosts various temporary exhibitions (with an admission charge).

To the east of Princes Street is **Calton Hill**, accessible by steps from Waterloo Place, and surmounted by the distinctive outline of the unfinished monument to Scotsmen who died in the Napoleonic Wars. It was designed in imitation of the Parthenon in Athens, but the end result was much less noble, becoming known as 'Edinburgh's Disgrace' because of the city's failure to raise the necessary funds to complete the building. Also on the hill are **Nelson's Monument**, with a good panorama from the top; the Playfair monument to Dugald Stewart, the John Playfair monument, and the old **Playfair Observatory** which houses the '**Edinburgh Experience**', a three-dimensional panoramic introduction to Edinburgh and its history.

North of Princes Street, at the corner of Queen Street and North St Andrew Street, is the grand, red sandstone building housing the **Museum of Antiquities** and the **Scottish National Portrait Gallery**. The former traces the history of life in Scotland from the Stone Age to the present day, while the latter displays portraits of Scotland's eminent figures, from early monarchs to 20th-century heroes like James Maxton and Hugh McDiarmid (admission free, open 10 a.m. to 5 p.m. Monday to Saturday, and 2 p.m. to 5 p.m. on Sunday).

In **Charlotte Square**, the core of the Georgian New Town, at number 7, is the **Georgian House**, a National Trust for Scotland-owned building showing a Georgian home typical of the late 18th century. Every detail of daily life has been illustrated and the result is a fascinating visit.

Beyond the City Centre

Beyond the city centre there are a number of places of interest. The **Printmakers' Workshop** at 23 Union Street, just off Leith Walk, is a former public wash-house containing a very smart gallery area and printmaking studio where you can see printmakers at work. Posters and prints made in the Workshop are on sale and it is open 10 a.m. to 5 p.m. from Monday to Saturday, and 2 p.m. to 5 p.m. on Sunday.

North of the New Town, the **Royal Botanic Gardens**, amongst the best in Europe, have an attractive display of flowers, trees and shrubs in their grounds, in addition to an aquarium and hothouses. The **Scottish National Gallery of Modern Art**, in Belford Road, north of Edinburgh's West End, has an impressive collection of 20th-century art, including works by Picasso, Braque, Matisse, Miró, Lichtenstein and Hockney. Sculptures by Henry Moore and Barbara Hepworth adorn the grounds. (Admission is free, and the gallery is open 10 a.m. to 5 p.m. from Monday to Saturday, and 2 p.m. to 5 p.m. on Sunday.)

A short walk from here lies **Dean Village**. Once home to Edinburgh's poorest, this is now one of the city's most exclusive residential areas, but amid the trendy flats are still the attractive water features and interesting architectural styles that make this worth a look. Back up to the west end of Princes Street sits **Edinburgh Dungeon**, the city's historical torture museum based on researched facts and enhanced with authentic sounds, smells and movement.

The **Royal Commonwealth Pool**, in Holyrood Park Road, hosted all of the water events at the Commonwealth Games when they were held in Edinburgh in 1970 and 1988, and currently houses Europe's biggest water-slide. **Ainslie Park Leisure Centre**, off Ferry Road, features swimming pools, flumes and a leisure complex. Three miles from the city centre, the **Royal Observatory** on Blackford Hill has an impressive visitor centre which explains the workings of one of the United Kingdom's most important space observation centres. Mary Queen of Scots sought refuge in **Craigmillar Castle**, three miles south-east of the city centre, when she feared for her life following the murder of Rizzio.

The main road west from the city, Corstorphine Road, leads to **Edinburgh Zoo**, one of the UK's largest (open every day of the year except Christmas Day). One of its most popular attractions, especially with children, is the Penguin Parade, which takes place each afternoon in the summer. It also boasts the biggest and best penguin enclosure in the world plus a new underwater viewing area to allow you to have a closer look. Some miles further on towards Glasgow, near the airport, is Ingliston, where you will find the **Scottish Agricultural Museum** as well as the renowned Sunday market. It is also the site of the **Highland Show** held in July each year. Ratho, directly south of Ingliston, is host to **Edinburgh Canal Centre** offering quiet cruises along the canal, east to Edinburgh or west to the Almond aquaduct with lunch and a full bar available. On the southern outskirts of Edinburgh lies **Hillend**, the largest artificial ski slope in Britain. It offers the views from the top of the chairlift (available to non-skiers) of the Pentland Hills, over Edinburgh and beyond. The **Edinburgh Butterfly and Insect World**, now Europe's largest, lies six miles south of the city, on the road to Dalkeith, and is home to more than 1,000 butterflies, fluttering around in sub-tropical conditions. There is also a children's adventure playground, garden centre and picnic area on site. Ten miles south of Edinburgh, **Penicuik** houses the Edinburgh Crystal Visitor Centre. Tours, shop, restaurant, picnic and children's play area are all available. Roslin, situated only a few miles from Penicuik, is home to **Roslin Glen Country Park** with the remains of an old gunpowder mill; **Rosslyn Chapel**, built in the 15th century has the most unique and stunning ornate stonework in the country, and **Rosslyn Castle**, where the past earls of Rosslyn once resided and part of it is still being used by the present earl. The **Penicuik to Bonnyrigg Walkway**, runs through Roslin, following the old railway line built by the Penicuik Railway Company in 1875, which once connected the existing towns of Midlothian. For more information on this Midlothian route contact the Recreation and Leisure Department of Midlothian District Council (Tel. 031 440 1352).

If the weather is kind, the closest beach to the city is at **Silverknowes** (bus number 14). From here it is a bracing walk to the old fishing village of **Cramond**. Two and a half miles to the east of the Forth Bridges, at South Queensferry, is situated Scotland's finest stately home, **Hopetoun House**. It was designed originally for the first Earl of Hopetoun by Sir William Bruce, the same architect who designed Holyrood Palace. There are paintings by Gainsborough, Raeburn and Canaletto, as well as woodland walks, a red deer park and nature trails to the west of the house. Dalmeny House, similarly situated at South Queensferry, is home to the Earl of Rosebery, and has an art collection and beautiful grounds open to the public. Under the north cantilever of the Forth Rail Bridge is **Deep Sea World**, the world's largest marine aquarium of its type. It is to be the future home to sharks and other fish, and visible to us through an acrylic tunnel along 120 metres of the seabed. It is due to open in the spring of 1993. If you prefer to be above the water, there are the Forth ferries summer cruises on board *The Spirit of Life* which regularly sails between Edinburgh and Fife, as well as daily lunchtime cruises around the Forth estuary to enjoy the wildlife and the famous bridges themselves.

The Kingdom of Fife

INTRODUCTION

Fife occupies most of the peninsula enclosed on the north by the Firth of Tay and on the south by the Firth of Forth. The region was an important one in Scotland's coal industry but today most of its pits, as in the rest of the country, have been closed down. It has much to offer the visitor though: along its coast are many popular holiday resorts and fishing villages, such as Elie, Anstruther, Crail and Pittenweem, and throughout, particularly in Dunfermline and St Andrews, it is a region steeped in history, with many interesting and well-preserved reminders of its past.

The appellation 'The Kingdom of Fife' dates from the fourth century AD, when the Romans left Scotland and the country was divided into seven kingdoms. Of those, Fife is the only one which has survived to the present day as an identifiable region. Indeed, plans to dissolve the name and divide the region between Lothian and Tayside were abandoned during the 1975 reorganization of local government due to the fierce resistance of the Fifers. The Fifers themselves are well known as determined and canny people, hence the saying 'You need a lang spoon to sup wi' a Fifer'.

The region is easily reached by road and rail across the impressive bridges over the Forth from Edinburgh and the Tay from Dundee. From the west, the A91 connects north-east Fife with Stirling, and the A876 crosses the Forth at Kincardine in the south-east corner of the region. There are also many roads branching from the M90 between the Forth Bridge and Perth which give access to all parts of Fife.

WHERE TO GO FOR WHAT

The best-known town in Fife is St Andrews on the north-east coast, famous as the world home of golf. It is also a very important historical town with much to interest the sightseer. Down the coast from here, between Lundin Links and Kingsbarns, is the East Neuk of Fife, a stretch of coast containing many picturesque fishing villages such as Pittenweem and Anstruther, whose pleasant sandy beaches have made them popular resorts for family holidays. The north-east corner of this region is decidedly the most attractive part, and this is where most visitors now spend their time. In addition to the attractions of St Andrews, visitors will find of interest Dunfermline, famous for its historic ruined abbey, and the quiet town of Falkland, home to the magnificent Falkland Palace and Gardens. Finally, admire the restoration work of the National Trust in the 17th-century village of Culross.

This chapter begins with Culross, on the shores of the Firth of Forth in the south-west corner of Fife, before following the coast towards St Andrews. **CULROSS** (pronounced 'cooruss') is unique in the extent to which its character and architecture have been preserved since the late 16th century when it had a flourishing trade in salt and coal, and enjoyed prosperous seafaring links with Scandinavia, Germany, and the Netherlands. When this trade came to an end, however, the local economy went into decline, and by the 19th century the once prosperous town was a backwater passed over by the industrial revolution. This period of neglect, however, appears to the visitor and historian of today as a stroke of good fortune, for it allowed the Culross of the 16th and 17th centuries to survive untouched by industrial redevelopment, and throughout the last 50 years or so the National Trust has been diligent in preservation and restoration work.

The entire village is a historical monument whose character can be discovered in the steep walk uphill through its narrow streets to **Culross Abbey**. Dating from the 13th century, its nave is in ruins but its central **tower** and choir have been incorporated into the adjoining parish church. Back down the hill is **Culross Palace**, built between 1597 and 1611 by Sir George Bruce, prominent in the town's salt and coal trade. **The Study** houses a museum and is open year round by arrangement (also from 2 p.m. to 4 p.m. Saturday and Sunday during April, June, July, August and October). The admission charge includes entry to the **Town House**.

The road east from Culross joins the A994 a few miles from
DUNFERMLINE. A busy town with a distinguished past, it is
the former seat of the kings of Scotland and the birthplace of the
American millionaire industrialist and philanthropist, Andrew
Carnegie. In the south-west of the town is the **Abbey Church**. The
foundations and the nave belong to the original abbey begun in
1128, while the choir was reconstructed as the parish church
between 1817 and 1822. During excavation work in 1818 the body
of Robert the Bruce was discovered and later reburied beneath the
pulpit where a memorial brass now marks the grave. The 11th-
century King Malcolm Canmore and his wife Margaret are buried
at the east end of the church, in what remains of St Margaret's
Shrine. Nearby are the ruins of the **Monastery** and the **Palace** –
connected to the abbey by means of an arch across the road – and
the magnificent gardens of **Pittencrieff Glen**, an extensive estate
attached to **Pittencrieff House**, which is now a local museum. The
estate was presented to the town by Andrew Carnegie in 1903.
Carnegie was born in 1835 in a weaver's cottage in Moodie Street
which has now been transformed into the **Andrew Carnegie
Birthplace Museum**. It preserves the humble residence of his
parents and chronicles his success as an industrialist in America,
where the family emigrated while he was still a child. Elsewhere is
Dunfermline District Museum with prominent displays on the
town's successful linen industry, and the restored 16th-century
Abbot's House in Maygate.

Accommodation is available for around £15 at the **Auld Toll
Tavern**, 119–121 St Leonards Street (Tel. 0383 721489); **The
Gables**, 121–123 New Row (Tel. 0383 735625/736294); and
Garvock Guest House, 82 Halbeath Road (Tel. 0383 734689).
The **Tourist Information** centre at Abbot House, Maygate (Tel.
0383 720999) runs an accommodation service, and is open from
Easter to the end of September.

A few miles south-east of Dunfermline is
ABERDOUR, a small holiday resort on the shores of
the Firth of Forth. It has pleasant beaches, a scenic golf course, and
with its sheltered harbour it has become a popular sailing centre.
Its chief historic sight is **Aberdour Castle** (closed in winter on

Thursday afternoon and all day Friday). The foundations and tower date back to the 14th century, the rest having been added in the 16th and 17th centuries. Nearby **St Fillan's Church** was founded in the 12th century with 16th- and 17th-century additions. There are boats from Aberdour harbour to the small island of Inchcolm and the relatively well-preserved **Abbey of St Columba**, founded as an Augustinian priory in 1123 and turned into an abbey in 1235.

The coastal road passes through Burntisland and Kinghorn on its way to **KIRKCALDY** (pronounced 'kirkawdy') which acquired prosperity and some renown in the manufacture of linoleum. It had the nickname 'Lang Toun' ('long town') because it occupied a narrow area running four miles along the coast. Nowadays it has broadened out, but the monicker is still in use. Its famous sons include the economist Adam Smith born in 1723, the site of whose birthplace in the High Street is marked by a plaque, and the architect Robert Adam born in 1728. A plaque in Kirk Wynd commemorates the employment of historian Thomas Carlyle as a teacher at the burgh school. **Kirkcaldy Museum and Art Gallery** has displays of local material and prominent among the artists represented are Scottish painters such as McTaggart and Raeburn in addition to work by Lowry and Fantin-Latour. The town is also famous for its **Links Market** reputedly the largest street fair in Britain. The ruins of **Ravenscraig Castle** at the north end of town date from 1460 and stand within **Ravenscraig Park**. **Burntisland Museum** reflects the bygone age of an Edwardian fairground. Walk through the sights and sounds of the town's fair as it was in 1910.

North from Kirkcaldy the A92 passes through the new town of Glenrothes and connects with the A912, which leads to the quiet village of **FALKLAND**, notable for the beautiful **Falkland Palace** and its gardens (open April to September, 10 a.m. to 6 p.m. Monday to Saturday, and 2 p.m. to 6 p.m. on Sunday; October, 10 a.m. to 5 p.m. and Sunday 2 p.m. to 5 p.m.). It was a popular retreat of the Stuarts, begun by James IV in the 15th century and completed by James V between 1525 and 1542. The Royal Tennis Court is still in use, and, dating from 1539, is the oldest in Britain.

The stretch of coastline between Lower Largo and Crail, opposite North Berwick on the other side of the Forth, is known as the 'East Neuk' (East Corner), and contains many quaint little ports easily reached by the A917. Turn left off the A917 and one soon reaches the tiny village of Kilconquhar and **Kilconquhar Estate and Country Club**. As well as 'Holiday Ownership', two-, three-, and four-bedroom holiday homes are available to rent for three, four or seven nights. There are around 55 villas set in over 50 acres of beautiful grounds. The spacious rooms are equipped with four-poster beds, jacuzzis and every piece of modern equipment in the kitchen. Two superb restaurants, swimming pool, tennis and squash courts, riding and a BMX track for children are some of the activities on offer. Prices from around £400–£1100 for seven nights depending on the size of the villa and the time of year. The fishing port of **PITTENWEEM** has been a royal burgh since 1542. The name is Pictish for 'the place of the cave', and relates to **St Fillan's Cave** near the harbour, above which are the remains of the 12th-century **priory**. At the east end of the harbour are **The Gyles**, an attractive group of 16th-century houses restored by the National Trust for Scotland. The **Kellie Lodging Gallery**, on the High Street, is host to temporary exhibitions of contemporary Scottish artists. Three miles north-west of Pittenweem is **Kellie Castle**, part of which dates back to the 14th century, although most of the present structure was built in the 16th and 17th centuries. It is notable for its fine plasterwork and painted ceilings and, along with its four-acre grounds, is open to the public. **Balcaskie House** and beautiful terraced gardens are well worth visiting. Not far up the coast is **ANSTRUTHER** or, to give it its full title: The United Burgh of Kilrenny, Cellardyke, Anstruther Easter and Anstruther Wester. Until the 1940s it was the main herring fishing centre in Scotland. Today it is the home of the **Scottish Fisheries Museum**, situated by the harbour. From here there are boat trips in the summer to the **Isle of May**, six miles offshore. The island was the location of the first lighthouse in Scotland in 1636 and contains the ruins of a **Benedictine priory**, founded by David I in 1153. On the East Harbour is the red **North Carr Lightship**, the last of its kind in Scotland and now home to a maritime museum. It is open seven days a week from Easter, between 11 a.m.–5 p.m.

Anstruther has a lot to offer the sporting visitor. **East Neuk Outdoors** at Cellardyke (open from 10 a.m. to 5 p.m., Tel. 0333 311929) offers a variety of activity holidays: abseiling, archery, canoeing, climbing, cycling, bird-watching, and so on. The town is also popular for wind-surfing and equipment is available for hire. **Anstruther Riding Centre** is at Cauldicots Farm (Tel. 0333 311923). **Anstruther Golf Club** (Tel. 0333 310224) has a nine-hole course.

Hotel accommodation is available at **Royal Hotel**, 20 Roger Street (Tel. 0333 310581), where prices start around £15; and **Beaumont Lodge Guest House** (Tel. 0333 310315), where prices begin at around £16. For an economical self-catering option, a family house in central Anstruther can be rented (Tel. 0702 75310). The four crown commended **Craw's Nest** (Tel. 0333 310691), offers accommodation from £30, as well as homestyle Scottish cuisine.

Tourist Information is at the Scottish Fisheries Museum.

Further up the coast **CRAIL** is a former smuggling centre and currently a popular holiday resort and fishing town. In Marketgate there is the **Tolbooth** and many well-restored houses from the 16th and 17th centuries, at which time it was a thriving fishing and trading port. Number 62 Marketgate is the address of **Crail Museum and Heritage Centre** (open for two weeks at Easter and from June to September. **Tourist Information** is available here). Local guides provide historic walks through the town, leaving from **Crail Museum**, from June to August every Sunday at 2.30 p.m. In the east of the town, the **Collegiate Church of St Mary**, where John Knox used to preach, was built in 1517 and includes parts of the 12th-century church which stood on the same site. Crail also has an 18-hole golf course at **Balcomie**. Just a few miles outside Crail, on the A917, is **Cambo Country Park** where you can see rare farm animals and enjoy the nature trails and seashore as well as the indoor and outdoor adventure playgrounds.

There is a good selection of reasonably priced accommodation, from between £12 and £25, at **Croma Hotel** (Tel. 0333 50239); **East Neuk Hotel**, 67 High Street (Tel. 0333 50225); **The Golf Hotel** (Tel. 0333 50206); and **Marine Hotel**, 54 Nethergate South (Tel. 0333 50207). For camping facilities there is space at

Sauchope Links Caravan Park (Tel. 0333 50460), for tourers and tents from March to October, charging between £6.50 and £8.50.

 ST ANDREWS is revered by golfers throughout the world as the home of the sport. The **Royal and Ancient Golf Club**, founded in 1754, is the ruling authority. It has four courses of which the New Course, the Jubilee Course, and the Eden Course are open to visitors without the need for introduction or membership. The famous Old Course is closed on Sundays and during March. **Strathyrum** course is due to open in summer 1993. The **British Golf Museum** (Tel. 0334 78880) opened in 1990, and is a 'must' for golfers interested in tracing the history of the game. Multi-media systems make this an interesting visit (open Thursday–Tuesday 10 a.m.–4 p.m. November, Thursday–Monday 11 a.m.–3 p.m. December to February, Thursday–Tuesday 10 a.m.–5 p.m. March–April and daily 10 a.m.–5.30 p.m. May to October).

Behind the Royal and Ancient Golf Club, on the green near the sea, is **Martyr's Memorial**, an obelisk dedicated to, and recording the names of, the Protestant martyrs burned for their faith near here during the Reformation. East from here, along the coast, are the ruins of **St Andrews Castle**. It stands on a rocky promontory and was founded in 1200 as an Episcopal residence by Bishop Rogers. Further east is the ruined **St Andrews Cathedral**, begun in 1160 by Bishop Arnold but not completed until 1318. Its destruction was partly due to the iconoclasm of the Reformers, incited by John Knox, and also the citizens of the town who removed stone from it to use as building material elsewhere. The practice was stopped in 1826 when new owners undertook to conserve what remained of the structure, which once formed the largest church in Scotland. Nearby are the ruins of the **Priory** of 1144. From here South Street runs west and, along with the adjoining side streets, this area contains many fine buildings from the 18th century and earlier. Notable examples are St Leonard's School, occupying the site and some of the 16th-century buildings of **St Leonard's College; St Mary's College** (1537); and **Holy Trinity Church** (founded 1412 but frequently altered). At the end of the street is the **West Port**, the main city gate, dating from 1589.

Throughout the town there are many admirable buildings belonging to **St Andrews University**, whose foundation in 1412 makes it the oldest university in Scotland, although today it is principally known as a little English enclave, due to the high proportion of its students who come from south of the border. **St Andrews Preservation Trust Museum** has displays of local material at 12 North Street, open July to September, Monday to Saturday 10 a.m. to 5 p.m. The new **St Andrews Museum** opened in July 1991 in Kinburn House. The museum features the story of the burgh from medieval times to the present day. Open all year. Along the road at number 93 is the **Crawford Centre for the Arts**, specializing in drama workshops and temporary exhibitions. The **Botanic Garden** is set in 18 acres with a large variety of plants, flowers, trees and glasshouses.

There is a swimming pool, squash courts, and snooker tables at **East Sands Leisure Centre**, and at **St Andrews Sea Life Centre**, The Scores, is a variety of marine life. **Craigtoun Country Park**, two miles south-west, is a 50-acre site with a wide range of attractions: boating lake, trampolines, gardens, miniature railway, and so on, which are free after paying the entrance charge. One mile east of Leuchars and six miles from St Andrews lies **Earlshall Castle and Gardens**. Built in 1546, the castle is still a family home. It boasts richly fitted main rooms including the long gallery with its magnificent painted ceiling. The gardens have topiary yews shaped in the form of chessmen.

In keeping with a resort of its size and popularity, St Andrews has a wide choice of accommodation. From around £19–£26 there is **Argyle House Private Hotel**, 127 North Street (Tel. 0334 73387); **Homelea Hotel**, 1 Pilmour Place (Tel. 0334 73252); and **Yorkston Hotel**, 68 and 70 Argyle Street (Tel. 0334 72019). From around £18 there are **Albany Private Hotel**, 56 North Street (Tel. 0334 77737) and **Arran House** (Tel. 0334 74724). For a touch of luxury, the **St Andrews Old Course Hotel**, Old Station Road (Tel. 0334 74371), overlooks the 17th fairway of the Championship Old Course. Leisure facilities are superb and include spa and pool. The two restaurants are of international standard, and accommodation is in the region of £125 plus. University accommodation is quite reasonably priced. **David Russell Hall**, Buchanan Gardens (Tel.

0334 72281) and **Hamilton Hall**, Golf Place (Tel. 0334 77641), charge around £17 per person. The nearest camping and caravan park is at Largo Road (Tel. 0334 73604) and charges between £7 and £8 per night for tourers and £6.50 for tents.

Tourist Information is available all year at 78 South Street (Tel. 0334 72021). North of St Andrews, off the back road from Leuchars to Tayport, lies the Forestry Commission's Tentsmuir Forest, an attractive picnic area noted for its wildlife interest and with access to a superb beach.

West of St Andrews on the A91 is **CUPAR**, the county town of Fife which retains many attractive buildings from the 18th and 19th centuries. **Sir Douglas Bader Garden** for the disabled is situated in Daffus Park. The garden has raised beds, rock gardens, shrub border, fountains, waterfalls and sheltered seating. Three miles west of Cupar is the **Scottish Deer Centre**. The centre offers visitors the unique opportunity to see deer at very close quarters. You can stroll round the walkways with raised viewing platforms or visit the indoor audio-visual shows and exhibitions, whilst children can play in the adventure barn or outside in the adventureland play area. A few miles south on the A916 is **Scotstarvit Tower** which dates from 1579. The village of **CERES**, east of here, is the home of the **Fife Folk Museum**, with displays on the county's domestic and agricultural past.

Two miles south of Cupar is **Hill of Tarvit House**. A beautiful Edwardian home, designed by Sir Robert Lorimer, the house is well worth a detour to see the outstanding collections of Chinese porcelain, paintings and furniture. In the care of the National Trust for Scotland, it opens between April and October, and time should also be allowed to visit the outhouses which are still intact, including the fine period laundry, and to appreciate the woodland walk to the hilltop viewpoint and beautiful gardens.

Perth and Perthshire

INTRODUCTION

With the Highland Boundary Fault running through the county, visibly separating the hilly Highlands from the rolling Lowlands, Perthshire's 2,000 square miles provide the visitor with scenery as varied as it is spectacular. The south-east is an area of gently undulating farm and woodland, while further north and to the west, the land is that of rolling hills and rugged peaks sheltering long wooded glens and peaceful lochs.

HISTORY

As the meeting place of Highland and Lowland Scotland, Perthshire's strategic importance has given it a prominent role in the nation's history. This was part of the Pictish kingdom and the northernmost boundary of the Roman Empire. In the mid-ninth century, Kenneth MacAlpine made Scone, near Perth, the capital of his newly formed joint kingdom of Scots and Picts. Later the separate kingdoms into which the country had divided following the Roman withdrawal became a united country under Duncan in 1034, and again Scone was declared capital. This was the place where monarchs from MacAlpine to Charles II were instated, and the essential part of the inauguration ceremony, the Stone of Scone, is still used as part of today's Coronation Ceremony Chair in Westminster Abbey following its theft from Scone by Edward I in 1296. Or rather, to say that the stone in Westminster is the self-same Stone of Scone deserves qualification. The Stone of Destiny, as it is also known, was a *cause célèbre* for six months in 1950–1 when it was repatriated as a symbolic act of national self-assertion by a group of young Scottish Nationalists. Before its return to London it was accidentally split and had to be placed in the care of a stonemason for repair. The story in circulation thereafter was that the stone eventually handed back was a fake and that the stonemason had placed within the fissure a note to that effect. No one has yet taken the necessary action to verify the story.

Outside the principal town, the glens in the north of the county were for a long time accessible only with the utmost difficulty. They therefore provided an ideal refuge from the Crown for the Highland clans who, safe from the interference of the King's officers, spent a great deal of time and blood feuding with each other. When industrialization came to Britain it largely passed by this part of Scotland, with the result that Perthshire's population today is scattered in small towns and villages which have preserved their rural character and charm.

COMMUNICATIONS

Perth, as the geographical centre of Scotland, is the meeting place for many major roads, particularly the M90 from Edinburgh and the A9 from Stirling, which give easy access to travellers from the south. From Glasgow or Aberdeen the car journey is only one and a half hours, and two hours from Inverness. There are InterCity rail links with Glasgow, Edinburgh, Inverness, Aberdeen, and Dundee, as well as London, Birmingham and other English towns.

WHERE TO GO FOR WHAT

For the keen sightseer there are many historic buildings and castles such as **Scone Palace** and **Huntingtower** and **Elcho Castles** near Perth, **Loch Leven** and **Burleigh Castles** near Kinross, **Ardblair Castle** (which cannot be visited without prior appointment) near Blairgowrie, and **Castle Menzies** near Aberfeldy. Golfers will be interested in the region's many courses, including the world famous **Gleneagles Hotel**. The terrain in the north combines spectacular scenery with stout exercise, and is ideal for hillwalkers. Particularly rewarding are **Schiehallion** and **Ben Lawers** which are both more than 3,500 feet high, and **Ben Vrackie** which is over 2,500 feet. The region's many lochs and rivers are ideal for water sports and there are popular centres at **Lochs Earn, Tay**, and

Rannoch. There are many excellent locations for the angler. Two deserving a special mention are the **River Tay**, Scotland's longest and noted for its salmon and trout, and **Loch Leven**, renowned for its unique variety of trout. Two scenic and historic routes through Perthshire provide alternatives to the major trunk roads. The Perthshire Tourist Route, following the line taken by General Wade's military road, loops off the A9 via Crieff and Aberfeldy, whilst the Deeside Tourist Route through Blairgowrie and Glenshee offers a superb alternative to the main Perth – Aberdeen road.

Beginning with Perth before going south to Kinross, the region will be covered here in a clockwise circuit finishing at Glamis.

The capital of Scotland until the mid-15th century, **PERTH** stands on the banks of the River Tay, beneath the hills of Kinnoull, Moncrieffe, and Kirkton. The town grew following Kenneth MacAlpine's foundation of nearby Scone in 846 as the capital of the joint kingdom of the Scots and Picts, but had to be re-established by William the Lion in 1210 following a flood in the same year which washed the original town away. North of the town centre, running along the river bank, is the **North Inch**, a large park with a range of sports, such as golf, rugby, football, cricket and bowls, and in the park lies the **Gannochy Sports Pavilion** which provides the opportunity for pursuing a number of indoor sports. And Perth's award-winning leisure pool and neighbouring curling ice rink provide family entertainment whatever the weather. Bell's Whisky is based in Perth, as is General Accident Insurance, and both companies have contributed many civic assets. Perth is indeed a prosperous town – voted in 1991 'the best place to live in the UK', after a survey checked all sorts of relevant factors such as schooling, property prices, health care, leisure facilities etc. Next to the sports centre, **Balhousie Castle**, originally dating from the early 15th century but subsequently rebuilt in Scottish baronial style, houses the **Museum of the Black Watch**, the regiment raised at Aberfeldy in 1739. Visitors to **Caithness Glass** in the north of the town can observe the process of glass-making and purchase some of the fine finished products. **John Dewar and Sons** whisky bottling plant offer free conducted tours, Monday to Friday all year. Back in Perth, **St Ninian's Cathedral**, the first cathedral built in Scotland since the Reformation, stands at the corner of Atholl Street and North Methven Street, built between 1850 and 1900.

The preacher John Knox was active in Perth at the time of the Reformation and as a consequence of his sermons the monasteries in the region were destroyed. One of these, Blackfriars Monastery, dating from 1231, is commemorated by a plaque on the corner of Charlotte and Blackfriars streets. South-east of here the **Fair Maid's House** in North Port is now a craft shop hosting occasional exhibitions of work by Scottish artists. The permanent collections at the nearby **Art Gallery and Museum** in George Street include displays on archaeology, natural history, art, local history, and the whisky industry. Two blocks south of here is **St John's Kirk**, where John Knox's iconoclastic ranting and raving issued forth from the pulpit in the mid-16th century. His virulent brand of rhetoric in 1559 sparked the destruction of the many august religious centres which had contributed to the early importance of Perth. In addition to Blackfriars Monastery mentioned above, his inflammatory sermons were responsible for the destruction of the town's Greyfriars, Whitefriars, and Carthusian monasteries. St John's Kirk was founded by David I in 1126, but has been restored and rebuilt many times between 1328 and 1926. The work of 1328 was undertaken at the behest of Robert the Bruce but was aborted after his death the following year. Near here is one of the oldest hotels in Scotland, the attractive **Salutation Hotel** dating from 1695, where Bonnie Prince Charlie rested in 1745. His particular room, number 20, is still in use. Tay Street runs along the river bank, passing the site of Greyfriars Monastery at Greyfriars Cemetery, before reaching the **Fergusson Gallery** in the Round House, formerly the city's waterworks and now a unique art gallery housing the J. D. Fergusson collection; nearby is the expansive park of **South Inch** whose current public amenities of boating, putting, and the children's playground are in sharp contrast to its former use for archery and witch burning. Heading north, on the other side of the river are the two acres of **Branklyn Garden**, in the care of the National Trust. An outstanding collection of alpines, rhododendrons and herbaceous plants can be seen here: open from

1 March to 31 October. **Bell's Cherrybank Gardens** also offers a floral treat with its national heather collection just off the Glasgow Road. The **Lower City Mills** (sign-posted as 'Working Water Mill' near the city centre), is a recently restored 18th/19th-century water-powered mill with a craft centre, gift shop and tearoom. For the more energetic, prepared for a 700-foot climb, **Kinnoull Hill** makes for a good walk and vantage point from which to see the town and surrounding countryside. The Forestry Commission have excellent trails through the woodland here.

Perth has plenty of accommodation to choose from. The **Queens Hotel**, Leonard Street (Tel. 0738 25471), charges upward of £38, as does the **Royal George**, Tay Street (Tel. 0738 24455), while **Lovat Hotel**, Glasgow Road (Tel. 0738 36555), is slightly cheaper. The new **Beaumont Hotel Garni**, 15 John's Place (Tel. 0738 441770) offers 4 star accommodation from £35, in the very centre of Perth. **Stakis City Mills** is a comfortable, well-appointed hotel in West Mill Street (Tel. 0738 28281) in the upper-middle price category. It has reliable quality and good catering options. The **Station Hotel** in Leonard Street (Tel. 0738 24141) offers accommodation from around £33. Once used by Bonnie Prince Charlie, **Salutation Hotel**, 34 South Street (Tel. 0738 30066), is one of Scotland's oldest hotels and has prices starting at around £16. It has been recently refurbished. In Dundee Road **Sunbank House Hotel** (Tel. 0738 24882) and **St Leonard's Manse** at number 112 (Tel. 0738 27975) are particularly good value at around £16. Overlooking the South Inch on St Leonard's Bank sits the **Parklands Hotel** (Tel. 0728 22451), a classical town house which has been restored by its present owners to create a country house hotel in the city. Bed and breakfast from £50 p.p. and it has an excellent dining room. Just outside the city is an excellent country house hotel: **Murrayshall House Hotel** (Tel. 0738 51171). Located just outside Scone, it boasts an award-winning chef and its own golf course. Exquisite food is served in the restaurant and it is a fine example of the de luxe country house genre. Another country house hotel close to Perth is **Ballathie House**, at Kinclaven, by Stanley (Tel. 0250 883268). Overlooking the Tay, this mid-19th-century mansion has 27 bedrooms, a fine restaurant, and offers Tay salmon fishing and field sports. **Huntingtower Hotel** is situated two miles from Perth (Tel. 0738 83771). This fine country house has just recently been refurbished, offering a choice of elegant rooms from £55. The restaurant serves traditional Scottish cuisine as well as provincial French. Activities such as fishing, hill walking, riding and golf can also be arranged.

If you are looking for a very luxurious and exclusive place to stay in Perthshire, **Duncrub Self-Catering Holidays** may be the answer. Three stone-built Scottish farm buildings set in beautiful countryside are available to rent and come complete with all home comforts. Phone 076 484 368 for more details.

One of the best-known restaurants in Perthshire is **Timothy's**, 24 St John Street (Tel. 0738 26641), which specializes in Danish food (closed for three weeks in July/August). The **Orchid Blossom Restaurant**, 224 High Street (Tel. 0738 38178), serves genuine Peking cuisine, while Italian fare can be had at **Italian Corner**, 33 Princes Street (Tel. 0738 29645). The city also boasts several good Indian restaurants. Fresh Scottish fish is on the menu at **Number Thirty-Three Seafood Restaurant**, 33 George Street (Tel. 0738 33771). An exceptionally good meal for a very reasonable price can be had at **Paco's Restaurant**, a bistro/de luxe burger house at 16 St John's Place (Tel. 0738 22290), or at **Littlejohn's**, 65 South Methren Street (Tel. 0738 39888).

The **Tourist Information** office is at 45 High Street (Tel. 0738 38353). It is open all year, and at high season from 9 a.m. to 8 p.m. each day.

Scone Palace, seat of the Earl of Mansfield and situated two miles north-east of Perth, is an essential item on the itinerary of any sightseer to Scotland. The site was in existence during Pictish times but its importance increased considerably when in the mid-ninth century Kenneth MacAlpine made Scone the centre of his new united kingdom of Scots and Picts and adopted the Stone of Destiny as the central element in the ceremonial enthroning of monarchs. In 1034 Scone became the capital of the newly unified Scotland under Duncan and the place where monarchs were crowned; this continued right up until Charles II. Most of the present structure of the palace dates from 1802, but this incorporates some of the 16th-century and some of the earlier buildings. The opulent apartments contain many pieces of antique French furniture including a writing table made for Marie Antoinette, a fabulous collection of ivories, and in the Long Gallery one can walk the same oak floor as the kings of Scotland on their way to be crowned. There are also paintings by, among others, Ramsay, Reynolds and Wilkie, and collections of 18th-century timepieces, porcelain and 16th-century needlework, the latter including embroidered bed hangings worked by Mary Queen of Scots. The **Woodland Garden and Pinetum** has one of the finest collections of specimen conifers in Britain, many of which were introduced by David Douglas, a local lad famous for his plant hunting expeditions to North America, and there is an adventure playground to occupy the children. **Moot Hill** in the grounds houses a 19th-century chapel but was formerly the site of the Stone of Destiny. The 12th-century abbey was destroyed in 1559 by followers of John Knox. (The palace and grounds are open from Easter to mid-October, Monday to Saturday, 9.30 a.m. to 5 p.m., and Sunday, 1.30 p.m. to 5 p.m. In July and August, Sunday opening is brought forward to 10 a.m.)

Three miles north-west of Perth is **Huntingtower Castle**, a 15th-century castellated mansion which changed its name in 1600 from the Castle of Ruthven. This was the scene of the nobles' conspiratorial Raid of Ruthven in 1582, when James VI was held against his will for 10 months. (Open from April to September, Monday to Saturday, 9.30 a.m. to 7 p.m., and Sunday 2 p.m. to 7 p.m.; and from October to March, Monday to Saturday, 9.30 a.m. to 4 p.m., and Sunday 2 p.m. to 4 p.m. Closed on 25, 26 December and 1, 2 January.)

Two miles East of Perth, just off the A85 at Walnut Grove, is the **Fairways Heavy Horse Centre**, both a working and breeding place for Clydesdale Horses. There are wagon rides pulled by a team of Clydesdales as well as two interesting displays on the blacksmith and the horses at work.

Six miles north of Perth on the A9 at Blackfoot is the **Highland Motor Heritage Centre** where you can see a selection of vintage cars in period setting and other such memorabilia.

Elcho Castle is a fortified 16th-century mansion beside the River Tay, three miles south-east of Perth, and open to the public.

A few miles further away, the village of **ABERNETHY** on the A913 is notable for its 11th-century **Round Tower** which stands 74 feet high and would have been used both as a belfry and a place of refuge.

Fourteen miles south of Perth on the M90 is **KINROSS** near the shore of **Loch Leven**, a nature reserve and important bird refuge. This is an excellent base from which to enjoy the attractions of the loch which offers good fishing, and is renowned for its particular breed of trout. A ferry from the town takes visitors to **Loch Leven Castle**, built on an island in the 14th-century, and place of Mary Queen of Scots' incarceration from June 1567 until her escape 11 months later. On the southern shore of the loch is **Vane Farm Nature Reserve**, noted for its wild geese and duck. The Nature Centre in a converted farm building has displays on the wildlife at home in the area. Just off the M90 at Junction 6 lies Heatheryford, where stocked trout lochs and a restaurant provide a pleasant day out.

Kinross has a good selection of accommodation. The **Green Hotel** (Tel. 0577 863467), from a little over £30, has its own 18-hole golf course. Nearby **Nivingston House** (Tel. 0577 850216) is a small country house hotel with a good restaurant. It is located near Cleish, a nearby village. Back in Kinross, from under £25 there are **Bridgend Hotel**, 257 High Street (Tel. 0577 863413), and **Granada Lodge Hotel**, Kincardine Road (Tel. 0577 864646). **Tourist Information** is at the service area, junction 6 of the M90 (Tel. 0577 863680), from Easter to October.

North-west from Kinross, **AUCHTERARDER** on the A9 is reached via the A91 and the A823. To the north-west, **Tullibardine Chapel** has remained almost entirely unaltered since its foundation in 1446. A little further on, the town of **DUNNING** is notable for its square tower of 1210. Auchterarder has a fine selection of antique shops and the surrounding countryside offers some splendid scenic walks. Its golf course is overshadowed by the four at the more famous name in golf, **Gleneagles Hotel** (Tel. 0764 62231) one mile south-west, which has long been known as *the* hotel of Scotland. Its 236 bedrooms are beautifully appointed, its restaurants are excellent, and the sporting facilities on offer (golf, shooting in the Jackie Stewart Shooting School, riding in the Mark

Philips Equestrian Centre, the country club and so on) are too numerous to be listed here. It is a fabulous resort and well worth coming to see if finances will not allow a stay.

Auchterarder has a fine selection of hotels including the luxurious **Auchterarder House** (Tel. 0764 63646/63647) whose restaurant is very highly recommended. Prices start at £70. More modest accommodation is available from around £50 at **Cairn Lodge Hotel**, Ochil Road (Tel. 0764 62634), and the **Hotel Collearn**, High Street (Tel. 0764 63553). The **Crown Hotel**, High Street (Tel. 0764 62375) and **Queens Hotel**, High Street (Tel. 0764 62493), charge from around £17. There is a touring caravan and camping site at **Nether Coul**, just outside town (Tel. 0764 63119).

Tourist Information is available all year at 90 High Street (Tel. 0764 63450).

A short distance north-east of Auchterarder, the small town of **CRIEFF** lies on the side of Knock Hill overlooking the River Earn, and its position on the edge of the Highlands offers the visitor splendid contrasts in scenery. Outside the Tourist Information Centre in High Street are the town's former stocks and the octagonal cross of 1688 bearing its former name of 'Burgh of Regality of Drummond'. Further along the street one can see the 17th-century **Mercat Cross**. Whisky connoisseurs will be interested in the guided tours provided at **Glenturret Distillery**, the oldest in Scotland. The town's pottery, **Thistle Pottery**, is also the oldest in the country and, together with the adjacent **Perthshire Paperweights** factory, can be found at the **Creiff Visitor Centre**. **Stuart Strathearn Crystal**, the town's glassworks, is open for the public to observe craftsmen at work. **Crieff Hydro Hotel** (Tel 0764 2401) is one of the best known hotels in Scotland. Family-run, it offers a wide choice of accommodation as well as a leisure complex, sports hall and such outdoor facilities as golf, tennis and riding, and is excellent value for money. **Tourist Information** is available all year at the High Street (Tel. 0764 2578).

Two miles south on the A822, **Drummond Castle Gardens**, but not the castle itself, are open to the public in summer and recommended for their Italianate landscaping and John Mylne's unusual sundial of 1630. Four miles north-west of Auchterarder,

Innerpeffray Library is the oldest in Scotland, having been founded in 1691 by David Drummond in the attic of the adjacent chapel before transferring to its present building between 1750 and 1758.

The road west of Crieff to Loch Earn passes through **COMRIE**, home of the **Museum of Scottish Tartans** which has a collection of over 1,300 patterns and a record of every known tartan. Surrounding the town is some magnificent countryside including **Dunmore Hill** to the north and the four miles of **Glen Lednock Circular Walk**. From here it is a short drive to the even more breathtaking scenery and the mountains around **Loch Earn** which rise to over 3,000 feet, notably in the form of Ben Vorlich and Stuc a'Chroin.

On the other side of Crieff, on a minor road off the A85, **FOWLIS WESTER** is a small, picturesque village and more interesting than its size would lead one to expect. The **Cross** from the eighth century indicates the longevity of the place as does the 13th-century **Church of St Bean**. The original was founded by St Bean in 720 and 1,250 or so years later the astronaut Alan Bean took a piece of the MacBean tartan to the moon.

Twenty-three miles north on a straight run from Crieff, via the Sma' Glen (especially picturesque when the heather is in bloom), **ABERFELDY** lies at the heart of the Perthshire Highlands surrounded by inspiring scenery which takes in mountain, loch, and riverside. The town stands near the banks of the River Tay, which, along with the loch of the same name six miles west, is a fertile fishing ground. Climbers will be interested to know that **Ben Lawers** on the loch's northern shore is the highest peak in the county at almost 4,000 feet. For those who enjoy the pleasure of a countryside walk, but in a more leisurely fashion than the ardent hillwalker, the **Birks o' Aberfeldy**, immortalized in a song by Robert Burns, are a short distance from the town, and **Drummond Hill Forest Walks** are at the east end of Loch Tay. Sightseeing in Aberfeldy should take in **Wade's Bridge** of 1733–5, named after its builder rather than its architect William Adam. A stone beside the bridge bearing a kilted figure commemorates Wade's raising of the Black Watch Regiment in 1739.

Tourist Information is available throughout the year at The Square (Tel. 0887 820276).

One mile to the west on the B846 is **Castle Menzies**, a fine example of a 16th-century Z-plan tower house. The castle is open from April to September and houses the **Clan Menzies Museum**. Further on, the road turns north and passes the small ruined keep of **Comrie Castle**, followed one mile later by **Garth Castle**.

The alternative westward route from Aberfeldy is along the A827, through the picturesque town of **KENMORE**, beneath **Drummond Hill** and along the northern shore of **Loch Tay**, famous for its salmon fishing. **Croft-Na-Caber** (Tel. 0887 830236) can offer a wide variety of activities in this area, especially watersports from sailing to waterskiing. Accommodation is either offered in a hotel or an Austrian-style chalet. A few miles north of the visitor centre **Glen Lyon** is the longest and also one of the most beautiful glens in Scotland, with the attractive village of **FOR-TINGALL** at its end. One enclosed yew tree in the churchyard here is reputedly over 3,000 years old. This, the beautiful thatched cottages, and the fact that this is claimed to be the birthplace of Pontius Pilate make it worth a visit. Make time for a spectacular detour: from Fortingall return to Kenmore via Loch Tay. An unclassified single-track road from Kenmore south to Amulree affords unrivalled elevated views.

East from Aberfeldy, the A827 joins the A9 heading north to **PITLOCHRY** which has been a popular Highland resort since Victorian times, and, like Aberfeldy, makes a good touring base for the magnificent countryside surrounding it. Many of the area's attractions involve its stretches of water. To the west, boats can be hired to appreciate the beauty of **Loch Faskally** which is well stocked with salmon and trout. It also features, at its southern end, a **Fish-Pass** or **Salmon Ladder**, which consists of 34 stepped pools allowing salmon to return upstream to their spawning ground each year between April and October. Visitors can get a close-up view of this phenomenon from the observation room. Adjacent is the **Loch Faskally Dam Visitor Centre** (open Easter to October) with an exhibition on the Tummel Valley hydro-electric scheme and also the life cycle of the salmon. At the southern end of Pitlochry off the main A9 road, is **Blair Atholl Distillery**, where there are guided tours and a chance to taste the best-selling Blair Atholl whisky as well as visit the gift shop and coffee shop. In the hills above

Pitlochry is **Eradour**, the smallest distillery in the world, where free guided tours and tastings are available.

Pitlochry has an extensive choice of accommodation. The **Atholl Palace Hotel**, Atholl Road (Tel. 0796 472400), is a majestic building set in 48 acres of parkland with a range of recreational facilities from sauna to pitch-and-putt course. Prices start around £25 and rise to over £50. The **Pitlochry Hydro Hotel**, Knockard Road (Tel. 0796 472666), stands in its own grounds with a commanding view across the Tummel Valley. Prices start at around £40. From around £20 there are **Adderley Hotel**, 23 Toberargan Road (Tel. 0796 472433); **Balrobin Hotel**, 14 Higher Oakfield (Tel. 0796 472901); **Fisher's Hotel**, 75–79 Atholl Road (Tel. 0796 472000). **Burnside Apartments**, 19 West Moulin Road (Tel. 0796 472203), offers the independence of comfortable, serviced apartments for two to six persons. There is also a good selection of guest houses offering cheaper accommodation. The three-crown commended **Carra Beag Guest House** (Tel. 0796 472835) charges from £16.35 per person and **Derrybeg Guest House**, 18 Lower Oakfield (Tel. 0796 472070) charges from £15. Caravans can be let for up to six persons at **Faskally Home Farm** (Tel. 0796 472007).

The woods just over one mile south-east of Pitlochry contain the **Black Spout** waterfall, while to the north, the **Dunmore Trail** up **Craigower Hill** offers a pleasant walk and a fine view from the top. **Linn of Tummel** is a 47-acre area of woodland to the north-west greatly admired by Queen Victoria on her visit in 1844.

North of the town, the B8019 heads west along the northern shore of Loch Tummel, passing **Queen's View**. More likely named after Mary Queen of Scots in 1564 than after Queen Victoria in 1886, this beauty spot gives an excellent view of Loch Tummel and the distinctive conical shape of **Schiehallion**, rising to over 3,500 feet in the distance. The nearby Forestry Commission **Tummel Forest Centre** is very interesting, with a slide-show and displays on local natural history and forest life in addition to suggested routes for walking through the forest. The B846 to Kinloch Rannoch leads you to the 22-mile circuit of Loch Rannoch. The main road runs along the north side and from the eastern end there are superb views west to Glen Coe and, again, Schiehallion.

The B8019 adjoins the A9 at the start of the **Pass of Killie-crankie**, a wooded gorge which in July 1689 was the site of an inconclusive battle between the Jacobite Highlanders and the English troops of King William III. Information on the Battle of Killiecrankie, along with that on the natural history of the area, is on display at the **Killiecrankie Visitor Centre** (open April to October). Further north along the A9, before coming to the small town of **BLAIR ATHOLL**, the road passes the stone marking the spot where the Jacobite commander Claverhouse fell. Housed in the Old School, the **Atholl Country Collection** (open May to October) is a display of material illustrating the history of the village, at the opposite end of which is the water-powered **Corn Mill** (open April to October) which dates from 1613 and is still working. The village is best known for **Blair Castle** (open April to October), home of the Duke of Atholl and the Atholl Highlanders, the only private army in Britain. The oldest part of the castle dates from 1269 although it has been enlarged and rebuilt many times since. Its contents include 300 years of family portraits, Jacobite relics, tapestries, firearms, and a collection of Victorian toys. There is also a deer park, nature trails and pony trekking, as well as a picnic area and licensed restaurant on the grounds.

A further three miles northward along the A9 a footpath leads from the road through woods to the spectacular **Falls of Bruar**, three waterfalls formed by the Bruar Water. Near the falls is the **Clan Donnachaidh Museum**; exhibits include items on the Jacobite Risings of 1715 and 1745. Open from April to October.

Returning south on the A9, 13 miles after Pitlochry comes the village of **DUNKELD**, whose chief characteristic is its splendid rural setting beside the River Tay. **Dunkeld Cathedral** dates from the 12th century, although most of the remaining structure dates from the 14th and 15th centuries. Nearby, visitors can admire, from the outside only, the **Little Houses** along Cathedral Street which were constructed in 1689 and so successfully restored by the National Trust in the 1950s that they are now let to tenants. **Dunkeld Bridge**, one of Telford's finest bridges, built in 1809, crosses the Tay here. A riverside path leads downstream to the famous **Birnam Oak**, last relic of Macbeth's

Birnam wood. The attractive 18th-century village **Cross** is the location of the **Scottish Horse Museum** (open from Easter to October) and the **Tourist Information** centre is open Easter to October (Tel. 0350 727688). Accommodation is available in the luxurious **Stakis Dunkeld House Hotel** (Tel. 0350 727771), which stands in 280-acre grounds overlooking the River Tay. Prices are upwards of £60. **Kinnaird House**, on B898 north-west of Dunkeld, home of Master chef John Webber, is well known for its gourmet food (Tel. 0796 482440).

Two miles north-east of the village is the Scottish Wildlife Trust's **Loch of Lowes Nature Reserve** (open April to September) which, in addition to the variety of waterfowl it shelters, offers visitors the rare opportunity, chance permitting, of observing ospreys from a hide. On the opposite side of the river to the village, **Hermitage Woodland Walk** runs for one mile and contains, in addition to its considerable natural beauty, the **Falls of Braan** and two 18th-century follies: the **Hermitage** or **Ossian's Hall**, and **Ossian's Cave**. Also here one can see exotic North American trees, which were among the first to be brought over to the UK. Note the huge Douglas Firs, planted after their discovery in North America in the mid-19th century and now the largest trees in Scotland.

Twelve miles east of Dunkeld on the A923, the principal distinction attached to **BLAIRGOWRIE** is the raspberry crop from the surrounding area which accounts for half of all those grown in Scotland. Set in 25 acres of woodland and parkland, grazed by Highland cattle lies **Kinloch House** (Tel. 0250 884237). This Scottish country house was built in 1840 and has an oak-panelled hall and first-floor galleries. Some of the 21 bedrooms have four-poster beds. Dinner, bed and breakfast is from around £65 per person. One mile before the town the road passes **Ardblair Castle** (open to groups by appointment only – Tel. 0250 873155), whose foundations date from the 12th century although the rest of the structure is mainly 16th-century. **Tourist Information** is available all year at 26 Wellmeadow (Tel. 0250 872960/873701). From Blairgowrie drive north on the A93 to the ski slopes of **Glenshee**, Britain's largest ski area, with 26 lifts and tows serving green to black runs. At nearby Glenisla cross-country skiing is available. If skiing does not interest you drive on a little further and explore the beautiful scenery of Glen Prosen and Glen Clara. **Glenmarkie Farmhouse** is ideally situated in Glenisla (Tel. 0575 82341) and offers traditional accommodation and home cooking from £12 per person.

Four miles south of Blairgowrie on the A93 near **MEIKLEOUR** is Meikleour House whose grounds are bounded by the world's largest **Beech Hedge**: planted in 1746, it is now 580 yards long and 100 feet high.

Five miles east of Blairgowrie, just off the A926, the town of **ALYTH** has the remains of an 18th-century church and **Alyth Folk Museum** which presents an account of the area's agrarian history. South of here on the A927, the **museum** at **MEIGLE** has an interesting collection of sculpted Celtic monuments from the seventh to tenth centuries.

Heading east again on the A94, the town of **GLAMIS** is renowned for the spectacular **Glamis Castle** (open Easter, and May to September). It has retained its regal connections up to this century, as the birthplace of Princess Margaret in 1930, having been the childhood residence of the Queen Mother. The castle and grounds are well worth an afternoon of any visitor's time and the home baking in the tearoom is well worth a detour. Most of the present structure was built in the 17th century, about 600 years after the reign of King Macbeth – who in reality, bore no relation to his fictional counterpart – and inside there is much for the visitor to admire in the furnishings and decor. Another link with the play can be seen elsewhere in Glamis, namely in the Manse garden where the **Malcolm Stone** is said to mark the grave of Malcolm II, believed to have died in uncertain circumstances in or near the castle in 1034. The **Angus Folk Museum** (open Easter, and May to September) occupies a terrace of restored 19th-century cottages and houses, with displays on bygone domestic and agricultural life in the area.

Aberdeen, Grampian Highlands and Dundee

INTRODUCTION

This chapter takes in the north-east of Scotland, an expansive area whose scenery is as magnificent as it is diverse, embracing the rugged Grampian peaks, the gently undulating farmland of Banff and Buchan, the glens and braes of Angus, and some excellent sandy beaches at Arbroath, Stonehaven, Aberdeen, and along the shores of the Moray Firth.

HISTORY

Aberdeen and Dundee are Scotland's third and fourth cities respectively, and each boasts a long and august past. **Dundee** was granted the status of a royal burgh by William the Lion late in the 12th century, but records indicate that it was the site of a settlement in Roman times, and the headquarters of Kenneth MacAlpine when his conquest of the Picts in 834 led to the formation of the first Scottish kingdom. In the 16th century, largely through the evangelical efforts of George Wishart, who was later to be burned at the stake for his faith, the city became the first in Scotland to embrace the principles of the Reformation. In the 17th and 18th centuries it provided staunch support to the House of Stuart. This was manifested, firstly, in the persecution by Viscount Dundee, Graham of Claverhouse (also known as 'Bonnie Dundee'), of the Covenanters, opponents to the introduction of Episcopalianism by James VII of Scotland and II of England; and half a century later, the Jacobites had a secure hold on Dundee for almost the entire duration of Charles Edward Stuart's campaign to regain the throne for the House of Stuart in 1745. Like most other towns and villages along the east coast, fishing was the staple occupation, and here the whaling industry developed in tandem with the textile industry, the latter employing the women while the men were absent in foreign waters. It was this economic combination that rescued the city when the weaving industry slumped. In 1822 a new fibre called jute was sent home by the East India Trading Company and was promptly dismissed as too difficult to work, until the discovery that it became much more manageable with the application of whale oil. As the world centre of jute manufacture, the city enjoyed unprecedented prosperity, and many of its finest buildings were built with the profits of this trade. Although never renowned as a great shipbuilding centre, the city did produce two famous vessels: *Discovery* and *Terra Nova* in which Scott sailed on different expeditions to the Antarctic. More detail on Dundee follows later in this chapter.

Aberdeen lies between the mouths of the rivers Don and Dee, an area which was first settled in prehistoric times, and was subsequently an important centre for the Romans, Picts, and Scots. The city was granted a charter as a royal burgh by William the Lion in 1179, since when it has enjoyed several periods of prosperity as a direct result of its position on the coast. As far back as the 13th century it was the main port in northern Scotland, and this allowed it to benefit greatly during the years of heightened seafaring trade between Scotland and the countries of the Baltic. The discovery of oil in the North Sea brought a timely fillip to the local economy when Aberdeen, again by virtue of its position on the coast, became the centre of Scotland's oil industry.

COMMUNICATIONS

The region is very well served by an extensive road network, with the A92 following the coast from Dundee to Aberdeen and beyond, while the area north and east of Aberdeen is dissected by a series of fast and efficient routes. InterCity trains from London King's Cross, including a sleeper service, call at Dundee and other towns on the coast on their way to Aberdeen. Inland, there is one branch line from Aberdeen, north-west to Elgin, Nairn, and Inverness. For a more touristic route, **Grampian Rail Tours** operate steam-hauled and regular rail excursions on board the classic, award-winning *Northern Belle*. Setting out from Aberdeen you can travel to Elgin and Inverness through some of the finest Grampian scenery and whisky country, and what's more, in grand style. For more information contact 11 Mavis Bank, Newburgh, Ellon, Aberdeen (Tel. 03586 89513).

Dundee airport currently receives business air flights from Aberdeen, Manchester and Esbjerg in Denmark, with the hope of establishing a London service in the near future, while Aberdeen airport has connections with most parts of Britain including Manchester, Birmingham, Norwich, Newcastle, and London, and many Scandinavian cities.

WHERE TO GO FOR WHAT

For sightseers, the individual style of the architecture of **Aberdeen**

FORFAR
and MONTROSE

1 Caird Hall
2 St Paul's Episcopal Cathedral
3 St Andrew's Church
4 Wishart Arch
5 City Churches
6 The Howff
7 Barrack Street Museum
8 McManus Galleries
9 War Memorial, Dundee Law
10 Mills Observatory
11 Mains Castle
12 RRS *Discovery*
13 Frigate *Unicorn*
14 University of Dundee
15 Jordanstone College of Art

is quite distinctive, along with the numerous surrounding historic castles, particularly Craigievar Castle, which dot the countryside to the west of the town. There is an abundant choice of golf courses throughout the region, the best known of which is CARNOUSTIE the championship course where the British Open was staged in 1975. Along the coast there is a good choice of family resorts such as **Arbroath, Montrose** and **Stonehaven**, between Dundee and Aberdeen, and **Findhorn, Lossiemouth, Buckie**, and **Cullen** on the shores of the Moray Firth.

Dundee

For many people, **DUNDEE** is characterized by jute, jam and journalism. Its pre-eminence in the production of jute has already been explained. It was in Dundee that marmalade was first made. In journalism, the city is the well-known home of the D.C. Thomson empire, famed publishers of many popular comics, magazines, and newspapers, the most notable being the *Dandy* and the *Beano*.

Arriving by road or rail from the south, the city is approached by a bridge across the Firth of Tay. Either provides an auspicious entrance to the city and each is a quite spectacular feat of engineering to behold. The **Tay Road Bridge**, built 1963–66 is 120 feet above the water and more than a mile long. Two miles to the west, the **Tay Rail Bridge** is even longer, running in a curve to a length of two miles and standing 20 yards west of its predecessor. The earlier rail bridge was built between 1871 and 1878, but, in the year following its completion, catastrophe struck when, on the night of 28 December, it collapsed during a storm. The train crossing the bridge at the time plunged into the Tay, resulting in the loss of 90 lives.

From the road bridge, one soon arrives at City Square where there are a number of handsome buildings; eminent among them are **Caird Hall**, covering two acres on the north side, and to the east, **St Paul's Episcopal Cathedral**. Next to the latter, at number 8 Castle Street, is the birthplace of one of history's underestimated heroes, James Chalmers, who, in 1834, invented the adhesive postage stamp. Seagate leads from the north-east corner of the square towards Nethergate, where one can admire **St Andrew's Church** of 1774, and **Wishart Arch** in the Cowgate. The latter dates from 1591, and is the only surviving city gate. From the north-west corner of City Square, Nethergate leads to a trio of churches under one roof, known as the **City Churches**. Although this rare amalgam is largely obscured by a shopping precinct, it is still possible to appreciate the salient feature, the 15th-century **St Mary's Tower**. A plaque in the adjacent pedestrian precinct honours William Lion Mackenzie, born in Dundee in 1795, later to become the first mayor of Toronto. North of the City Churches, beyond **The Howff** (Dundee's burial ground for the 300 or so years before 1857), **Barrack Street Museum** has extensive displays on local and natural history. East of here, in Albert Square, a statue of

Robert Burns welcomes visitors to the **McManus Galleries**, housing paintings by Flemish, Dutch, French, and British artists – with considerable attention paid to the Scottish Colourist School – in addition to displays illustrating the city's economic history. South of here, the **Seagate Gallery and Printmakers Workshop** stages many visiting exhibitions, especially of contemporary art from the UK and abroad. Just west of the city centre, on West Henderson's Wynd, is situated the newly restored **Verdant Works**, a 19th-century flax and jute mill, now home to a living museum of Dundee's textile industry.

The city has generous areas of parkland. About a mile northwest from the City Square is **Dudhope Park**, within which stands the 14th-century Dudhope Castle (no admission) currently undergoing restoration. **Dundee Law**, rising to 517 feet, overlooks the park, giving splendid views of the city from its summit, on which stands Dundee War Memorial. One mile to the west, **Balgay Hill** is surmounted by the **Mills Observatory**, containing a planetarium and exhibitions on the themes of astronomy and space travel. **Caird Park**, north of Kingsway, includes the ruins of the 16th-century **Mains Castle**, recently restored and now a popular restaurant. Three miles north-west of the city centre is **Camperdown House and Country Park**. The latter, occupying 395 acres, contains many rare species of trees, a golf course, tennis courts, horses for hire, and an adventure playground. The early 19th-century mansion contains a restaurant and information centre. A few miles north of Dundee is **Clatto Park**, which offers a number of water-based activities for children of eight years and over. Four miles northwest of the city centre is **Templeton Woods**, 120 acres of woodlands with guided walks and trails through the forest.

West of the road bridge, on Discovery Quay, can be found one of Dundee's most exciting new attractions – **Discovery Point** – due to open in the summer of 1993. Based around the **Royal Research Ship** *Discovery* which took Captain Scott on his famous expedition to the Antarctic, Discovery Point's 29,000 square feet of space will have exhibitions, audio-visual displays, the original wooden ship – which visitors will be able to explore – and many other exciting features. Contact the Dundee Tourist Board (Tel. 0382 23141) for more details. Victoria Dock provides a permanent mooring for the

Unicorn, a 46-gun wooden warship, whose launch in 1824 makes it the world's fourth oldest ship still afloat. West of here, off Riverside Drive running along the waterfront, the **University Botanical Garden** charges adults £1 and children and senior citizens 50p for admission to its collection of native and exotic plants, landscaped garden, and hothouses.

Dundee has an unusual attraction which is particularly popular with children: **Shaw's Dundee Sweet Factory** where confectionery can be seen being made using old-fashioned methods and machinery. The **Olympia Leisure Centre** on the waterfront can provide fun for children and adults alike. It has Scotland's largest leisure pool as well as water slides, a rapid river, a health suite and a restaurant.

At the top of Dundee's range of hotels are the **Angus Thistle Hotel**, 101 Marketgate (Tel. 0382 26874), and the **Stakis Earl Grey Hotel**, Earl Grey Place (Tel. 0382 29271), charging upward of £60. The **Queen's Hotel**, 160 Nethergate (Tel. 0382 22515), is slightly cheaper. From around £25 there is a choice of the **Carlton House Hotel**, 2 Dalgleish Road (Tel. 0382 462056), the **Craigtay Hotel**, 101 Broughty Ferry Road (Tel. 0382 451142), and the **Tay Hotel**, Whitehall Crescent (Tel. 0382 21641). A few miles to the north-west of Dundee on the B954 lies the little village of AUCHTERHOUSE. Here you will find a small luxury hotel the **Old Mansion House** (Tel. 082626 366). Converted by its present owners from a 16th-century baronial home, the hotel has six bedrooms, ten acres of grounds, outdoor swimming pool, croquet lawn and tennis court, excellent dining and wine cellar recognised by the 'Taste of Scotland' guide. Prices from £30. Local guest houses are worth considering and a full rundown of these is available from the Tourist Information Centre, 4 City Square (Tel. 0382 27723). The one crown commended **Cullaig Guest House**, Upper Constitution Street (Tel. 0382 22154), offers comfortable rooms in a family-run Victorian town house from £12 per person. The **University of Dundee** also has reasonably priced accomodation (Tel. 0382 23181), with a choice of self catering flats from £35 per person, and serviced accommodation from £13.50. **Duncan of Jordanstone College of Art**, 13 Perth Road (Tel. 0382 23261), similarly offers low-cost accommodation in **Duncan House** on

Blackness Road overlooking the River Tay, set in its own gardens. From mid-July to mid-September, a two-person flat costs around £80; a three-person cottage around £135; and rooms from £35 to £62.

Dundee is not a great culinary centre but there are some decent restaurants. **Miguel's Restaurant** is a seven-day, Italian kitchen in picturesque Broughty Ferry at 128/130 Gray Street (Tel. 0382 730201). In town a good Chinese Cantonese meal can be found in **Hosikai's**, at 121 St Andrews Street (Tel. 0382 24021). Finally, the **Rep Theatre** has a good restaurant. (Tel. 0382 200813).

The **Tourist Information** office is open all year at 4 City Square (Tel. 0382 27723).

On the eastern outskirts of Dundee is the Victorian resort of **BROUGHTY FERRY**, the 'posh part' of Dundee, which enjoys an attractive location, with fine sandy beaches stretching the two miles along the coast to Monifieth. There is free admission to **Broughty Castle** (open all year, Monday to Thursday and Saturday, 10 a.m. to 1 p.m. and 2 p.m. to 5 p.m., Tel. 0382 76121), built in the 15th century, and currently housing a museum explaining the ecology of the Tay, along with displays on Dundee's maritime history. The **Eduardo Alessandro Gallery** displays exhibitions of local and up and coming artists, and can be easily found at 30 Gray Street (open October to May, Monday–Friday 9.30 a.m. to 5 p.m. [half-day on Wednesday]; and from June to September, Monday to Saturday 9.30 a.m. to 5.30 p.m.). To the north is **Claypotts Castle**, a remarkably well preserved tower house, dating from the 16th century, and well worth a visit (open April to September, Monday to Saturday, 9.30 a.m. to 6.30 p.m., and on Sunday 2 p.m. to 6.30 p.m.).

A few miles along the coast from Broughty Ferry, the town of **CARNOUSTIE** is notable for its golf courses, which include the **Carnoustie Championship Course**, on Links Parade (Tel. 0241 53249), which hosted the British Open in 1975, and hopes to do so again in the near future. At Ardestie and Carlungie, off the A92 west of Carnoustie, are the '**Earth Houses**', remains of surface dwellings and souterrains that date from around AD 300. West from Carnoustie on the A930 is Barry village, home to **Barry Mill** a working water mill now open daily to visitors, 11 a.m. to 1 p.m. and 2 p.m. to 5 p.m. from Easter to October. **Tourist Information** is available all year round at 24 High Street (Tel. 0241 52258). Six miles on, **ARBROATH** is a pleasant seaside town of paramount importance in Scotland's history. It was in **Arbroath Abbey**, still impressive, although now a ruin in the town centre, that the Estates of Scotland met in 1320 to formulate the Declaration of Arbroath affirming Scotland's independence from England, and to proclaim Robert the Bruce king. The document by which independence was asserted was a letter sent to Pope John XXII, although it took four years for Rome to acknowledge it, and another four for England's Edward III to do likewise. On a less momentous note, the town is renowned for its unique 'smokies', smoked haddock.

The library in Hill Terrace houses **Arbroath Art Gallery**, which concentrates on local artists in its frequently changing exhibitions. Local history is on display at the **Signal Tower Museum**, Ladyloan, with particular attention to the fishing and flax industries. The **Cliffs Nature Trail**, running one and a half miles along the red sandstone cliffs between King's Drive and Carlinheugh Bay, allows visitors to observe a variety of birdlife and marvel at the fascinating rock formations. **St Vigean's Museum**, one and a half miles north of the town, occupies a converted cottage just off the A92, and houses a collection of Pictish stone sculptures and early Christian gravestones. **Kerr's Miniature Passenger-Carrying Railway**; one fifth of the full size runs for 400 yards alongside the main Aberdeen to London line. These miniature steam and diesel locomotives were established in 1935.

Arbroath has a modest selection of hotel accommodation, all of which is very reasonably priced. From around £25 there is **Hotel Seaforth**, Dundee Road (Tel. 0241 72232), where guests have the use of a snooker room, gymnasium, and jacuzzi; and **Windmill Hotel**, Millgate Loan (Tel. 0241 72278). From £20, there are: **Rosely Hotel**, Forfar Road (Tel. 0241 76828); **Towerbank Hotel**, James Street (Tel. 0241 72203); and **Cliffburn Hotel**, Cliffburn Road (Tel. 0241 73432). There are two caravan parks in Arbroath: the **Red Lion Caravan Park**, Dundee Road (Tel. 0241 72038), charging from £5 for tourers and motors, and **Seaton Estate**

Caravan Park, Seaton House (Tel. 0241 74762), which costs from between £5 and £6 including tent pitches. The **Tourist Information** centre, Market Place (Tel. 0241 72609/76680), is open all year.

Seven miles north from Arbroath, the A92 passes within sight of the ruins of **Red Castle,** a 15th-century structure in Lunan Bay, whose name is an apt, if unimaginative, reflection of the distinctive red sandstone in which it was fashioned. Five miles further on, a bridge crosses the strait separating the sea from Montrose Basin, a 2000-acre tidal basin which is a nature reserve and home to an extensive variety of birds, to reach the town of **MONTROSE**. This busy port prospered during the early years of Scotland's trading links with the Baltic countries, and it retains much of the fine architecture from this and later periods, particularly in the spaciously elegant High Street. Buildings of particular merit in this thoroughfare are the **Old Church,** and the 18th-century **Old Town Hall**. Nearby Panmure Place is the location of the **Museum and Art Gallery** which concentrates on local history. The sculptor William Lamb lived and worked in Montrose until his death in 1951, and his work is on display where it was fashioned by him in the **William Lamb Memorial Studio,** 24 Market Place. Three miles west on the A935, is the beautiful William Adam-designed **House of Dun,** which overlooks the Montrose Basin, and is notable for its fine plaster-work (open May to October, Monday to Sunday, 11 a.m. to 5.30 p.m.). Three miles north-west of the town, along the A937, is the **Sunnyside Museum**. Part of Sunnyside Royal Hospital, the first hospital in Scotland for the mentally ill, the museum houses displays illustrating the history of psychiatry in this country. Following the coast northwards, on the A92, is the **St Cyrus Nature Reserve**. As well as having a wide selection of plant and birdlife, the visitor centre has exhibits on local history, natural history, salmon fishing and wildlife. There is also a salt-water aquarium and an audio visual display open April–October, Tuesday to Sunday, 9 a.m. to 5 p.m. Further along the coast by Johnshaven is **Damside Garden Herbs,** which colourfully illustrates the history of herbs and herb gardens in its various traditional styles of gardens. Additionally, there is an arboretum showing the life-cycle of trees, and a local crafts shop and restaurant, both demonstrating the utility of herbs (open April–September, daily 11 a.m. to 7 p.m., closed Mondays).

Nine miles west of Montrose, **BRECHIN** is notable for its **Round Tower**. Dating from the 11th to 12th centuries, it is one of only two in the whole of Scotland (the other in Abernethy), built in a style which is otherwise unique to Ireland. Five miles north-west of here, either side of the road from Little Brechin to Bridgend, are the **White and Brown Caterthuns**, the remains of Iron Age hill forts. Six miles north of Brechin, just off the B966, stands the 16th-century **Edzell Castle and Gardens** (open from April to September, Monday to Saturday, 9.30 a.m. to 7 p.m., and Sunday 2 p.m. to 7 p.m.; and October to March, Monday to Saturday, 9.30 a.m. to 4 p.m., and Sunday, 2 p.m. to 4 p.m.). The ruined castle is of less interest than the magnificent walled garden, which is well worth a detour, with sculptures and other Renaissance features unique in Scotland. Beyond Edzell and north into GLEN ESK, a former shooting lodge houses the **Glen Esk Folk Museum**, which has displays of everyday life from 1800.

At the junction of the A94 and the A92 is the popular seaside resort of **STONEHAVEN**, offering various outdoor pursuits including golf, sea angling, boating, and wind-surfing. The town is composed of two easily discernible parts: the Old Town, built around the harbour, and beyond this the New Town, which dates mainly from the 19th century. The former is the more interesting of the two, and it is here, on the quayside, that visitors will find the 16th-century **Tolbooth**, now housing the local history museum, which pays special attention to Stonehaven's fishing industry. Immediately south of the town, perched on a promontory near the A92, are the extensive ruins of the 13th-century **Dunnottar Castle**. Standing 160 feet above the sea, it makes a spectacular sight and has an equally impressive history. Impregnable to William Wallace in 1297, it was the last place to fall to Cromwell's army in 1652, and even then, surrender did not come until after eight months under siege. Open daily from April to October, and Monday to Friday from November to March.

Stonehaven has a good selection of hotel accommodation, among the best of which are **Heugh Hotel**, Westfield Road (Tel. 0569 62379), an impressive baronial structure standing in its own grounds, charging from around £35. **Muchalls Castle** by Stonehaven (Tel. 0569 31170), built in 1624, offers a choice of elegant rooms with *en-suite* facilites, canopied beds and royal connections. The **Commodore Hotel**, Cowie Park (Tel. 0569 62936), is situated near the beach and charges upward of £25. From around £15–20, there are: **Eldergrove Hotel**, Arduthie Road (Tel. 0569 62265); **Marine Hotel**, Shorehead (Tel. 0569 62155); and **Station Hotel**, Arduthie Road (Tel. 0569 62277). The **Queen Elizabeth Caravan Park** (Tel. 0569 64041) has room for tourers and motor caravans, and costs from £4.50 to £7.50. The **Tourist Information** centre at 66 Allardice Street (Tel. 0569 62806) is open from Easter to October.

Aberdeen

From Stonehaven, the A92 leads, in 10 miles, to **ABERDEEN**. In recent years the city has been synonymous with Scotland's North Sea oil industry, but there have been residents at the mouth of the Dee since prehistoric times, and Aberdeen's prosperity predates the 13th century, by which time it was the main port in northern Scotland. For the visitor today, Aberdeen's elegant architecture provides abundant evidence of its distinguished and prosperous past. However, lest the mistake be made, it must be added that there is a lot more here than history and stone. The city has won national awards for floral displays in its many parks and gardens. For the golfer, there are eight courses to choose from, and the two miles of beach extending north of the harbour are among the best in Scotland.

EATING OUT AND NIGHTLIFE

When it comes to nightlife and dining out, Aberdeen has the choice and variety appropriate to any busy and prosperous city. The magnificent **His Majesty's Theatre**, in Rosemount Viaduct, next to Schoolhill, hosts plays and opera, while the diverse programme at the **Music Hall**, Union Street, includes regular visits from pop bands and the Scottish National Orchestra. Live music for the youth audience is available at the

ABERDEEN

1 Provost Ross's House and
  Aberdeen Maritime Museum
2 Mercat Cross
3 Town House
4 Tolbooth
5 Marischal College and
  Aberdeen University including
  Mitchell Hall and Marischal Museum
6 Provost Skene's House
7 Kirk of St Nicholas
8 James Dun's House
9 Art Gallery
10 His Majesty's Theatre
11 Music Hall (1820)
12 St Mary's Cathedral
13 King's College + Visitor Centre
14 Cruickshank Botanic Gardens
15 St Machar's Cathedral
16 Brig o'Balgownie (Auld Brig)

BALGOWNIE ROAD

BALGOWNIE GOLF COURSE

Footpaths: no vehicular access
from Chanonry

RIVER DON

SEATON PARK

KING STREET

KING'S LINKS

CHANONRY

BEACH ESPLANADE

ST. MACHAR DRIVE

HIGH ST.

KING STREET

POWIS PLACE

WESTBURN DRIVE

WESTBURN PARK

HUTCHEON STREET

WESTBURN ROAD

NELSON STREET

KING STREET

GEORGE STREET

QUEEN'S LINKS

BEACH ESPLANADE

To: Castle Fraser
Grampian Transport Museum
Kildrummy Castle
Craigievar Castle
Pittodrie House
Glenfiddich
and Strathisla
Distilleries

SCHOOL HILL

UNION STREET

TRINITY QUAY

UPPER DOCK

MARKET STREET

FISHMARKET

QUEENS ROAD A944

HOLBURN STREET

GREAT WESTERN ROAD A93

Crathes Castle

ESPLANADE WEST

VICTORIA BRIDGE

RIVER DEE

13 14 15 16

BON ACCORD SHOPPING
CENTRE (pedestrianised)

GEORGE STREET

WEST NORTH STREET

KING STREET

ST ANDREW'S CATHEDRAL

BLACKFRIARS STREET

UPPER KIRKGATE

BROAD STREET

CASTLE ST.

MARISCHAL ST.

ROSEMOUNT VIADUCT

SCHOOLHILL

i

UNION TERRACE

UNION TERRACE GARDENS

UNION BRIDGE

UNION STREET

COLLEGE STREET

UPPER DOCK

P&O FERRY
TERMINAL

HUNTLY STREET

GOLDEN SQUARE

MARKET STREET

TRINITY QUAY

UNION STREET

BRIDGE OF DEE
(BRIG O' DEE)

GUILD STREET

RAILWAY STATION

BUS STATION

FISH MARKET

ALBERT

TOURIST INFORMATION
CENTRE

Lemon Tree and **Café Drummond**, 1 Belmont Street. If you fancy a karaoke evening pop into **Café Bardot**, 491 Union Street. **The Cocky Hunters** at 504 Union Street was awarded the 1992 'Evening Express Pub of the Year Award', host to live bands most evenings and ceilidhs every Sunday. Popular with all age groups is the **Prince of Wales**, on St Nicholas Lane with an excellent selection of beers and real ales as well as offering good bar lunches. Discos and nightclubs include **Mister G's** and the **Cotton Club**. For 'older' people there is **Eagles Night Club**, 42 Union Street and for a younger crowd there is the **Hoochie Coochie Club** at Windmill Brae. **Café Ici** is an all-day bar and restaurant for smart young professionals. **Poldino's**, 7 Little Belmont Street, is an Italian restaurant with a strong recommendation, where a typical bill of £25–30 for two represents good value. **Dolce Vita** is much the same, but more expensive. **Inversneckie**, on the Prom, serves good, basic fare enhanced by the impressive views out to sea. **Burger King** is at 5 West North Street and 221 Union Street. An alternative for fast food is **Radar's Eating House** at 9 Belmont Street.

A 'What's On' monthly guide can be picked up from the Tourist Information Centre in Broad Street, giving the latest information on shows, exhibitions and the best restaurants. For daily information there is a 'What's on' line you can call (Tel. 591477). For Aberdeen's many festivals, see the Socialite section.

ACCOMMODATION

FIRST CLASS
The best hotel in the city centre is the very elegant **Caledonian Thistle Hotel**, Union Terrace (Tel. 0224 640233), which charges upward of £65. In addition to a choice of bars, it has a highly commendable restaurant, open to non-residents, which is noted for its Scottish cuisine. The same standards, and prices, are also to be found at the **Copthorne Hotel**, 122 Huntly Street (Tel. 0224 630404), which houses Poachers restaurant and Tiffin's café bar, and at **Stakis Tree Tops Hotel**, Springfield Road (Tel. 0224 313377). The latter is in a rural setting, with landscaped grounds, 10 minutes' drive from the city centre.

BUSINESS CLASS
In the city centre, the **Swallow Imperial Hotel**, Stirling Street
(Tel. 0224 589101), offers a good standard of accommodation and
service. Prices here are upward of £40, as they are at the **Aberdeen
Marriott**, Riverview Drive, Dyce (Tel. 0224 770011), and at
Prince Regent Hotel, 20 Waverley Place (Tel. 0224 645071).

ECONOMY AND LISTED
Aberdeen has a wide range of low-price hotels and guest houses
offering a high standard of comfort and service. From under £30
there are **Russell Private Hotel**, 50 St Swithin Street (Tel. 0224
323555); **St Magnus Court Hotel**, 22 Guild Street (Tel. 0224
589411); the family-run **Mannofield Hotel**, 447 Great Western
Road (Tel. 0224 315888), and in the city centre, **Brentwood Hotel**,
101 Crown Street (Tel. 0224 595440), which has 60 bedrooms, a
bar, and brasserie. University of Aberdeen, **Kings College** (Tel.
0224 272664), offer reasonable accommodation from £20.45.
Caravan and camping parks include: **Marywell Park Homes** on
Stonehaven Road (Tel. 0224 781973) which overlooks the city
from sheltered farmland location, charges £5–£8 per night for
tourers, motor caravans and tents; **Hazlehead Caravan Park
Campsite**, three miles from the city centre, adjoining a golf course
and public park (Tel. 0224 647647), charges £6.20 for tourers and
motor caravans and between £3.10 and £6.20 for tents.

ADDRESSES

Tourist Information is available all year from the City of Aberdeen
Tourist Board, St Nicholas House, Broad Street (Tel. 0224
632727), who also offer an accommodation booking service. An
information stand is situated in the Travel Centre in the railway
station.

SIGHTS

The compact city centre can be quite easily covered on foot, starting in Shiprow, curving away from Market Street, north-east of the railway station. **Provost Ross's House** dates from the 16th century when it was the home of a wealthy merchant, although it owes its name to the Lord Provost who lived here in the 18th century. The latter had profitable shipping interests, and it is therefore only appropriate that this building should now house the **Aberdeen Maritime Museum**. At the north end of Shiprow is Castle Street, where the **Mercat Cross** of 1686, with its base containing the images of Scottish monarchs from James I to James VII, used to provide the meeting place for the city's merchants. The **Town House** on the corner of Broad Street dates from 1868, but incorporates the tower and spire of the earlier Tolbooth, which served as the site of public executions up to 1867.

At the opposite end of Broad Street is the magnificent **Marischal College**, a visually stunning example of the locally quarried stone which gave Aberdeen the sobriquet, 'the Granite City'. Marischal College was founded on this site in 1593 by George Keith, the 5th Earl Marischal, occupying the buildings of Greyfriars monastery which had been defunct since the Reformation. Though the university was already founded in 1495 at King's College, Marischal amalgamated with King's College in 1860 to form Aberdeen University. From the mid-19th century it was substantially altered and enlarged, culminating with the present pinnacled façade of 1906, by which time the building had grown to become the second largest granite structure in the world (after El Escorial in Spain). Devote considerable time to admiring the exterior, before going inside to the **Mitchell Hall** – which is open to the public when not in use by the university – and the **University of Aberdeen Marischal Museum** which has displays of anthropological artefacts from ancient to modern times. The Scottish prehistoric weapons and archaeological remains are particularly fascinating. A short distance from King Street, which is perpendicular to Castle Street, is **St Andrews Episcopal Cathedral**. This houses a permanent exhibition on Aberdeen which should be of interest to the keen historian.

Across the road from Marischal College is **Provost Skene's House**, built in the 16th century and named after Sir George

Skene, who became Lord Provost a number of years after his family took residence in 1654. Today the house is home to the city's folk museum and has rooms furnished in Georgian and Victorian styles. The **Kirk of St Nicholas**, on Schoolhill, was built between the 12th and 15th centuries, and was for long the largest parish church in Scotland. Today its carillon of 48 bells is the largest in Britain. North from here, Schoolhill is the location of **James Dun's House**, the 18th-century residence of the master and rector of Aberdeen Grammar School, and now a museum mounting frequently changing exhibitions. There is an impressive permanent collection of art from the 18th to 20th centuries, with the emphasis on more recent work, at the **Art Gallery** on the corner of Schoolhill and Blackfriars Street. The wide range of the exhibition includes works by Raeburn, Augustus John, Reynolds, Toulouse-Lautrec and a fine selection of 20th-century British art. Nearby is **His Majesty's Theatre**, built in 1906, standing opposite Union Terrace, which runs the short distance south to Aberdeen's main thoroughfare. Continuous with Castle Street, Union Street, begun in 1800 and named after the political union binding the parliaments of Great Britain and Ireland, is a mile-long testament to the elegance of 19th-century architectural style. Specific examples worth highlighting are, west of here, the **Music Hall** of 1820, and on Huntly Street, just off Union Street, **St Mary's Cathedral** of 1859–69.

A walk round Aberdeen's busy HARBOUR AREA will be greatly enhanced by a prior visit to the Maritime Museum (see above) in Shiprow. From here the adjacent Market Street gives convenient access to the harbour's north-west corner at Upper Dock, before passing the Fish Market, the largest in Scotland, extended in 1982. Just before Victoria Bridge, North Esplanade West bears right, leading to Riverside Drive, where a peaceful walk through **Duthie Park** allows visitors to enjoy its gardens, exotic birds, aquarium, 'Mountain of Roses' – a glorious array of over 100,000 bushes – and winter gardens. The latter draws many tourists keen to enjoy the banks of exotic flowers, wonderful spring flower displays, the Japanese water garden, the cactus house, and the music every weekend. Beyond the park, Riverside Drive follows a bend in the

Dee until the latter is crossed by the early 16th-century **Bridge of Dee**, whose 400-foot span is supported by seven arches and decorated with engravings showing a series of heraldic crests. Follow the A944 west out of the city centre and you will find **Hazlehead Park**, the largest in Aberdeen. The park's amazing maze is the only one in Scotland with over a mile of paths. There is also a children's corner with farm animals, as well as an adventure playground and walks in the aviary.

OLD ABERDEEN, one and a half miles north of the city centre, was not incorporated with the rest of the city until 1891, and today it retains an identity which detaches it from the rest of bustling Aberdeen – this is largely due to the air of reverence and contemplation that the many university buildings and the cathedral inspire, making it a pleasant place to stroll.

South of St Machar Drive, **King's College** was founded in 1495 predating Marischal College, its counterpart in the composite body of Aberdeen University, by nearly 100 years (see above). The earliest part of the building dates from the 16th century, although its present appearance owes much to the many later additions, such as Cromwell's Tower of 1658. The chief attraction, however, is the Chapel – constructed 1500–05, and rebuilt after storm damage in 1633 – which went from being Catholic to Protestant, and now stages interdenominational services on Sundays during term time. The new **King's College Visitor Centre** is situated within the 19th-century library building, helping you to enjoy your visit further with a video on life during the university's five-hundred-year past. There is also a gift shop and coffee lounge.

Heading north from St Machar Drive, Chanonry passes the university's **Cruickshank Botanic Gardens** – containing a variety of shrubs, alpine plants, and different types of heather in its rock and water gardens – before reaching **St Machar's Cathedral** (open daily 9 a.m. to 5 p.m.). A magnificent granite edifice with traces of sandstone, the oldest parts of the existing structure date from the 14th century, with many additions made in the 200 years that followed. The nave has remained intact since its construction in the 15th century. A fascinating feature of St Machar's is the magnificent oak heraldic ceiling added in 1520. A little less than a mile to the north-east, on the other side of Seaton Park, the River Don is spanned by the **Brig o' Balgownie**, or **Auld Brig**, the latter appellation hinting at its status as the oldest bridge in Scotland, having been built in the early 14th century, completed on the orders of Robert the Bruce. The water beneath it is said to be inhabited by witches, and be warned, for the soothsayer Thomas the Rhymer said that it would collapse in the event of it being crossed by an only son riding a mare's only offspring.

West from Aberdeen

All over this corner of Scotland there are many interesting places within easy reach from Aberdeen. A number of trails meander through the region each with a theme designed to lead you through the best of the spectacular countryside. On the world's only **Malt Whisky Trail** you can visit famous distilleries – Glenfarclas, Glenfiddich, Glen Grant, Glenlivet, Strathisla, Tamdhu, Tomnavulin and Cardhu. All the distilleries welcome you for a tour with knowledgeable guides. Follow the **Coastal Trail** with its fascinating fishing heritage from Dundee to Inverness. It runs for over 200 miles through some of the most spectacular coastal scenery. A very different trail is the **Castle Trail**. Nine of the most interesting castles and houses are featured on the trail – Huntly Castle, Fyvie Castle, Haddo House, Tolquhon Castle, Corgarff Castle, Castle Fraser, Craigievar Castle, Leith Hall and Kildrummy Castle. The **Quality Trail**, usually featuring internationally renowned manufacturers from the Grampian region, is currently being redeveloped and enlarged to involve more partners and a greater variety of attractions to highlight the high quality of the region's products. You can also take the **Victorian Heritage Trail** through the splendour of Royal Deeside visiting Balmoral Castle, Crathie Kirk, Ballater, Cambus O'May suspension bridge, the Queen's View, Drum Castle, Fasque House, Fettercairn, Banchory, Glen Muick, Royal Lochnagar Distillery and Linn of Dee. An interesting circuit of the area due west can be made, going out on the A944 and returning by the A93.

At Maryculter, five miles west of Aberdeen, just off the South Deeside Road (B9077), is a marvellous day's outing for the children. **STORYBOOK GLEN** is Scotland's answer to Disneyland – 20 acres of every imaginable nursery rhyme character and now with the additional attraction of Cinderella and her fairytale castle – set in glorious Deeside scenery (open from 1 March to 31 October, from 10 a.m. to 6 p.m.; and from 1 November to 28 February, weekends only, 11 a.m. to 4 p.m.). Fifteen miles along the A944, the B993 branches off and leads to the National Trust's 16th-century **Castle Fraser**, one of the most spectacular of the castles of Mar (open May, June and September, Monday to Sunday, 2 p.m. to 6 p.m., July and August 11 a.m. to 6 p.m. gardens open all year). The most interesting features are the Great Hall, and the exhibition on the other castles in the area.

Further along the A944 is the attractive town of **ALFORD**, home of the **Grampian Transport Museum**, near which is the terminus of the **Alford Valley Railway** which runs on a two-foot gauge track to Haughton Country Park, one mile away (runs daily from June to August; and on Sunday only during April, May, September and the first half of October). The town has a dry-ski slope offering all-year-round skiing. Six miles south of Alford is **Craigievar Castle**, a masterpiece of the Scots baronial style. Finished in 1626 for one William Forbes, the present-day structure is virtually unscathed by the last 350 years. Inside is some wonderful panelling, exceptional plaster ceilings, and outside is a good picnic and woodland walk area (open from May to September).

A few miles south of Mossat, the ruined **Kildrummy Castle**, dating from the 13th century, was once controlled by Edward I, and later housed the wife and children of Robert the Bruce during his exile on Rathlin Island in 1306. It was largely destroyed in revenge for it having been the place where plans for the Jacobite rebellion of 1715 were finalized. Next to the castle stands a first-rate country house built in 1900, **Kildrummy Castle Hotel** (Tel. 09755 71288), one of Scotland's best kept secrets, with gardens administered by a local trust as part of estate grounds. Costing considerably less than comparable hotels, the accommodation and cuisine are of a very high standard, and families are made particularly welcome.

Travelling west from here to Cockbridge leads you to the A939 road to the **Lecht** ski area. The terrain is wide and open and the runs shorter, compared to other resorts in Scotland, providing ideal slopes for novices and families. Five miles away the **Glenmulliach Nordic Ski Centre** at Tomintoul provides high-level forest trails. **Tomintoul Museum** on The Square has local history displays, a reconstructed farm kitchen and a blacksmith's shop, as well as interesting displays on the local wildlife and environment. It is also the site of the Tourist Information Centre (open April, May and October, Monday to Saturday 9.30 a.m. to 5.30 p.m., Sunday 2 p.m. to 5.30 p.m.; June and September, Monday to Friday, 9.30 a.m. to 6 p.m., Saturday 9.30 a.m. to 1 p.m. and 2 p.m. to 6 p.m., Sunday 2 p.m. to 6 p.m.; July and August, Moday to Friday, 9 a.m. to 6.30 p.m., Saturday 9 a.m. to 1 p.m. and 2 p.m. to 6.30 p.m., Sunday 11 a.m. to 1 p.m. and 2 p.m. to 6.30 p.m.).

South from Kildrummy the A97 comes to an end at the junction with the A93, 13 miles west of which is **Balmoral**, the private residence of the Royal Family (open from May to July, Monday to Saturday, 10 a.m. to 5 p.m. except when in use by members of the House of Windsor). Prince Albert bought the estate in 1852 when it was called Bouchmorale and had the castle rebuilt by William Smith. Of particular interest are the works of art decorating the ballroom, while its extensive grounds and gardens offer visitors attractive country walks and pony-trekking.

A few miles west of Balmoral on the A93 lies **Craigendarroch Hotel and Country Club** at BALLATER. This luxury, 50-bedroom country house hotel with its time-share lodges, stands on 28 acres of wooded and landscaped gardens. The atmosphere is intimate but friendly, the service magnificent. Many of the bedrooms have balconies offering wonderful views of the Dee Valley. The hotel has three restaurants including the elegant 'Oaks Restaurant' (also open to non-residents) which serves *cuisine moderne* together with traditional Scottish dishes, using the finest fresh local produce. The adjoining country club provides many sport and leisure facilities – two indoor pools, spa bath, sauna and steam room, squash, snooker, trimnasium, solarium and health and beauty salons. Craigendarroch also has a floodlit dry ski slope, curling rink and tennis court. Nearby outdoor pursuits include walking, mountaineering, clay pigeon shooting, gliding and riding. Skiing at Aviemore and the Lecht are within easy reach. The lodges are also available for three-, four- and seven-night breaks. The **Dee Valley Confectioners** can also be found at Ballater in Station Square, where you can watch sweets being made in the traditional manner.

Near Balmoral is the **Royal Lochnagar Distillery** where there is an excellent visitor centre (open all the year round), and interesting tours of the small distillery followed by a dram of the Highland Malt Whisky. The A93 continues westwards to the village of BRAEMAR, the site of the famous **Braemar Highland Gathering** and the new **Highland Heritage Centre**. Here you can learn more about the gathering, the history of the village's close royal connections, and the landscape of the area. **Braemar Castle** can certainly not be missed, built in the early 17th century by the Earl of Mar and later rebuilt as a Hanoverian garrison post. A striking turreted residence with an underground pit prison, it has an interesting assortment of historic relics from throughout the ages. Branching off the main road and further up the Dee is the **Linn of Dee** where the river cascades down through a series of enormous potholes. This is a good base for walks into the majestic Cairngorms – either serious hillwalking or short strolls through the pinewoods along the river. Returning to Aberdeen the A93 passes through Aboyne where the **Balnacoil Hotel** (Tel. 03398 86806) recently reopened. It's a delightful, small, country house hotel perched on the banks of the River Dee. First-class, imaginative cuisine is served in both the dining room and the Stalkers lounge bar.

The 42-mile return journey to Aberdeen takes in the magnificent 16th-century, **Crathes Castle** (open during Easter, and from April to October, daily from 11 a.m. to 6 p.m. The grounds are open all year, daily from 9.30 a.m. to sunset). This outstanding National Trust property is notable for the painted ceilings in its Chamber of the Nine Nobles, Green Lady's Room, and Chamber of the Nine Muses, as well as its licensed restaurant recognised by the 'Taste of Scotland' guide. Its 600-acre grounds contain nature trails, a visitor centre, and formal gardens. Two miles further on, the attractive town of **BANCHORY** offers visitors a number of relaxing recreations, such as sea trout and salmon fishing, golf, and footpaths through natural woodlands. **Banchory Museum** in the Burgh Buildings on the High Street is also worth a visit. Exhibits include costumes, ceramics, photographs and local history displays (open every afternoon except Thursday, 2 p.m. to 5.20 p.m.). Another fine building, at Drumoak by Banchory, is **Drum Castle**, a 13th-century tower house adjoining a Jacobean mansion house with Victorian additions (open April to September, 2 p.m. to 6 p.m.)

North-west from Aberdeen

North-west from Aberdeen, the A96 passes the small town of Inverurie, two miles from which is the unspoilt village of Pitcaple, location of the commendable country house hotel, **Pittodrie House** (Tel. 04676 81444) where dinner with wine, bed and breakfast cost between £136 and £210 per night for two. Huntly, along with Keith and Dufftown, is part of a small triangular grouping of venerable towns of interest to the visitor. **HUNTLY** grew as a town in the 16th century, although **Huntly Castle** has been here since the 12th century and is today the chief attraction for the town's visitors (open from April to September, Monday to Saturday, 9.30 a.m. to 6.30 p.m.; and Sunday, 2 p.m. to 7 p.m.; and from October to March, Monday to Saturday, 9.30 a.m. to 4 p.m., and Sunday, 2 p.m. to 4.30 p.m., closed Thursday afternoons). The remaining structure is largely the work of several periods of rebuilding between the 15th and 17th centuries. The **North-east Falconry Visitor Centre** lies just three miles northwest of Huntly and offers a unique experience of seeing falcons, owls and magnificent eagles take part in flying demonstrations each day, providing excellent video and photographic opportunities. There is a café and picnic area, and a souvenir and gift shop. **DUFFTOWN**, like Keith, is an important town in the Malt Whisky Trail (see above and chapter on 'Aviemore and Spey Valley'), and in addition to **Glenfiddich Distillery**, providing excellent free guided tours throughout the year, is famous for **Balvenie Castle**, an attractive ruin, overlooking the distillery (open from April to September, Monday to Saturday, 9.30 a.m. to 7 p.m., and Sunday 2 p.m. to 7 p.m.). The Speyside Way has a spur linking Craigellachie with Dufftown, and a second spur runs from Ballindalloch to Tomintoul.

An exceptionally good new hotel opened here in 1990 – **Craigellachie**, Speyside (Tel. 0340 881204). An 1893 country house hotel, restored to its former glory and in the heart of the 'Malt Whisky Trail', 12 miles south of Elgin. Its 30 bedrooms, excellent restaurant, and period public rooms make this a wonderfully relaxing place to enjoy fishing and game sports for a few days. Whisky dominates this part of Scotland, and every few miles one sees the distinctive chimney of a malt distillery. Tours and free samples abound – drivers beware! The **Speyside Cooperage** can be found in the very heart of the malt whisky country where you can observe the complete whisky barrel process from the 'Acorn to Cask' exhibition, and by watching the skilled coopers at work. There is also a gift shop specialising in quality goods crafted from wood (open Easter–October, Monday to Saturday 9.30 a.m. to 4.30 p.m. and Sunday by appointment, October–Easter Monday to Friday, 9.30 a.m. to 4.30 p.m.). Local history dominates the exhibition at **Dufftown Museum** in the Square. **KEITH** is the home of Chivas Brothers' **Strathisla Distillery**, and although it can claim to be one of the oldest in Scotland, dating back to 1786, it is not the only one in Scotland to have been described as the oldest.

The principal town among the many strung along, or near, the Moray coast, is **ELGIN**. Its outstanding feature is the ruined **Elgin Cathedral**, a magnificent structure which gained lavish praise in its day, was founded in 1224 as the seat of the Bishop of Moray, but from 1270 onward, when it was badly damaged by fire, it was visited by frequent misfortune. The cycle of destruction and repair came to an end when Cromwell's troops vandalized the west windows in the mid-17th century. The town's main thoroughfare, High Street, contains a number of elegant buildings, including **St Giles Church** of 1828, and **Elgin Museum**. From the east end of the High Street, Abbey Street leads to the restored **Greyfriars Chapel** which incorporates the remains of the 15th-century

Franciscan friary. In Oldmills Road, in the west of the town centre, is the restored 17th-century meal mill, **Old Mills**.

Elgin has a good selection of hotel accommodation. At the top of the range is the **Mansion House Hotel**, The Haugh (Tel. 0343 548811). A grand baronial design of the mid-19th century, it stands in generous grounds overlooking the River Lossie, only a quarter of a mile from the town centre. Prices are upward of £57. Guests at the **Eight Acres Hotel**, Sheriffmill (Tel. 0343 543077/8), have access to the hotel's own swimming pool, sauna, snooker room, and squash courts. Prices start from £33. From around £25 or less there are: **City Hotel**, High Street (Tel. 0343 547055); **Laichmoray Hotel**, Maisondieu Road (Tel. 0343 540045); **Park House Hotel**, South Street (Tel. 0343 547695); and **Royal Hotel**, Station Road (Tel. 0343 542320). There is a good selection of bed and breakfast accommodation in and around Elgin. For non-smokers, **Mrs Isobel McGowan**, 63 Moss Street (Tel 0343 541993), offers rooms from £9.50. For a little extra, **Mrs Anne Munn**, Caronvale, 18 South Guildry (Tel. 0343 546864), charges between £11.20 and £15.50. The **Tourist Information Centre**, 17 High Street (Tel. 0343 543388/542666), is open all year.

In addition to its elegance and sedate charm, Elgin occupies a strategic location for the tourist, offering, as it does, quick and easy access to Inverness, Nairn, and the battlefield of Culloden Moor to the west (see chapter on 'Inverness, Loch Ness and Nairn'); the Malt Whisky Trail and the Spey Valley to the south-west (see chapter on 'Aviemore and Spey Valley'); and a host of seaside towns and resorts along a short stretch of sandy coastline. Notable among the latter are such popular family resorts as **FINDHORN**, **LOSSIEMOUTH, BUCKIE**, and **CULLEN**.

Inverness, Loch Ness and Nairn

INTRODUCTION

Inverness, capital of the Highlands, is a convenient base from which to tour the area and is an attractive town whose previous conservative image has undergone a dramatic change, as substantial development and growth has taken place in recent years. It affords access to many miles of unspoilt, breathtaking countryside, castles and historical monuments.

Inverness is easily reached by car, train or plane. The airport is only seven miles from the town and receives flights from London (80 minutes), Glasgow (40 minutes), and Edinburgh (30 minutes). There are direct train services from Glasgow, Edinburgh, and Euston and King's Cross in London. Travelling by car, there are good road links from Glasgow and Edinburgh.

HISTORY

This is the part of Scotland where the final battle of the Jacobite rebellion of 1745 took place, and the visitor touring the area will be frequently reminded of this episode in history. The Jacobite aim of returning the crown to the House of Stuart finally came to an end in April 1746 at the sad and bloody battle of Culloden, located between Inverness and Nairn, where the Jacobite troops under the command of Charles Edward Stuart, or 'Bonnie Prince Charlie', were savagely routed by the Hanoverian forces under the Duke of Cumberland. It was the last battle to be fought on British soil and ended not only the Stuart hopes of acceding to the throne, but also saw the end of much of the traditional Highland way of life. The Act of Proscription of 1747, which aimed to subdue the Highlanders who were none too enamoured with the Union, outlawed Highland dress, but its repeal in 1782 was followed by the greater and more damaging iniquity of the Highland Clearances. Crofters had paid rent on their land not in cash but in armed service to the landowner. As warring in the Union became a thing of the past, this payment in kind was rendered obsolete and the landowners found that a more profitable use for their land was in selling or leasing it to English and Lowland sheepfarmers. To make way for the new occupants, the Highlanders were callously evicted and turned out of their crofts, rarely with much more than the clothes they wore. By 1860, their dispersal to the cities, and emigration to Canada and Australia, had left the Highlands almost bereft of population.

WHERE TO GO FOR WHAT

Culloden Battlefield has monuments to the Jacobites who died, and the excellent exhibition in the visitor centre, which tells the story of the battle and Clearances, is recommended to the sightseer with a keen interest in history. There is also a newly installed **raised map** which, it is hoped, will give blind and partially sighted visitors the chance to 'view' the battleground. Just south of the battlefield, **Clava Cairns** are thought to be as much as 4,000 years old, and represent one of the two most important archaeological sites on the Scottish mainland. Sixteen miles east of Inverness, **Nairn** has miles of sandy beach, several golf courses (one of championship standard), and many colourful parks and gardens, all of which combine to make it a popular resort for family holidays.

INVERNESS is a pleasant town standing either side of the River Ness and surely one of few locations in the world where it is possible to land a salmon right in the town centre. As its sobriquet 'Capital of the Highlands' suggests, it is well positioned to act as a base for touring the magnificent Highland countryside which is only a short drive away.

Most of the town occupies the right bank of the river where **Inverness Castle** commands a prominent position looking down on the Ness. The present building, housing the law courts and local government offices, dates from the 19th century but stands on the site of a much older and battle-scarred castle built in the 11th or 12th centuries. The exhibitions in **Inverness Museum** and **Art Gallery** concern not only the town but also the Highland region, with fine collections of Highland silver bagpipes, Jacobite relics and many views of old Inverness. The impressive Gothic-style **Town House** of 1880 hosted the first cabinet meeting outside London when Lloyd George and his ministers gathered there in September 1921 to discuss the Irish question. North of this trio of buildings, Church Street runs through the heart of the town with the **Steeple** of 1791 grabbing the visitor's attention at the corner with Bridge Street. **Abertarff House** further north near Fraser Street was built in 1592 and restored in 1963 by the National Trust for Scotland, whose offices it now contains. The **High Parish Church** retains its 14th-century tower, the rest of the building having been rebuilt in 1772. Standing opposite is a fine example of 17th-century domestic architecture, **Dunbar's Hospital**, restored since its construction in 1688 as an almshouse. Half a mile north on Cromwell Road, only a clock tower remains of **Cromwell's Fort** (built 1652-7), the rest having been destroyed during the Restoration.

On the opposite bank, near the river, **St Andrew's Cathedral** of 1868 is said to lack a spire due to the money for its construction running out. The **Loch Ness Monster Video Show** is housed in Kiltmaker Building, and features archive film video and pictures. The hill half a mile south of here, **Tomnahurich** (Hill of the Fairies), is a cemetery which gives an impressive view of the town from its summit. **Ness Islands** near here are linked to each other and the river's banks by a series of bridges to form an attractive and unusual public park. For the children, **Bught Park** has one of Scotland's top BMX tracks. Training sessions are available. There is also a boating pond and children's play area. For a guided walk around historic Inverness, there are tours leaving from **Inverness Castle** at 10.30 a.m. every Sunday from April to September, and other times by arrangement.

In the centre of town the **Caledonian Hotel** (Tel. 0463 235181) provides good accommodation from around £55. Beside the river,

Brae Ness Hotel, Ness Bank (Tel. 0463 712266) serving good home-cooking, and **Columba Hotel**, Ness Walk recently refurbished and overlooking the castle (Tel. 0463 231391), have prices from under £30. Outside the town, the de luxe **Culloden House Hotel** (Tel. 0463 790461) is an elegant Georgian maison whose fine cuisine receives the recommendation of Egon Ronay. Prices are suitably luxurious. For good bed and breakfast accommodation, try the **Cedar Guest House**, 33 Kenneth Street (Tel. 0463 230477), centrally situated charging from £13 and credited with two crowns. Close to the city centre, is the three-crown commended **Aberfeldy Lodge Guest House**, 1 Southside Road (Tel. 0463 231120), charging from around £18. For caravan and camping facilities, there is **Bught Caravan and Camping Site** (Tel. 0463 236920), charging £6.20 for tourers and motor caravans, and £3.10 for tents; **Bunchrew Caravan and Camping Park**, Bunchrew (Tel. 0463 237802), costs from £6.33 for tourers, motor caravans and tents. Caravans can be let. Additionally, there is **Torvean Caravan Park**, Glenurquhart Road (Tel 0463 220582), with space for tourers from £6.50 and caravans to let. The **Scottish Youth Hostel Association** provides hostel accommodation at 1 Old Edinburgh Road (Tel 0463 231771). It is open all year round except 2 January to 1 February; prices from £6.20 per night. The **Inverness Student Hotel**, 8 Culduthel Road (Tel. 0463 236556), offers reasonably priced self-catering accommodation.

Among the town's top restaurants is **Dunain Park Hotel** (Tel. 0463 230512) one mile along the A82. The award-winning Egon Ronay recommended set-dinner menu at around £25 a head will satisfy gourmet tastes. **Loch Ness House Hotel and Cluny Restaurant**, Glenurquhart Road (Tel. 0463 231248), and **Redcliffe Hotel**, 1 Gordon Terrace (Tel. 0463 232767), both feature traditional Scottish cuisine from haggis to salmon. **Janey's Wholefood Café**, 89 Academy Street (Tel. 0463 710877), is Inverness's first vegetarian restaurant and has a very relaxed and informal setting.

For evening entertainment, there is the **Eden Court Theatre**, Bishops Road (Tel. 0463 239841), offering a variety of drama, opera, jazz and specialist events, while the **Riverside Cinema** (Tel. 0463 221718), shows award-winning films. The **Inverness Jazz**

Platform (Tel. 0403 790137) offers regular jazz concerts through-out the year. For more traditional Scottish entertainment, **Cummings Hotel**, 14a Church Street (Tel. 0463 2325311), hosts the well-established Scottish Showtime from Monday to Saturday at 8.30 p.m., during June to September, with traditional songs, music and dancing. The **Beaufort Hotel**, Culduthel Road (Tel. 0463 222897), provides the venue for the folk-singing club every Sunday at 8.30 p.m. The **Market Bar**, Market Lane off Church Street, hosts similar folk entertainment Tuesday to Sunday. And, there is of course, the **Folk Festival** from 17 to 19 April.

Tourist Information is available all year at Castle Wynd (Tel. 0463 234353).

Loch Ness is only six miles away and one of the best ways of getting there is to take a boat cruise from the outskirts of the town, along the Caledonian Canal and the length of the loch. **Jacobite Cruises**, Tomnahurich Bridge, Glenurquhart Road (Tel. 0463 233999), run cruises three times per day. There are also various minibus tours which run twice daily from the Tourist Information Centre.

Taking the car round the banks is an equally enjoyable means of exploring the natural beauty of **LOCH NESS**, a 24-mile long narrow stretch of water whose depth is reckoned to be equal to the height of the hills around it. Circumnavigating Loch Ness by road makes a total journey of about 70 miles through some of the most spectacular scenery – travel anti-clockwise for the best views. The A82 runs south-west from Inverness along the loch's northern shore. The first notable stopping point is the village of **DRUM-NADROCHIT** which is the location of the **Loch Ness Monster Exhibition**. The exhibition has an extensive display on the monster legend, sightings, and the various attempts to confirm the existence of the creature. The **Art Gallery** on the Green offers the chance to view paintings by Highland artists. Crafts and paintings are on sale. Two miles further on, the ruins of **Urquhart Castle** stand on a promontory commanding an excellent view of the loch, which may explain why more sightings of the monster have been reported here than from anywhere else (open April–September, Monday to Saturday, 9.30 a.m.–6 p.m. Sunday, 9.30 a.m.–6 p.m.; October–March, Monday to Saturday, 9.30 a.m.–4 p.m. Sunday,

2 p.m.–4 p.m.). After the **Cobb Memorial**, a cairn commemorating John Cobb who died on the loch in 1952 while trying to break the world waterspeed record, the road comes to the picturesque village of **INVERMORISTON** with its **Old Bridge** over the River Moriston in an idyllic setting. At the south-western extremity of the loch, **FORT AUGUSTUS** is a popular holiday resort built on either side of the Caledonian Canal. Formerly known as Kilcumein, it was renamed in 1729 after the fort built here by General Wade, itself named in honour of William Augustus, Duke of Cumberland and a prominent figure on the government side in the war against the Jacobites under Bonnie Prince Charlie. The remains of the fort were, in 1876, incorporated into **Fort Augustus Abbey**, now run as a boy's school. Their church is always open to visitors. A four-mile trail through **Inchnacardoch Forest** starts just south-west of the town. Cabin cruisers can be hired from **Abbey Cruisers** (Tel. 0320 6316).

Tourist Information is available in the car park from Easter to October (Tel. 0320 6367).

The return route along the opposite shore is by means of the B862 and the B852. As the road climbs to over 1,100 feet it passes the panoramic vantage of **Suidhe Chumein Viewpoint**.

Joining the B852 soon leads to the **Falls of Foyers Woodland Walk**, through the village of Foyers and on to **INVERFARIGAIG** where there is a Forestry Commission visitor centre near the start of the steep **Farigaig Forest Trail** offering superb views of Loch Ness. To the north-east of the village, the Iron Age **Inverfarigaig Fort** stands on a rock above the mouth of the River Farigaig. For the eight miles from here to Dores, the road skirts the water's edge and passes many tempting picnic sites, before rejoining the B862 and back to Inverness.

The A862 west from Inverness runs along the southern shore of the Beauly Firth for much of the 10 miles to **BEAULY** whose dominant feature is the ruined **Beauly Priory** of 1230, notable for the three rare triangular windows in the south wall and the window arcading in the south transept. Four miles from Beauly on the A831 Cannich Road is **Aigas House and Field Centre**, home to many art and sculpture exhibitions. There are also nature and woodland trails within the grounds and guided field trips into the hills and glens to observe the wildlife. Loch fishing for rainbow and brown trout is available, as well as bed and breakfast accommodation.

The main road east to Nairn, the A96, is less interesting than the quieter B9006 which, not far from Inverness, runs through the site of **Culloden Battlefield**. The battle took place on 16 April 1746 under the command of the Young Pretender, Charles Edward Stuart, on one side and the Duke of Cumberland on the other. Stuart's troops numbered 5,000 and marched from Inverness to meet the 9,000 Hanoverians under Cumberland coming from Nairn. The casualty figures indicate the extent of the rout: 1,200 of the Young Pretender's men killed in comparison with 76 from the enemy side. Cumberland, however, was not content with so conclusive a victory, and insisted on the wanton slaughter, which continued for several days, of any wounded who had taken refuge in the surrounding woods. Even civilian spectators of the battle who had come out from Inverness were murdered by his men. Where the fighting was concentrated there now stands the **Memorial Cairn** of 1881, the **Irish Memorial** of 1963 honouring those nationals who took part on the Jacobite side, and the **Graves of the Clans** scattered on either side of the road. The **Well of the Dead** is a spring in a clearing where wounded Highlanders were said to have been mercilessly killed while trying to drink. The whole area is now owned by the National Trust for Scotland whose **Visitor Centre** (open all year except January, 9 a.m.–6.30 p.m.) provides information on the battle and its historical significance by way of an exhibition and audio-visual display.

A minor road across the River Nairn a short distance beyond the battlefield leads to one of the most important archaeological sites in mainland Scotland. **Clava Cairns** are three large burial mounds surrounded by standing stones, thought to have been in place since 2000–1500 BC. Returning to the B9006, and then taking the B9090, leads to **Kilravock Castle** and its attractive gardens, dating from the 15th century (open from May to September but not on Sunday. Admission by scheduled tour. Tel. 06678 258 for times).

More interesting is **Cawdor Castle** (open from May to October, daily from 10 a.m. to 5.30 p.m.) a little further along the road, although it is not the same one which Shakespeare had the three witches promise to Macbeth. That earlier castle stood about a mile away; the present one was founded about 300 years after Macbeth, the oldest part being the tower of 1372 while the rest dates mostly from the 16th century. Inside, an exhibition of miscellany includes tapestries, portraits, and 18th- and 19th-century kitchen equipment. The extensive gardens include woodland and a nature trail, and the small planned village of Cawdor is one of the most attractive in the Highlands.

Five miles on, the B9090 reaches **NAIRN**, where long sandy beaches, links, and two golf courses combine to make it a popular family resort, which was the summer haunt of Charlie Chaplin during his regular visits to the area. The Fishertown area, now characterized by its picturesque restored cottages, was formerly the province of the town's English-speaking community while the rest of Nairn was home to Gaelic-speakers. Information on these bygone days and other aspects of the town's past features beside an exhibition on the local fishing industry, in the **Fishertown Museum** in King Street. More local history is on display in **Viewfield Museum** which also houses relics from Culloden. The **Highland Railway Museum** on the station platform has a collection of old railway memorabilia. **Nairn Leisure Park** at The Links, can provide endless amusement with facilities for table-tennis, croquet, indoor draughts and chess, as well as an adventure fort and fitness trail outdoors. A popular BMX track is situated on The Riverside, and during the summer, youngsters aged between 8 and 15 years have activities arranged throughout the day by a beach leader at the **Nairn Summer Activities Centre**. For discovery walking tours around Nairn for day or half-day walks, contact Tel. 54935.

In keeping with its popularity with visitors, Nairn has a wide choice of fine hotels. **Golf View Hotel**, Seabank Road (Tel. 0667 52301), is a four-star Egon Ronay recommended hotel overlooking the sea and the hills of the Black Isle. Prices start at £48. **Carnach Country House Hotel**, Inverness Road (Tel. 0667 52094), stands in eight acres of grounds overlooking the Moray Firth. Prices start below £30, as they do also at **Alton Burn Hotel** (Tel. 0667 52051) and **Royal Marine Hotel** (Tel. 0667 53381). From under £20 there are **Hermitage Hotel**, Cawdor Road (Tel. 0667 53089), in five acres of grounds and **Invernairne Hotel**, Thurlow Road (Tel. 0667 52039); **Braeval Hotel**, Crescent Road (Tel. 0667 52341), prices from £25. There are also quite a few camping and caravan parks in and around the area. These include: one mile from Nairn, **Delnies Woods and Tourer Park** (Tel. 0667 55381), charging between £4 and £6.50 for tourers and motor caravans, and **Lochloy Holiday Park**, East Beach (Tel. 0667 53764), charging between £5 and £9 for tourers, motor caravans and tents.

The **Tourist Information** office at 62 King Street is open from Easter to October.

There are a number of interesting excursions which can be easily made from Nairn. Eight miles to the west, **Fort George**, standing on a narrow strip of land jutting out into the Moray Firth, is one of the most impressive examples of 18th-century military architecture to be seen anywhere in Britain (open from April to September, Monday to Saturday, 9.30 a.m. to 7 p.m., and Sunday, 2 p.m. to 7 p.m.; and from October to March, Monday to Saturday, 9.30 a.m. to 4 p.m., and Sunday, 2 p.m. to 4 p.m.). The fort was built to accommodate 2,500 men, and today the barracks are still in use. **Fort George Military Museum** houses material relating to the regiment of the Queen's Own Highlanders (Seaforth and Camerons).

On the way to Brodie Castle the A96 runs through the village of **AULDEARN**, notable for the 17th-century **Boath Doocot** (dovecote). Seven miles east of Nairn, **Brodie Castle** had been a family possession since the land was first granted to the Brodies in 1160. The original castle was burned in 1645 during the Civil War and today's magnificent structure is the work of the 17th and 19th centuries. A fine collection of paintings hangs inside, including work from 17th-century Holland, 18th-century England and the French Impressionists. The extensive grounds are open all year and include a woodland trail, lake and adventure playground. (The castle is open from 1 April to 30 September,

Monday to Saturday, 11 a.m. to 6 p.m., and Sunday, 2 p.m. to 6 p.m., and during October on Saturday, 11 a.m. to 6 p.m., and Sunday, 2 p.m. to 6 p.m.)

Three miles west of Forres, off the A96, is **Darnaway Farm Visitor Centre**. This is an interesting exhibition of the forests and farms of Moray Estates, with cow-milking demonstrations, nature trails, a play area, woodland walks and so on. Open from June to September.

The **Highland Golf Trail** features 76 golf courses. Choose from small picturesque nine-hole courses like Fort Augustus to the 18-hole championship links of Nairn and the choice of two challenging courses at Inverness. Green fees start around £5 per day. The **Loch Ness Monster Trail** takes in the many attractions around the famous loch other than monster-spotting. The total journey covers about 70 miles and includes Inverness, Dochgarroch, Lochend, Abriachan, Drumnadrochit, Lewison, Milton, Invermoriston, Fort Augustus, Whitebridge, Foyers, Inverfarigaig and Dores.

Aviemore and Spey Valley

INTRODUCTION

From modest origins in a burn near the loch of the same name, the River Spey gathers and flows north-east to the Moray Firth, between the serried peaks of the Grampian and Monadhliath mountains, through picturesque towns and villages, rolling woodland, and heather-tinted hills. Although its beauty is eclipsed in places by that of the Tay and the Dee, overall, the 98 miles of the Spey are of a more consistent character. The motorist can join it near its source and accompany it all the way to the sea, while the railway line escorts it from Newtonmore to Aviemore on a stretch flanked by the towering bulk of the Cairngorm and Monadhliath ranges.

All of the towns in the area lie in a line, fairly close together, along the banks of the Spey, and all are convenient bases for skiing in the Cairngorms. The oldest town is Kingussie, capital of the historic district of Badenoch, and heart of the Comyns' territory, the powerful family who ruled here until their defeat by Robert the Bruce in the 14th century. Until the arrival of the railway in the mid-19th century, Aviemore was little more than a few close buildings. It then grew as a quiet holiday resort until the mid-1960s when the development of the Aviemore Centre transformed it into a thriving, year-round holiday centre, with top hotels, restaurants, and sports facilities. Grantown-on-Spey is a spacious and elegant town which has retained much of its Georgian character since its development in the latter part of the 18th century. The many tourists it attracts today were preceded by members of Victorian society, who came here on the fashionable medical advice which regarded the change of air as a mild panacea.

Travel to and within the region is easy, with the A9 from Perth, and the InterCity railway line from London Euston, running through the main towns of Newtonmore, Kingussie, Aviemore and the village of Carrbridge. From Aviemore it is only a 45-minute drive along the A9 to the nearest airport at Inverness, which receives flights from Aberdeen, Edinburgh, Glasgow, Stornoway, Orkney, Shetland, and London.

The Spey Valley offers the holidaymaker many and varied pursuits. The **River Spey**, after the Tay and the Tweed, is the third most important in Scotland for salmon fishing. A specially adapted boat, ramps, runways and toilet facilities have recently been introduced on the River Spey to give disabled people access to the fishing. At **Lochs Insh and Morlich** there are watersports centres for canoeing, sailing and wind-surfing, while the rugged peaks of the **Cairngorms** offer a challenge to the experienced climber and hill walker. In addition to its popularity as a wintersports centre, **Aviemore** has many amenities and evening entertainments with which to keep its summer visitors busy.

WHERE TO GO FOR WHAT

Starting in the north-east of the region, and following the road south-west along the banks of the Spey, the first town on the tourist's itinerary is **GRANTOWN-ON-SPEY**, an attractive summer and winter resort with good fishing, and an 18-hole golf course. To the north of the town, **Castle Grant**, for several centuries the principal seat of the Clan Grant, retains its keep from the 15th century, while the rest of the present structure was added by Robert and John Adam in the 18th century. The interior contains decorative work by Robert Adam and period furnishings, but unfortunately the castle is no longer open to the public. At the present time a scheme is planned to restore the castle and create a luxury hotel and heritage centre. **The Heritage Exhibition** has claimed the north-east corner of the Square, at the Courthouse from May to October. Set up by the Grantown Museum and Heritage Trust, there are plans to establish a major museum and visitor centre in Grantown. A new fishery has also opened at Craggan, one mile south of Grantown, where children and adults alike are invited to catch their own trout of up to 4lbs in weight. Open May to September. At the end of June there is the chance to spectate at the annual Highland Games which takes place at Black Park. Even better, **Grantown Festival** fortnight takes place between 1 and 15 August.

The town is situated amidst beautiful woodlands. The most attractive are situated between Grantown and the river about half a mile from the town. The woods belong to the Earl of Seafield's family and contain many paths and tracks for walks. Grantown in equidistant from the Cairngorm ski slopes and the Lecht Ski Centre near Tomintoul and therefore is an ideal resort for a winter break.

In keeping with its popularity, Grantown offers a wide choice of accommodation. Close to the town centre are the **Seafield Lodge Hotel**, Woodside Avenue (Tel. 0479 2152), and **Grant Arms Hotel** in the town square (Tel. 0479 2526). both of which charge from around £25. From around £20 there are **Spey Valley Hotel**, Seafield Avenue (Tel. 0479 2942), and **Ravenscourt House Hotel**, Seafield Avenue (Tel. 0479 2286). Comfortable bed and breakfast accommodation from £12 per person is available at **The Anvil**, 16 Castle Road (Tel. 0469 3371), and **The Hawthorn**, Old Spey Bridge (Tel. 0479 2016). Caravan facilities are provided at the **Grantown on Spey Caravan Park**, Seafield Avenue (Tel. 0469 2474), **Toperfettle Farm** (Tel. 0479 2710), **Mrs Rae**, 7 Wade Road (Tel. 0463 221681), and **Mrs M. Shand** (Tel. 0469 2473), all offering caravans to hire between £78 and £260 for two to eight persons a week. The **Tourist Information** centre is at 54 High Street (Tel. 0479 2773) and is open all year.

Visitors to Grantown are well placed to follow the **Malt Whisky Trail**. The A95, crossing the border into Moray, leads to several distilleries offering a guided tour, explanation of the production process, and a little something to sample at the end. Opening times vary but it is well worth visiting the following: **Glenfarclas Distillery**, Ballindalloch (Tel. 08072 257), 17 miles from Grantown, just off the A95; **Cardhu Distillery**, Knockando (Tel. 03406 204), on the B9102; **Glenfiddich Distillery**, Dufftown (Tel. 0340 20373), at the intersection of the A941 and B9009; **Glen Grant Distillery**, Rothes (Tel. 03403 413), north-west of Dufftown on the A941; and **Strathisla Distillery**, Keith (Tel. 05422 7471), north-east of Dufftown on the B9014. East from Grantown, the A95 and B9008 lead, first of all, to the **Glenlivet Distillery**, Glenlivet (Tel. 05422 6294), and then the **Tomnavoulin-Glenlivet Distillery**, Tomnavoulin (Tel. 08073 442).

Three miles south-west of Grantown, at Dulnain Bridge, the road forks, with the southern route, the A95, soon passing the **Speyside Heather Centre** which, in addition to 300 varieties of heather, has an extensive collection of conifers, trees and shrubs. **Muckrach Lodge Hotel** (Tel. 047958 257) at Dulnain Bridge is a former Victorian shooting lodge set in 10 secluded acres. The hotel offers an imaginative repertoire of Scottish and French cuisine; dinner, bed and breakfast from £53 p.p. Also near here is the fabulous **Muckrach Castle**, a restored 16th-century castle on three storeys, available for letting through the agents Strutt and Parker (Tel. 031-226 2500). Sleeping eight adults in four bedrooms at prices from £410–£765 a week, this castle is well worth considering for a stylish base in the Highlands. The oddly-named village, **BOAT OF GARTEN**, is the terminus for the steam-powered **Strathspey Railway** which runs on five miles of track between here and Aviemore (Tel. 0479 810725 for details). The Royal Society for the Protection of Birds owns **Loch Garten Nature Reserve** to the east of the village, famous for its summertime ospreys which were extinct in Scotland until their arrival here in 1959. The birds' eyrie can be viewed from fixed binoculars in the special observation hut. **Heatherlea** is a traditional Highland guest house, Deshar Road (Tel. 0479 83674), and an ideal base for professionally guided bird-watching holidays with the very latest information and advice on hand. Weekly packages cost in the region of £250, including six days' bird-watching with guide, accommodation, all meals and transport. The **Boat Hotel** (Tel. 047983 258) is situated overlooking the golf club. The hotel offers 6 miles of fishing on the Spey and dinner on board its own carriages of the steam train on the Strathspey railway. Bed and breakfast from £40 per person. July 11 is the date for the **Boat of Garten Gala** for some typical Scottish entertainment.

The alternative route from Dulnain Bridge is along the A938, through the village of DUTHIL, site of the burial ground of the chiefs of Clan Grant, to **CARRBRIDGE**, where the considerable height of the **Bridge of Carr**, built in 1717, was necessary in order to overcome the frequent problem of flooding. The **Landmark Visitor Centre** has three screens on which it presents programmes describing the main events of Highland history, and includes admission to the **Scottish Forestry Heritage Centre**, which tells the story of the timber industry. The pine forest and tree-top trails allow the visitor to the nature centre to see the wildlife at close range. The **Slochd Nordic Ski School**, outside the village on the way to Inverness, hires mountain bikes and around this area are to be found quiet tracks in splendid countryside (Tel. 047984 666). The **Pony Trekking Centre** (Tel. 047984 602) provides one- or two-hour treks across moorland and forests. There is also the well-established **Carrbridge Ceilidh Week** to look out for in September. The **Tourist Information** centre on the main street (Tel. 047984 630) is open from May to September.

AVIEMORE is the principal town in the region, famous as an all year round outdoor sports centre, with skiing from mid-January until mid-April, but with much to offer visitors in summer. In the 1960s its transition from being a small, but pleasant holiday resort to being a thriving, modern tourist centre came with the development of Europe's first purpose-built leisure and sports centre, the **Aviemore Centre** (Tel. 0479 810624). The complex incorporates a choice of accommodation on the site (some of which is listed below), a theatre, cinema, shops, restaurants, and many sporting facilities, such as tennis and squash courts, a curling rink, and a dry ski slope. Additionally, there is the **Aviemore Kart Raceway** for those of eight years or over, from 10 a.m. until late. Aviemore is also headquarters of **Highland Discovery Tours**, a minibus company dealing in small person-alised tours around the Highlands (Tel. 0479 811478).

Hotel accommodation at the Aviemore Centre includes **Stakis Badenoch Village Lodges** (costing from £25 per lodge) and the **Stakis Badenoch Hotel** (Tel. 0469 810261), and **Stakis Four Seasons Hotel** (Tel. 0479 810681), both of which charge upward of £40. The **Aviemore Highlands Hotel** (Tel. 0479 810771) charges from around £25, while the **Mercury Hotel** (Tel. 0479 810781) is slightly cheaper. Elsewhere in the town there are **Alt-Na-Craig Hotel** (Tel. 0479 810378) and **Balavoulin Hotel** (Tel. 0479 810672), both of which are situated on Grampian Road and charge from around £20. For two-crown commended bed and breakfast accommodation, **Craiglea Guest House** (Tel. 0469

810210), and **Kinapol Guest House**, Dalfaber Road (Tel. 0479 810513), charge from £12 upwards. For comfortable self-catering accommodation in this area, try **Alvie Manse** (Tel. 0479 810248). Caravan and camping facilities are available from **Campgrounds of Scotland**, Coylumbridge, one mile south of Aviemore (Tel. 0479 810120), charging between £4 and £5 including tents. **Dalraddy Caravan Park**, three-and-a-half miles south of Aviemore, charges slightly higher prices of £6.25 for tourers and motor caravans and between £5–5.50 for tents. The **Stakis Aviemore Centre Park** (0479 810751), has facilities for tourers and motors from £5.50 to £6.50. There are no facilities for tents. The **Tourist Information Centre** is on Grampian Road (Tel. 0479 810363) and is open all year.

The road going across the Spey and into Glen More Forest Park (see below) reaches in one mile the old village of **INVERDRUIE**, where the **Cairngorm Whisky Centre** has a video programme and museum explaining how the spirit is produced, in addition to a tasting room for giving the finished product careful consideration and a foodhall offering an unusual range of Higland produce. **Rothiemurchus Estate** has many attractions, including Highland cattle, red deer, extensive woodland and a trout farm. Information on what to see, and tours of the estate, are available from the **Visitor Centre**. Why not try fun 4 × 4 off road driving. **Highland Drovers** (Tel. 0479 83329) can provide all kinds of amazing rough-terrain vehicles and track rides near Boat of Garten.

Aviemore's chief asset is its proximity to the **Cairngorm Mountains**, rising to the south-east of the town, and, with six peaks above 4,000 feet, it is the highest mountain mass in Britain. There are many possible routes for climbers and hillwalkers of varying degrees of experience and stamina, information on which is obtainable from the Tourist Information centre in Aviemore.

On the north-west slopes, facing the town, **Glenmore Forest Park** is an area of magnificent woodland covering 4,000 acres, and home to an abundance of wildlife such as red deer, reindeer, wildcat, golden eagle, ptarmigan, and caper-cailzie. At the heart of the park is **Loch Morlich**, a rewarding stretch of water for anglers which also offers watersports enthusi-asts the chance to hire equipment and take instruction in sailing, wind-surfing and canoeing from **Loch Morlich Watersports Centre** (Tel. 0479 810310). There are signposts directing visitors to **Reindeer House** just beyond the loch, where they may accompany the keeper on his daily check of Britain's only herd of reindeer (Tel. 0479 86228).

The road through the park comes to an end at the **Cairngorm Chairlift** which operates throughout the year, carrying passengers to the **Ptarmigan Observation Restaurant** which, at 3,600 feet, is the highest diner in Britain, with breathtaking views to the west and north-east. From here, there is a footpath leading up the remainder of the 4,080 feet to the summit of Cairn Gorm.

On the return journey towards Aviemore, take the B970 south from Inverdruie, followed a mile later by the branch road, to **Loch-an-Eilean**, an outstanding beauty spot with a nature trail and **Visitor Centre** explaining the ecology of the area. Standing on an island, **Loch-an-Eilean Castle** was built in the 15th century and was accessible by a causeway until the loch was dammed in the 18th century. Back on the B970, it is a short distance to Loch Insh, passing on the way **Inshriach Nurseries** where over 600 species of alpine plants are cultivated. **Loch Insh** offers anglers the chance to land brown trout, sea trout, and salmon, while **Loch Insh Watersports**, Insh Hall, Kincraig (Tel. 0540 651272), hires out equipment for wind-surfing, sailing, and canoeing, and also offers tuition. **KINCRAIG**, by the west shore of the loch, is notable for its 250-acre **Highland Wildlife Park** which is divided into two sections: the one for pedestrians includes wolves, bears, wildcats, and eagles, while the area restricted to vehicles is home to deer, bison, and Highland cattle. The **MacPherson Monument**, an obelisk just off the A9 on the way to Kingussie, stands in honour of the 18th-century poet, James MacPherson, born in nearby Ruthven (pronounced 'riven') and best known for 'Ossian', the epic verse which he claimed to have discovered and translated from Gaelic into English. The work was greatly admired by many, including Napoleon Bonaparte. It was, however, not the complete text MacPherson claimed it to be, but snatches of ancient works revised and largely supplemented in his own hand.

KINGUSSIE lies at the intersection of the B970 and the A9, pleasantly situated by the river and convenient for the Cairngorms. Like its neighbour, Newtonmore, the town has a formidable reputation for consistently fielding successful teams playing the ancient Gaelic sport of shinty. The partly outdoor **Highland Folk Museum**, in Duke Street, has exhibits representing traditional life in all parts of the Highlands. An 18th-century shooting lodge houses the indoor exhibits and you can also see a black house from the Island of Lewis, farming equipment, weapons, costume, and musical instruments. There is now a **Heritage in Action** programme which invites you to come and see real Highland characters at work, either behind the spinning wheel, or baking over the peat fire in the black house. These occasions take place in July and August every day except Sunday, helping to bring history alive.

Kingussie has a moderate selection of accommodation, of which the following charge from around £20 or less: the **Columba House Hotel**, Manse Road (Tel. 0540 661402); **Homewood Lodge** (Tel. 0540 661507) and **Scothouse Hotel** (Tel. 0540 661351) both in Newtonmore Road. The **Craigan Darroch Guest House**, High Street (Tel. 0540 661235) and the **Sonnhalde Guest House**, East Terrace (Tel. 0540 661266), offers three-crown commended accommodation from £12 upwards. The **Tourist Information** office in King Street (Tel. 0540 661297) is open from May to September. Recommended by the *Good Food Guide*, **The Cross**, 25–27 High Street (Tel. 0540 661166), is one of the finest restaurants in the area. Dinner for two, without wine, will typically cost £47 mid-week and £59 for a seven-course meal on a Saturday night. The restaurant has three bedrooms, a bonus for those who do not wish to drive.

To the south-west of the town, across the river, **Ruthven Barracks** stand on the site of a medieval stronghold belonging to the former rulers of the area, the Comyn family. The stark, redoubtable barracks were built by the Crown in 1718 to control the Highlanders, and were extended in 1734. In 1745 they fell at the second attempt to the army of Charles Edward Stuart, whose few remaining troops gathered here after Culloden. Their response to orders, briefly instructing them to save themselves by means of their own devising, was to blow up the barracks and scatter.

As mentioned above, **NEWTONMORE** is renowned for its shinty team, the arch rival to that in Kingussie, two miles away. It is also home to an excellent ski school which can provide equipment and ski lessons for groups and individuals (Tel. 0540 3 433/447). Golfers are also well catered for with an 18-hole course and golf driving-range suitable for beginners (Tel. 0540 673732). Pony trekking is available at the **Newtonmore Pony Trekking Centre**, The Birches, Boavista Road (Tel. 0540 661705). **Waltzing Waters**, Europe's most elaborate water, light and music spectacular is to be found at Balavil Brae, Newtonmore. In the Waltzing Waters theatre, visitors are entertained by thousands of dazzling patterns of moving water synchronized with fine music. A different musical selection is provided each day of the week (Tel. 0540 3 673752). Highland **pottery** can be seen being made at Church Terrace, with domestic and giftware items on sale (open May to October, 9 a.m. to 7 p.m., November to April 10 a.m. to 5 p.m.). The chief tourist attraction is the **Clan Macpherson Museum** (open from May to September), and the town hosts the Clan Gathering and Highland Games on the first Saturday in August. Visitors will encounter more Macpherson history if they continue west for two miles, where they will come to the cliffs of **Creag Dhubh**, beside the A86. It was in a cave here that Cluny Macpherson, the chief of the clan, hid for nine years after Culloden, despite the reward of £1,000 offered for his capture.

Ross and Cromarty

INTRODUCTION

Ross and Cromarty covers an extensive area spanning the width of the country. The Black Isle peninsula in the east is an area of rolling farmland and woodland with good beaches and a variety of seabirds to be observed along its coast. The most notable seaside resorts are **Fortrose** and **Rosemarkie**. In the west the scenery features spectacular hills and peaks, and the adjacent nature reserves of **Beinn Eighe** and **Torridon Estate** are strongly recommended visits for nature lovers.

Although communications are sparse, both the east and west coast are easily reached from Inverness. For those who enjoy the scenic route, make the journey from Inverness cross-country to Kyle of Lochalsh, in South-west Ross. The road runs beside what British Rail calls the 'Great Scenic Railway' and whether travelling by car or train, the magnificent hills and peaks of Ross and Cromarty, which continue into South-west Ross, make it one of the most memorable journeys in Britain.

This chapter covers the two coastal stretches: starting in the Black Isle in the east and heading north, then going over to Ullapool in the west and following the road south.

One trail is to be found in this area: the **Wester Ross Coastal Route** which helps the visitor make the most of the varied scenery of Wester Ross. It runs from Lochcarron to Achiltibuie.

WHERE TO GO FOR WHAT

Kessock Bridge crosses the Beauly Firth from Inverness giving quick and easy access to the peninsula misleadingly named the Black Isle. **FORTROSE** is an attractive resort with pleasant coastal scenery and beaches. Along with Dornoch further north, Fortrose claims to be the town where Scotland's last witch was burned and a memorial stone on the golf course marks the exact spot. A less macabre item for the sightseer is the ruins of the 13th-century **Fortrose Cathedral**, and adjacent to it the **Chapter House** from the same period. To the north, ROSEMARKIE possesses an unassuming charm and from **Chanonry Point**, there is a splendid view across the water to Fort George. Chanonry Point was the place where the Brahan Seer was burned in a barrel of tar in the 17th century. Many of his prophecies have come true, not least those he made as unpleasant as his own death.

At Rosemarkie you will find the **Fairy Glen**, a narrow valley full of wild cherry trees and waterfalls. Rosemarkie's cliffs featured in the writing of the geologist Hugh Miller (1802–56), born further up the coast in **CROMARTY**, where visitors can look round his birthplace, **Hugh Miller's Cottage**, which now houses an exhibition of his life and work as a geologist, stonemason, and writer. The **Fishertown Craft Centre** at 47/49 Shore Street, sells pottery which has been made on the premises, as well as the paintings on exhibit. Buildings of special interest amidst the town's narrow streets and old cottages are the **Court House** and **East Church** from the 18th century and the **Cross** dating from the 16th century, but repaired in 1772. The **Court House** is home to the 1991 Scottish Museum of the Year, with computer-controlled animated figures and a tape tour of Cromarty (open daily Easter to October, 10 a.m. to 6 p.m.; winter 12 p.m. to 4 p.m.). The **Gaelic Chapel** which stands on a hill above the town was built for Highlanders, dispossessed by the heinous Clearances in the 18th century and attracted to Cromarty by the prospect of work in the town's mills. Next to the chapel is a statue of Hugh Miller who carved many of the tombstones in the churchyard. To the west, **Udale Bay** combines with **Nigg Bay** across the Cromarty Firth to form a nature reserve attractive to many migratory wildfowl and waders. The **Royal Hotel**, Marine Terrace (Tel. 03817 217), occupies an attractive location overlooking the harbour and the beach and charges from around £25.

The B9163 along the southern shore of the Cromarty Firth leads to the busy town of **DINGWALL**, birthplace of Macbeth and an important Norse colony (whence the name derives: 'Thing Volle' meaning 'Council Place'). The **Town House** is the principal place of interest and houses a small local history museum, with a fascinating military collection including material related to General Sir Hector

MacDonald, as well as displaying permanent exhibitions on local history and temporary exhibitions throughout the year. Nearby DELNY is the setting for a good self-catering centre **Delny Highland Lodges** – chalets of a woodland estate, very reasonably priced and offering lots for the family to do (pony-trekking, fly-fishing, etc). Open all year (book through Hoseasons). A few miles west on the A834, **STRATHPEFFER** owes its elegant appearance to its popularity in Victorian times as a spa resort. In the Square, the **Pump Room** was where visitors came to take the water during the resort's heyday. Visitors can still sample the sulphur waters in the **Water Sampling Pavilion** in the Square. The renovated railway station is home to the **Highland Museum of Childhood** which tells its story with displays and recordings. The **Ben Wyvis Hotel** (Tel. 0997 421323) is very pleasantly situated in six acres of landscaped garden with prices from around £18. There is a wide choice of attractive hotels from under £20, one of which is the **Strathpeffer Hotel** (Tel. 0997 421200) and the **Gardenside Guest House** (Tel. 0997 421242). Holiday caravans to let are available from **Mrs G. Aird of Redbank**, Achterneed (Tel. 0997 421312), starting from £75 a week for up to six persons.

North from Dingwall on the A862 and A9 after four miles Cnoc Fyrish (1483 feet) can be seen crowned by an 18th-century folly, **Fyrish Monument**. It was erected by Sir Hector Munro to provide work for the unemployed and recalls his fighting days in India. It is a replica of the gateway of a captured Indian town. The road carries on through the industrial town of Invergordon to **TAIN** on the Dornoch Firth. The 16th-century **Tolbooth** here, in addition to being a striking building, was the centre of administration for the Highland Clearances and prison for those crofters who failed to comply with issued injunctions for them to leave their land. The **District Museum and Clan Ross Centre** has a display on less ignoble features of the town's past, going back to the days of its occupation by Norsemen, and includes displays on the Clan Ross and interesting artefacts on the crafts and industries of Easter Ross. There are also the ruins of **St Duthac's Chapel** dating from the 11th or 12th centuries and **St Duthac's Church** from the mid-14th century. The **900 Roses Garden** was laid out to celebrate the 900th anniversary of the Burgh receiving its Royal charter. To find out more about Tain's heritage, try the **Tain Town Trail** which takes you around its most important landmarks with the aid of nine illustrated displays.

In the north-west of the region the fishing industry has always been important, and nowhere more so than in **ULLAPOOL**, a town founded in 1788 by the British Fisheries Society. Nowadays it is also prospering as a bustling tourist centre and port for the car ferry to Lewis. **Lochbroom Museum** (open from April to October) contains material relating to Wester Ross, covering subjects such as the Clearances, geology and wildlife. There are regular boat excursions to the nearby group of islands, the Summer Isles (contact MacKenzie Marine, Ullapool. Tel. 0854 612008).

Ullapool's extensive choice of accommodation includes the **Royal Hotel**, Garve Road (Tel. 0854 612181), very pleasantly located on the shores of Loch Broom and charging from between £35 and £40. From around £15–25 there are the **Caledonian Hotel** (Tel. 0854 612306), **Ferry Boat Inn**, Shore Street (Tel. 0854 612236) and **Riverside Hotel**, Quay Street (Tel. 0854 612366). The **Altnaharrie Inn** (Tel. 0854 83230) is a small hotel reached only by the hotel's private boat. It is Egon Ronay recommended and open April to October. All six bedrooms have *en-suite* facilities, but children are discouraged. Dinner, bed and breakfast costs from £100. **Ardmair Point Caravan Site and Boat Centre**, three-and-a-half miles north of Ullapool (Tel. 0854 612054), offers camping and caravan facilities from £5, as well as sail boarding and canoeing, and the hire of fishing boats. **Broomfield Holiday Park**, Shore Street (Tel. 0854 612020), situated in Ullapool, also offers camping and caravan facilities from £4 to £8. **Ullapool's Tourist Information** office is open from Easter to November (Tel. 0854 612135).

Ten miles north from Ullapool on the A835, a single-track road branches north-west, enabling visitors to view the spectacular mountain scenery of Coigach, passing Ben More Coigach, Ail Beag and the distinctive Stac Polly, and which leads after 15 miles to **ACHILTIBUIE** and the fine **Summer Isles Hotel** (Tel. 085482 282). Here visitors can enjoy an excellent standard of accommodation, along with dinner with wine, and breakfast for two at a cost of around £122 per night. Achiltibuie, from where boats leave for the

Summer Isles and sea angling trips (contact Ian Macleod on Tel. 085482 200), has two noteworthy sights: the **Hydroponicum**, at the Summer Isles Hotel (mentioned above), a soil-less plant-growing garden; and the **Smokehouse** where you can watch the smoking of fish, game and meat. The views on the Smokehouse Road over the mountains are fabulous.

Returning from Achiltibuie a detour to **Lochinver** is a must. Turn left, still on a single-track road and follow the hilly road with many sharp twists and turns through Inverkirkaig to Lochinver. The views are magnificent especially where the road hugs the coast. A few miles from Lochinver the B869 takes you to the cliffs and the white sand of secluded **Achmelvich Bay**.

Ten miles south from Ullapool, the A835 passes within sight of the **Falls of Measach** which pour down 120 feet into **Corrieshalloch Gorge**, a spectacular sight at one mile long and 200 feet deep.

A short distance south, the A832 branches west and edges the coastal shores of Little Loch Broom, Gruinard Bay, and Loch Ewe before coming to the village of **POOLEWE**. The village is notable for **Inverewe Garden** (open all year, Monday to Sunday, 9.30 a.m. to sunset). Located on a promontory obtruding into Loch Ewe, the garden benefits from the warming effect of the Gulf Stream, making possible the growth of a variety of plants native to more exotic climes. Among the eucalyptus and rhododendrons there are giant forget-me-nots from the South Pacific, Himalayan lilies and many species from South America.

A few miles further south is the resort of **GAIRLOCH**, set amid some magnificent coastal scenery with fine beaches and a golf course. The hire of small boats, sailing dinghies, Canadian canoes and sea kayaks is available from **West Highland Marine Ltd** on the harbour (Tel. 0445583 291). Skippered trips and boats for sea angling can also be arranged. The **Gairloch Watersports Centre** (Tel. 0445 2131), can offer windsurfing instruction, board hire, water skiing and canoeing. Group accommodation is also available. **Gairloch Cruises** offers one and two hour pleasure cruises and sea angling which can be arranged by booking at the Post Office on the pier. **Highland Trails** offers guided tours using Honda 4-wheel drive all-terrain vehicles to explore the **Flowerdale Forest** and its wildlife. Book at the Post Office (Tel. 0445 2175).

The award-winning **Gairloch Heritage Museum** is in a former farm steading, and illustrates the past through to the present times of Gairloch Parish. The adjoining **Steading Restaurant** serves good food all day (Tel. 0445 2449). **Ru'a Reidh Exploration Centre** runs weekly activity programmes at a cost of £110 to £250 (Tel. 044585 263). The town's generous choice of accommodation includes the Victorian **Shieldaig Lodge Hotel** (Tel. 0445 83250) from around £30, and the slightly more expensive **Gairloch Hotel** (Tel. 0445 2001). From around £20 there are **Creag Mor Hotel** (Tel. 0445 2068), overlooking the old harbour, and **Millcroft Hotel** (Tel. 0445 2376). There is also the **Whindley Guest House**, Auchtercairn (Tel. 0445 2340), which has views over the bay towards Skye. For comfortable bed and breakfast accommodation, the two-crown commended **Charleston Guest House**, Shore Street (Tel. 0445 2497), offers rooms from £15 upwards. **Sands Holiday Centre** three miles on the B8021 towards Melvaig (Tel. 0445 2152) provides facilities for tourers, motor caravans and tents from £6 to £7.50. **Gairloch Holiday Park**, Strath (Tel 0505 614343), charges from £2.50.

The road cuts back from Loch Gairloch to the magnificent scenery around the southern half of Loch Maree before reaching **Beinn Eighe National Nature Reserve**, information about which can be gained at **Aultroy Visitor Centre**, one mile north-west of Kinlochewe. Almost adjacent is another nature reserve, **Torridon Estate** which, in addition to its immense natural beauty, is home to a variety of wildlife such as deer, mountain goats, wildcats and eagles. **Torridon Countryside Centre** (open from May to September) provides invaluable information on the area's wildlife, hillwalks and climbs, and houses a deer museum.

Caithness and Sutherland

INTRODUCTION

The very north-east corner of Scotland is formed by Caithness, a land of rolling, barren moor and peat bog. The northern coast has a more interesting appearance than the east, although visitors will have to branch off from the main road to gain sight of the sandy beaches and the striking cliff and rock formations that make this one of the UK's most dramatic and unspoilt areas.

The sparse population of Caithness today belies the fact that this part of Scotland was the first to be inhabited. The 18th- and 19th-century Highlands Clearances depopulated large parts of the region. Along with Orkney and Shetland, the far north of the mainland was for many centuries under Norse occupation, although little evidence of this survives other than in place names such as Wick, meaning 'bay', and Lybster, meaning 'farmstead'. There are, however, many remains attributable to earlier settlers. The area is well endowed with prehistoric monuments – such as the **Grey Cairns of Camster** north of Lybster and the **Hill o' Many Stanes** near Clyth – and the sightseer will find much of interest in the unspoilt countryside as indeed will the nature lover. Around the coast there is rare wildlife such as puffins at **Dunnet Head**, and inland one may be lucky enough to catch sight of an eagle, an osprey, or a red squirrel.

The area is easily reached by road or rail, but once there, communications across the region are sparse. The A9 skirts the east coast all the way north from Inverness to John o' Groats from where the A836 heads west to Thurso and on to the north coast of Sutherland. The other major roads run diagonally from Latheron and Wick in the east to Thurso and nearby Castletown in the north. Rail links in Caithness are limited, there being only one line running up the east coast from Inverness to Thurso and Wick.

Caithness

The route for this chapter begins in the south-east and follows the coastal road to Thurso in the north. The A9 enters the former county, now the district, of Caithness a few miles north of Helmsdale at the **ORD OF CAITHNESS** where there are spectacular views of the coastline and frequent sightings of red deer early in the morning and at night. Further on, north of Dunbeath, the **Laidhay Croft Museum** occupies a mid-19th-century croft, situated three miles south of Latheron where visitors can see the **Clan Gunn Heritage Centre**. Half a mile after **LYBSTER** leave the A9 by Watten Road to see the **Grey Cairns of Camster**, two burial chambers thought to date as far back as the fourth millennium BC. Return to the A9 and three miles after the village of Clyth, just off the main road, is the **Hill o' Many Stones**, an unexplained prehistoric arrangement of over 200 small stones in the form of a fan. Three miles further on is one of the most unusual sights in Caithness – the **Whaligoe Steps**. Fisherwomen used to carry loaded creels up the 365 steps. The ruins of **Castles Girnigoe and Sinclair** lie perched on the clifftop out to the north of **WICK**, a town with a busy harbour and airport. **Wick Heritage Centre** in Bank Row has an exhibition on the local herring fishing industry and domestic life, while **Caithness Glass Visitor Centre** allows visitors the opportunity to observe from start to finish the traditional process of glass-blowing. Open at the airport industrial site, seven days a week, Easter to summer and six days at other times, 9.00 a.m.–4.30 p.m. all year.

The best choice of accommodation in Caithness is to be found in Wick and Thurso. In Wick there is the **Nethercliffe Hotel** (Tel. 0955 2044) and the **Mackays Hotel** (Tel. 0955 2323) from £20. The **Mercury Hotel**, Riverside, situated in the centre of town (Tel. 0995 3344), charges slightly higher prices of £30 upwards. Bed and breakfast accommodation is available from **Harbour Guest House**, 6 Rose Street (Tel. 0995 3276), and costs from £11.

Tourist Information is available all year from the office in Whitechapel Road (Tel. 0955 2596).

Mid-way between Wick and John o' Groats on the A9 is the **John Nicolson Museum** (open from June to August) with special attention among its displays to the Iron Age legacy in the region. The A9 reaches the north coast at **JOHN O' GROATS** which, contrary to popular opinion, is not quite the northernmost part of

Britain. Nevertheless, the reputed **Last House Museum Shop** is here. The museum features many old photographs and other artefacts from John o' Groats' past. The Last House craft and souvenir shop is next door.

In summer there are boat excursions to **Duncansby Head**, noted for its birds and cliff scenery, and to the island of **STROMA**, which attracts many seals. The **Tourist Information** centre is open from Easter to October (Tel. 095581 373). A few miles along the A836 a side road leads you to the **Castle of Mey**, built in the late 16th-century. The Queen Mother bought it in 1952, carefully restored it and it is now her official Caithness residence. The gardens only are open a few days in summer.

To the west, the A836 soon reaches Dunnet from where there is a road to the coast and **Dunnet Head**, an impressive sandstone promontory which rises to over 400 feet and represents the northernmost point of mainland Scotland. Returning to the main road and continuing westward one soon arrives at **THURSO** on the banks of the river of the same name which, incidentally, is Norse in origin, meaning 'Thor's River'. The area near the harbour is an attractive and well-restored part of town and the location of the ruined **St Peter's Church**, part of which dates back to the Middle Ages. In the Town Hall, **Thurso Heritage Museum** is open from June to September for visitors to see its exhibition of local domestic and agricultural life. The A882 leads to **Scrabster**; from here ferries sail to Orkney.

The town has a good selection of reasonably priced hotels. From between £15 and £30 there are **Ormlie House Hotel** (Tel. 0847 62733); **Pentland Hotel** (Tel. 0847 63202); **Royal Hotel** (Tel. 0847 63191); and the **St Clair Hotel** (Tel. 0847 63730/66482). There is a wide range of bed and breakfast accommodation available. Two approved one-crown establishments are **Mrs Murray**, 1 Granville Crescent (Tel. 0847 62993), and **Mrs M. Sinclair**, Shinval, Glengolly (Tel. 0847 64306), two miles from Thurso, both charging from £11 per person. For camping and caravan facilities, try the **Thurso Caravan and Camping Site**, Scrabster Road (Tel. 0995 3761). It overlooks Thurso Bay and charges between £4.45 and £5.50 for motor caravans, tourers and tents. Holiday caravans can be let for four to eight persons from £60 to £180 per week, at the **Thurso Municipal site**, 15 Shore Street (Tel. 0847 63524).

Tourist Information is available in the car park, Riverside, from Easter to October (Tel. 0847 62371).

Sutherland

In addition to covering a considerably greater area, the scenery of Sutherland is markedly different from neighbouring Caithness with which it is frequently mentioned as though the two form an inevitable pair. In the main, Sutherland is dominated by upland moor and bog with wooded valleys and lochs entering from the coast, and mountains rising in the west. In common with Caithness it has a sparse population (in fact, the least densely populated area of western Europe), the same Norse connection – the name Sutherland ('south land') was coined by the Norsemen from their vantage in Orkney – and similar attractions of wildlife and prehistoric monuments.

Sutherland's points of interest are thinly scattered around its coastline and so we shall begin in the south-east at the Dornoch Firth and travel in an anti-clockwise circuit to the south-west.

Five miles north of Bonar Bridge by the A836, the spectacular **Falls of Shin** are part of a notable beauty spot where leaping salmon are a frequent sight. The small village of Lairg is at the foot of Loch Shin. Here you will find many gentle walking routes and hill lochs abundant with trout. The selling of lambs from all over the north of Scotland also takes place here. East of here the road joins the A9 and comes to the quiet and unspoilt resort of **DORNOCH**. In the town square, **Dornoch Cathedral** dominates and dates from 1224 although extensive restoration work was carried out in the 17th and 19th centuries. **Dornoch Craft Centre and Town Jail** is a rare combination of a restored 19th-century jail and a centre for the production of tartan cloth, kilts, and soft toys. The town's miles of sandy beach and superb links golf course make it a popular holiday resort. North of Dornoch is **Loch Fleet**, which attracts many species of birds. The ruins of 14th-century **Skelbo Castle** lie on the shores of the loch. The **Royal Dornoch Golf Club** is reckoned by some to be in the top 12 courses in the world. It welcomes all visitors, and there are lunches, high teas and snacks available Tuesday to Sunday. Pony trekking and tuition is available at the **East Sutherland Riding Stables**, Skelbo Farm (Tel. 0408 633045).

Dornoch has the largest choice of accommodation in Sutherland. The **Royal Golf Hotel** (Tel. 0862 810283) is near the golf course and charges from around £48. Also near the course are **Dornoch Castle** (Tel. 0862 810216), **Dornoch Hotel** (Tel. 0862 810351), and **Burghfield Hotel** (Tel. 0862 810212), all charging around £26 and each offering a variety of activities including golf.

Caravan and camping facilities are provided for at the following sites: the **Sea View Farm Caravan Park** (Tel. 0862 810294), which costs from £4 for motor caravans, tourers and tents; the **Dornoch Caravan and Camping Site** (Tel. 0862 810732), and **The Links**, Cairnmuir (Tel. 0549 2136), both offering caravans to hire.

Tourist Information is available in the town square all year round (Tel. 0862 810400).

Twelve miles north, off the A9 near Golspie, **Dunrobin Castle and Gardens** has been the seat of the earls, later dukes, of Sutherland since its foundation in the 13th century. The present structure dates mainly from the mid-19th century and in addition to the collection of fine paintings and furniture in the house, the grounds contain a Victorian Museum and steam-powered fire engine (open May, Monday to Thursday 10 a.m. to 12.30 p.m.; June to mid-September, Monday to Saturday, 10.30 a.m. to 5.30 p.m., and Sunday 1 p.m. to 5.30 p.m.; and October, Monday to Saturday 10.30 a.m. to 12.30 p.m., Sunday 1 p.m. to 4.30 p.m.). There are horse and carriage tours which leave from in front of the castle. Pony and trap-driving lessons for beginners can be arranged in Rogart. For more information Tel. 0408 469.

The small town of **BRORA** is a famed centre for the spinning of Shetland wool. **Hunters of Brora** promises to be an enjoyable visit, as the finest remaining example of a fully integrated woollen mill.

Guided tours are at 11 a.m. to 3 p.m. from Monday to Friday. There are two brochs nearby. The first can be seen from the road by visitors entering the town from the south at Strath Steven while the second, standing a more impressive 30 feet in diameter, is three miles north. A stone beside the A9 close to the unremarkable fishing port of Helmsdale records the spot where the last wolf in Scotland was killed in 1700. The **Clynelish Distillery Visitor Centre** is conveniently situated on the A9, north of Brora. There are free guided tours and malt whisky tastings from Monday to Friday, 9.30 a.m. to 4.30 p.m. The A9 then continues up the coast into Caithness and the area covered in the previous part of this chapter.

The alternative route to the north coast of Sutherland bypasses Caithness by taking the A897 from Helmsdale. Before going through the open moorland of Strath Ullie, stop at Helmsdale to visit the award-winning **Timespan Centre**, an exciting exhibition of the Highlands' past and present with audio-visual displays and a riverside herb garden (open Easter to October, Monday to Saturday, 10 a.m. to 5 p.m.; Sundays 2 p.m. to 5 p.m., 9 a.m. to 6 p.m. during July and August). Helmsdale is also the home of the company Hidden Hills, who operate unique guided tours into the hidden parts of Sutherland, to observe the wildlife and ancient ruins *en route* (Tel. 04312 640). **St Donan Fisheries** (04312 886) can arrange bird-watching trips by boat to the sea-bird colonies on the cliffs to the east of Helmsdale, and sea angling aboard the MV *Danny Boy*. Continue on to the green, cultivated land of Strath Halladale where many crofters were evicted from their land here, as elsewhere in the north, and the sad and despicable history of the Clearances is told in **Strathnaver Museum**, occupying the 18th-century Farr Church near BETTYHILL on the northern coast. The village has a **Tourist Information** centre open from May to September (Tel. 06412 342).

Nearby, the **Invernaver National Nature Reserve** has the country's finest collection of northern flora in addition to being the breeding ground for birdlife such as the greenshank, ring ouzel, and linnet. The village of **TONGUE** on the east side of the **Kyle of Tongue** is dominated by the ruins of the

14th-century **Castle Varrich**, while on the opposite side there are quiet sandy beaches beneath the cliffs and rocks. West of Loch Eriboll, **DURNESS** is Scotland's most north-western settlement and has a splendid stretch of beach at Balnakeil Bay and golf course. The former radar station has been converted into a craft village, open Easter to October. One mile to the east is the spectacular **Smoo Cave**, three great hollows in the limestone rock of which the first is 200 feet deep and 120 feet high and accessible from the beach; access to the others is by boat from the first hollow. There is also a combined ferry and minibus service to the lighthouse and magnificent views at **CAPE WRATH**, a mile from which are **Clo-Mor Cliffs**, the highest cliffs in mainland Britain and home to thousands of puffins, guillemots and kittiwakes. Following the coastline south brings you to the spectacular beach of **Sandwood Bay**, apparently the haunt of mermaids and the ghost of a bearded sailor.

From Durness the road south-west is through remote and barren terrain. The **John Ridgway Adventure School** can be found in Ardmore, Rhiconich, offering various adventure courses, and cruises to St Kilda and the Outer Hebrides with the Atlantic rower and Round-the-World Yachtsman. From **SCOURIE** on the west coast there are boat trips to **Handa Island Nature Reserve**, home to many and varied seabirds. May and June are the best months to see the birds. The A894 south runs through the small village of **KYLESKU** from where there are boat trips to the southern end of **Loch Glencoul** and **Eas-Coul-Aulin**, which at 650 feet is the highest waterfall in Britain. Further south the road connects with the A837 running west to **LOCHINVER**, popular because of its scenic coastal setting, harbour and magnificent surrounding countryside. It is also famed for its Highland pottery. Guided tours around the Highland Stoneware are available, where you can see the pottery-making process right up to the delicate stage when the individual pieces are hand-painted (open Monday to Saturday 9 a.m. to 5.30 p.m.). There is a good choice of accommodation. From under £31 there are **Culag Hotel** (Tel. 05714 270) and, on the far side of Loch Assynt, **Inchnadamph Hotel** (Tel. 05712 202). **Inverlodge Hotel** (Tel. 05714 496), comes very highly commended, offering rooms from £55. There is an excellent restaurant and all the rooms enjoy a sea view. For less expensive accommodation there is the two-crown commended residence of **Mr and Mrs McBain**, Ardglass, (Tel. 05714 257), where rooms cost from £12. **Tourist Information** at this popular and attractive town is available from April to October (Tel. 05714 330).

Orkney

INTRODUCTION

At its closest point, Orkney is only six miles from the Caithness coast. Of its 67 islands, less than one-third are inhabited and, like Shetland, the largest and most populous of these is called Mainland. It contains the capital, Kirkwall, and the main point of arrival, Stromness, where there is a regular car ferry to and from Scrabster, near Thurso. The journey takes about 1 hour 45 minutes. In summer there are also regular crossings between John o'Groats and South Ronaldsay. There are coach and rail services to connect with sailings. British Airways and Loganair operate regular flights to Kirkwall from Glasgow, Aberdeen, Edinburgh and Inverness, with connecting services from Birmingham, Manchester and London.

Although they are separated by a distance of 60 miles, or so, Orkney and Shetland have a great deal in common in terms of culture and history, particularly their Scandinavian heritage. An important difference, however, is the greater concentration of archaeological material on the islands of Orkney, particularly Mainland, and it is renowned as the most important location of prehistoric remains in Britain. Of the many fascinating relics, the most remarkable is the well-preserved Stone Age village of Skara Brae on the west Mainland coast. At midsummer it never gets properly dark and bowls and golf are played at midnight.

WHERE TO GO FOR WHAT

MAINLAND is not only the largest of Orkney's islands, but it covers an area greater than that of all the others added together. **KIRKWALL**, the Orcadian capital, is a busy port which has always been an important site due to the natural protection afforded by its bay. **St Magnus Cathedral** was founded in 1127, and, apart from the one in Glasgow, it is the only pre-Reformation cathedral in Scotland whose structure remains intact. Its size alone makes it an imposing sight, enhanced by its grand Norman design, cruciform plan, and building materials of grey flagstone and red and yellow sandstone. In the choir are the remains of the founder, Rognvald III, and his uncle, the cathedral's patron saint, Magnus. The St Magnus Festival is from 18–23 June. The nearby 16th-century **Bishop's Palace** stands on the site of an earlier building of which part of the ground floor structure remains. King Haakon of Norway died here in 1263 following his defeat at the battle of Largs. On the other side of the road, the **Earl's Palace** is an excellent example of Scotland's Renaissance architecture, built between 1600 and 1607 for the former Earl Patrick Stewart of Orkney, infamous for his dishonesty and cruelty. **Tankerness House** in Broad Street is a fine restoration of an Orcadian merchant laird's home, typical of the 16th to 18th centuries. It dates from 1574 and houses a museum illustrating 5,000 years of life in Orkney. Open, along with its gardens, throughout the year. The **Kirkwall Heritage Trail** begins at Harbour Street and leads through the town's quarter-mile conservation area. For more details, Tel. 0856 872856. There are two whisky distilleries in the area worth visiting: travelling east out of town you will find the **Highland Park Distillery** which dates from 1798. It has its own visitor centre with an audio-visual presentation of Orkney; **Scapa** is the other distillery, and tours are available from mid-June to mid-September.

Hotels in Kirkwall include the **Kirkwall Hotel**, Harbour Street (Tel. 0856 872232), which costs from between £32 and £38. The **Ayre Hotel**, Ayre Road (Tel. 0856 873001), charges from £30 upwards, while a room at the **Albert Hotel** (Tel. 0856 876000) will cost from £35. From under £25 there are **Lynnfield Hotel**, Holm Road (Tel. 0856 872505), and the **Royal Hotel**, Victoria Street (Tel. 0856 873477). From around £18 there are **St Ola Hotel**, Harbour Street (Tel. 0856 875090), and **West End Hotel**, Main Street (Tel. 0856 872368). For comfortable bed and breakfast accommodation, there is **Mrs Braun**, Shearwood, ten minutes from town (Tel. 0856 3494), charging from £11, and many others – contact the Tourist Office for more information. The **Pickaquay Caravan and Camping Site**, Pickaquay Road (Tel. 0856 3535), provides facilities for motor caravans and tourers from £4.20, and between £2.60 and £3.55 for tents.

Kirkwall's **Tourist Information** centre is on Broad Street (Tel. 0856 872856), and at the Stromness Ferry Terminal (Tel. 0856 850716). Both are open all year, though the latter has reduced hours during October to April.

A number of interesting historical sites lie close to the A965 to Stromness. **Grain Earth Houses** (named after the local estate of Grain), just to the west of Kirkwall, and those at RENNIBISTER, four miles further on, are excellent examples of their type. There is no certain knowledge of the age or function of earth houses (also known as souterrains), although it is estimated that these underground structures, consisting of a long, narrow passage leading to a chamber, could have been used as storehouses, refuges, or winter dwellings. They date, at the latest, from the Iron Age.

Further on, **Maes Howe** is regarded as being the best example of a Stone Age chambered cairn in Europe. The names means 'greatest mound' and it consists of a mound of stones 24 feet high and over 300 feet in circumference covering a burial chamber, now artificially lit and bearing some fascinating runic inscriptions made by intruders in the 12th century. Five miles from Stromness, only four of the **Standing Stones of Stenness** remain, but there is evidence of others which show them to have formed a monument similar to Stonehenge, dating from about 2500 BC. Nearby is the **Ring of Brodgar**, formed originally from about 60 stones of which 27 have survived. Just before the road reaches Bridge of Waithe is **Unstan Cairn**, where the largest collection of Stone Age pottery on a single Scottish site was discovered during excavations in 1844, now on display at the National Museum of Antiquities in Edinburgh. The only other Orcadian town after Kirkwall, **STROMNESS**, is notable as the docking point for the car ferry taking visitors to and from the island, and it was long important as the last port of call before the transatlantic voyage. It was also the site of the Hudson Bay Company, and its main street on the harbour was a prime position for local traders, hence its growth to the present length of one mile. At the southern end is **Stromness Museum**, which has a maritime and natural history collection, and the **Pier Arts Centre**, a set of 18th-century restored buildings, with modern art permanently on display. There are also visiting exhibitions throughout the year. **Stromness Heritage Trail**, begins at John Street and leads you to the heritage landmarks of the town, for what should last more than an hour. For more details Tel. 0856 872856. The **Orkney Traditional Folk Festival** is something else to look out for, and is held in Stromness in late May every year.

The Stone Age settlement of **Skara Brae**, seven miles north of Stromness beside the B9056, is a remarkable relic, having been buried under sand for 5,000 years until uncovered by a storm in 1850. The extent to which the minutiae of daily life have been preserved suggests that the village was buried suddenly while still in occupation. At **BIRSAY BAY** are the ruins of the **Earl's Palace**, built in the 16th century by Earl Robert Stewart on the site of an earlier 12th-century residence of the Earls of Orkney. A causeway near here gives access to the island of **BROUGH OF BIRSAY**, on which are the ruins of early Christian and Norse settlements. Opposite the island of Rousay at **AIKER-NESS** stands the **Broch of Gurness**. South-west from here along the B9057 is a sign giving directions to **Click Mill**, still in use and notable as the last example in Orkney of a horizontal watermill.

Of the islands to the north of Mainland, **ROUSAY** has a large number of prehistoric sites, the most notable of which is **Midhowe Cairn** on the south-west coast. Of the type known as a stalled cairn, it is 76 feet long and seven feet wide and contains 12 burial stalls on each side. Nearby is **Midhowe Broch**, the best-preserved structure of its type in Orkney. Among the many other cairns on the island, the most interesting are **Blackhammer, Knowe of Yarso**, and **Taversoe Tuick**, all on the south shore. The sign posted, one-mile-long **Westness Walk** travels along the coast and takes in the wildlife, wild flowers, folk history and archaeological remains. It begins from either Westness Farm or Midhowe Cairn. For more details tel. 0856 072856. Between Rousay and Mainland, the uninhabited island of **EYNHALLOW** contains the ruins of the 12th-century **Eynhallow Church** and has excellent trout lochs and some of Europe's most important seabird cliffs. The island of **WYRE** has one of the oldest stone castles in Scotland in the form of **Cubbie Roo's Castle**, built in the 12th century by the Norse robber Kolbein Hruga, whose son, Bishop Bjarni, is thought to have built the now ruined **St Mary's Chapel** later that century. On EGILSAY, the **Church of St Magnus**, although dating from the 12th century, was still in use up to the last century and today is missing only its roof. SHAPINSAY is only 25 minutes from Kirkwall by daily ferry. **Balfour Castle** is the fine castle worth visiting. The island of WESTRAY contains the extensive ruins of **Noltland Castle**, most of which date from the 16th century, though it also incorporates part of the original building of 1420. Due west of here is **Gentlemen's Cave** where a number of Jacobites went into hiding after Culloden. The two stone houses at **Knap of Howar** on the adjacent island of PAPA WESTRAY are reckoned to be as much as 5,000 years old, and are believed by some to be the oldest standing houses in Europe. The island is also home to the largest colony of Arctic tern. SANDAY is notable for **Quoyness Chambered Tomb**, a cairn 60 feet in diameter, thought to date from 2900 BC. Sheep still roam the beach on North Ronaldsay and eat seaweed.

The area of water enclosed by Mainland and the islands to the south is called **Scapa Flow** and was a busy naval base in both world wars. The British ships HMS *Vanguard* and HMS *Royal Oak* were sunk by torpedo here in the First and Second World Wars, respectively. Also, after the German surrender in 1918, the 70 ships which made up the majority of her fleet were escorted to Scapa Flow before being scuttled by their crews. Seven of these still lie on the sea bed where they went down and are a popular attraction for divers – in fact, the area is considered Europe's premier dive site.

The **Churchill Barriers** were built to stop German submarines getting into the Scapa Flow naval anchorage. Now, with roads on top, they have become causeways linking Mainland, Lamb Holm, Glimps Holm, Burray, and South Ronaldsay. In two Nissen huts, LAMB HOLM retains the **Italian Chapel** built from scrap metal by Italian prisoners of war. **St Margaret's Hope** at the north end of SOUTH RONALDSAY is the location of **Orkney Wireless Museum** (open from April to September), containing domestic sets from the 1930s in addition to the principal exhibition of wartime communication instruments from Scapa Flow.

On the western side of Scapa Flow, **HOY** is the highest island in Orkney and best known for the **Old Man of Hoy**, a 450-foot stack off the north-west coast. The cliffs running north from here are quite spectacular, especially **St John's Head** which, at 1140 feet, is the highest vertical cliff in Britain. Both of these outstanding geological sights can be taken in by regular boat trips from Stromness and the car ferry to Lyness from Houton. Along with extensive areas of mountain and moorland, they form part of the **North Hoy Nature Reserve**. Several miles inland, just south of the Linksness to Rackwick road, is the **Dwarfie Stane**, a Stone Age burial chamber cut into a huge block of sandstone. It is the only one of its kind in Britain and is thought to date from the third millennium BC.

Shetland

INTRODUCTION

Shetland is the northernmost point of the British Isles and its
identity, as well as its location, is almost as close to Norway as it is
to Scotland. Along with the isles of Orkney, with which there is
much in common historically and culturally, Shetland was
annexed by King Haarfagr in 875 and from then until 1468 was a
dominion of Norway. In 1468 the islands were put up as collateral
by Christian I of Norway and Denmark in the absence of a dowry
for the marriage of his daughter Margaret to James III. Although
they were annexed by Scotland in 1468 and fully assimilated in
1615, they remain, theoretically, 'in hock'. Today, the islands'
Scandinavian influence is evident in various forms, from place
names to the dialect; from the law to the festivals such as 'Up Helly
Aa', held in Lerwick every January.

Shetland lies 60 miles north of the Orkneys and consists of
almost 100 islands, of which only 17 are inhabited. The most
important is Mainland, containing Shetland's capital, Lerwick,
and the airport at Sumburgh which receives daily flights from
Glasgow, Edinburgh, Inverness, Aberdeen, and Kirkwall in
Orkney. From Tingwall airstrip there are flights to the other
Shetland islands of Fair Isle, Whalsay, Fetlar, and Unst. The car
ferry between Aberdeen and Lerwick takes around 14 hours.

As far as livelihood goes, the situation for the Shetlander is the
reverse of that of his Orcadian neighbour. In Shetland, the staple
income is still from the sea, supplemented by working the land,
knitwear and now tourism, although the latter is in no way an
intrusive industry here. The name, however, which comes from
the Norse 'Hjaltland' ('High Land'), is widely associated with a
particular breed of pony reared all over the islands, while Shetland
knitwear, particularly from the remote Fair Isle, far to the south, is
equally famous.

In recent years the discovery of oil in the North Sea around
Shetland has resulted in considerable oil-related development.

Although the oil has brought prosperity to the islands, the islanders themselves have been canny enough to accept their improved financial circumstances whilst retaining the essential character of the place, with its distinctive traditions.

WHERE TO GO FOR WHAT

For the visitor, the most important island is **MAINLAND**, whose principal attractions are concentrated in the narrow southern half. From north to south it is 50 miles long, and roughly in the middle is the Shetland capital of **LERWICK**. This is a busy, maritime town whose fortunes have improved with the North Sea oil installation further north in Sullom Voe, to which Lerwick acts as service and supply base. Built up neither by Scotsmen nor Norsemen, but by Dutch fishermen working Bressay Sound early in the 17th century, the port today is used by boats from all over Europe which gives the town quite a cosmopolitan character. In 1653, Cromwell's fleet arrived to build the defensive structure now known as **Fort Charlotte**. It was burned along with the rest of the town by the Dutch in 1673 and repaired in 1781. In Hillhead Street one finds the 19th-century **Town Hall** and its stained glass windows depicting the history of Shetland, while the same theme is covered in more detail in **Shetland Museum**, opposite. One mile south-west of the town is **Clickimin Broch**, standing 17 feet high on the site of an early Iron Age fortification. As far as architecture is concerned, there is little that stands out. The buildings as a whole are remarkably close, designed as such to shelter the streets from the biting cold wind that is wont to blow in from the North Sea. Lerwick is perhaps best known for its annual fire festival, Up Helly Aa – a vivid manifestation of the Norse influence on these islands: on the last Tuesday in January, a Viking chieftain and a replica long boat lead a torch-bearing procession through the streets. The ritual, intended to welcome the return of the sun, culminates in setting light to the Norse galley. Visitors can take to the sea in a 40-foot replica of a Norse longship, the *Dim Riv*, which cruises the harbour on Wednesday evenings in summer, weather permitting. The unique sport of haggis-hurling takes place at the end of May each year and should not be missed. The **Lerwick Regatta** happens later, in the middle of August.

Lerwick has the best choice of accommodation in Shetland. At the top of the range is the **Shetland Hotel**, Holmsgarth Road (Tel. 0595 5515) and the **Lerwick Hotel**, 15 South Road (Tel. 0595 2166), from around £33. Overlooking the harbour is **Kveldsro Hotel** (Tel. 0595 2195), from around £30, while for a little less there are the **Grand Hotel** (Tel. 0595 2826) and **Queen's Hotel** (Tel. 0595 2826), both on Commercial Street. From under £18 there are **Glen Orchy Guest House**, 20 Knab Road (Tel. 0595 2031), and **Alder Lodge Guest House**, 6 Clairmont Street (Tel. 0595 5705). One of Shetland's best hotels, the four-crown commended **Busta House Hotel**, is situated north-west of Lerwick at Brae (Tel. 080622 506). This attractive 18th-century country house has a relaxing location and spectacular views over Busta Voe. All rooms have *en-suite* facilities, colour TV, direct dial phone and hairdryer. The restaurant specializes in fresh local produce. Prices start from around £38 per person for a double room. Specially prepared holiday packages either by sea or by air, including car hire from the airport or ferry terminal, dinner and bed and breakfast can also be arranged. Packages to suit motorists are also available.

For simple accommodation at a good price, try *böds* or camping barns. These once housed fishermen and their equipment during the fishing season, but they now provide basic self-catering accommodation in attractive locations. Prices begin as low as £2.50 per person per night. Booking is through **Shetlands Islands Tourism** (Tel. 0595 3434). The **Clickimin Caravan and Campsite**, Lochside, Lerwick, provides an ideal sheltered setting and charges between £4.75 and £6.50 for tents and touring caravans. **Lerwick Youth Hostel**, is found at Isleburgh House, King Herald Street (Tel. 0595 2114). It is ideal for groups, but advance booking is advised. Prices are between £3.60 and £4.50.

The Tourist Information Centre in Lerwick is at Market Cross (Tel. 0595 3434) and at a seasonal information desk at the ferry terminal.

Seven miles west of Lerwick, on the opposite coast, is the former Shetland capital of **SCALLOWAY**, principally of interest for

Scalloway Castle open January to December, seven days a week, from 9.30 a.m. to 5 p.m. whose medieval style was out of fashion on construction in 1600. A mere 15 years later it fell into disrepair when its owner, Earl Patrick Stewart, was executed. **Scalloway Museum** occupies a converted shop in Main Street and includes, among the local artefacts, information on the work of the Norwegian resistance fighters based in the town during the last war. Their clandestine move across the North Sea to here created the phrase: 'to take the Shetland bus'. The museum is open May to October, Tuesday, Wednesday, Thursday, Saturday and Sunday only. The **Scalloway Fire Festival** takes place around 10 January, and the town's **summer gala** is held around 8–11 July.

The main road south from Lerwick, the A970, passes close to **SANDWICK** on the west coast, from where there is a ferry service to the island of **MOUSA**, notable for **Mousa Broch**. Standing over 40 feet high and 50 feet in diameter, it is the best-preserved example of this type of Iron Age fortification, peculiar to Scotland. An interior staircase gives access to the top of the tower.

On the opposite coast, and a short way south, **ST NINIAN'S ISLE** is not an island at all, but a peninsula attached to the mainland by a very narrow strip of sand. Near the isthmus are the foundations of a **12th-century chapel** where excavations in 1958 uncovered the remains of a pre-Norse church, a Bronze Age burial ground, and a hoard of Celtic silver, dating from the eighth century and now on display in the National Museum of Antiquities, Edinburgh. A short distance south of the site is a **Holy Well**. Crossing back to the opposite coast, on an unclassified road off the A970, the **Shetland Croft House Museum** is an authentic crofter's house, furnished as it would have been in the mid-19th-century, and complete with outbuildings and a working watermill. It is open from May to September. You will also find the RSPB nature reserve at **Loch of Spiggie**.

One of the most important archaeological sites in Britain is **Jarlshof**, just beyond the A970 at Sumburgh Head, where there are the remains of five distinct settlements, built on top of each other from the Bronze Age to the 16th century. The wealth of historical data is interpreted and explained in the museum on the site, which is open throughout the year (closed on Tuesday, Sunday and Wednesday afternoon in winter).

At 2 p.m. daily, **Shetland Sea Charter's** boat to the Laerling leaves Lerwick Victoria Harbour on a three-hour cruise to Noss and Bressay. The cost is £10 a head but it's very good value. Passengers are taken to see the gannet colonies, seals and view at close quarters the abundant birdlife of the islands. Tickets are available from the Tourist Office. Noss is a National Nature Reserve, home to a variety of birdlife, and is worth visiting in order to see its spectacular 600-foot cliffs. It is open from mid-May to late August.

The remaining islands of Shetland are wonderful places for an 'escape-from-it-all' holiday. UNST, YELL, WHALSAY and FET-LAR are all paradise to the keen ornithologist.

Trout fishing in Shetland has been given a boost by the new week-long **Glenmorangie Shetland Brown Trout Festival**, held around 23–30 May. Into its second year, there are three fishing competitions, with over 365 trout lochs to chose from, a trout fishing road show and the inevitable whisky tasting.

The Outer Hebrides

INTRODUCTION

The Outer Hebrides form the second stretch of Scotland's Western Isles and are separated from the Inner Hebrides by the treacherous stretch of water known as The Minch. The Outer Hebrides are themselves called the 'Western Isles', locally and within Scotland. Although they lack the extremes of rugged scenery of much of the Western Highlands, the Outer Hebrides have their own distinctive character. The west coast consists mainly of sandy grassland known as 'machair', which, with the advent of summer and the blooming of the flowers, becomes a riot of colour, making May and June the most attractive months to visit. Most of the thinly-spread population is to be found in the west, the east coast tending to be rather bleak.

Island life is still traditionally linked to fishing, crofting and, in the north, the weaving of the world famous Harris tweed. A long-standing religious divide separates the staunchly Protestant north, where there is a strict respect for the Sabbath, and the more relaxed Catholic south. One of the most distinctive features of these islands is the language – Gaelic is spoken everywhere and many of the islands' roadsigns are given in both Gaelic and English. But don't worry about not being understood – everyone can speak English too.

There are regular scheduled air services from Glasgow and Inverness, as well as an inter-island service between Stornoway, Balivanich and Barra. However, some of these operate only once or twice a week (although most fly a couple of times daily), and on Barra the schedule is governed by the tide, as the plane lands on the beach (contact Loganair: Tel. 041-889 3181).

The most common way of reaching the islands is by ferry. Caledonian MacBrayne operate services to Barra and South Uist from Oban (taking five and seven hours, respectively); to North Uist and Harris from Uig on Skye (one hour 45 minutes); and to Stornoway from Ullapool (three and a half hours). A ferry timetable is essential, since the schedule is complicated and there are no ferries at all on Sundays, to Stornoway or Tarbert. Smaller, locally operated ferries run between the islands and their times are dependent upon the tides. Seasickness tablets are useful to have with you, especially on the longer journeys.

WHERE TO GO FOR WHAT

This chapter looks at the string of islands from south to north, starting with **BARRA**, the smallest of the six main islands and a stronghold of the great MacNeil clan throughout the Middle Ages. The only hill, Heaval, rises to 1,200 feet in the centre of Barra, and is skirted by the only road which encircles the island in a 12-mile round trip. One thousand species of wild flowers have been identified on the island. The ferry docks at the once-prosperous herring port of CASTLEBAY (BAGH A CHAISTEIL), which derived its name from the restored **Kisimul Castle**, dating from about 1120, which stands on a small islet in the bay, and which can be reached by boat (open May to September Wednesday, Friday and Saturday afternoons only); the charge for boatman and admission to the castle is £2.00. From around £21 a night, the **Clachan Beag Hotel** (Tel. 08714 279) is quiet and friendly, offering five comfortable rooms and good food. Its pleasant sun lounge has glorious views over the castle and the bay. **The Castle Bay Hotel** (Tel. 08714 223) offers accommodation from £25 upwards.

North-west from Castlebay, the circular island road leads to TANGASDALE and **Hallaman Bay**, one of Barra's beautiful west coast beaches. The **Isle of Barra Hotel** is situated here (Tel. 08714 383), offering rooms from £25.

The road continues through the machair until it reaches NORTHBAY (BAGH A TUATH), where a single-track road winds towards EOLIGARRY (EOLAIGEARRAIDH), and the sandy beach of TRAIGH MHOR, which is the island's airstrip. Nearby is **Cille-Bharra** cemetery, resting place of the novelist Sir Compton Mackenzie, who immortalized Barra as the island of 'Toddy' in his novel *Whisky Galore*. The story is based on an actual event in the

Second World War when a ship with a cargo of whisky was wrecked on the neighbouring island of Eriskay.

Beyond Northbay, the coastal scenery becomes more rocky, and has many tiny coves with pale, sandy beaches. Above the hamlet of **BREVIG (BREIBHIG)** is a standing stone, and below the summit of Heaval is a white marble statue of the Virgin Mary. The summit of the hill, which can be ascended with moderate effort, has breathtaking views over the bay. Every year a fell run is held from Castlebay to the top and back with the fastest runners completing the course in under half an hour.

From Castlebay it is only a short journey by a causeway to the island of **VATERSAY**, a tranquil place supporting a tiny population and a lot of cattle. Off the island's easternmost tip is the tiny islet of UINESSAN where visitors can see the **burial place of Mor nan Ceann** (Mor of the Heads). Its name comes from the wife of a chieftain who according to legend, sought preference for her son over his stepbrothers, and achieved this by having the latter executed.

Lying between Barra and South Uist, the rocky island of **ERISKAY** has been immortalized in the song 'The Eriskay Love Lilt'. In 1745, it was visited by Bonnie Prince Charlie – his first port of call in the islands to which he would return a year later as a fugitive. The only remarkable features of the island, apart from the birdlife, is the church altar, which is made from the debris of one of the island's many wrecks, the only bar on the island, '**Am Politician Lounge Bar**' (popular for seafood meals), and the island's own breed of Eriskay ponies.

On the island of **SOUTH UIST**, the car ferry from Barra and Oban berths in the town of **LOCHBOISDALE (LOCH BAGHASDAIL)**, although there is little on the island to attract visitors, apart from those looking for a very peaceful holiday, or the keen ornithologist or fisherman. There are two small hotels the AA two-star **Lochboisdale** (Tel. 08784 332), providing bed and breakfast from around £24, and the **Borrndale Hotel**, Daliburgh (Dalibrog), close by, charging from £25. Only one road leads out of town to join the main road running the length of the island. To the south lies Garynamonie (Gearraidh na Monadh) and Pollachar, where there is a small, quiet beach, and an inn which has good views of Barra. A couple of miles to the east, the hamlet of LUDAG is the end of the road and departure point for the ferry to Barra and Eriskay. Journey times are posted daily on the pier.

Travelling north, the disparate character of the east and west of this island is starkly apparent, with the fertile machair to the left and the rocky outcrops of Arnaval and Beinn Mhor masking the sea to the right. A string of crofting villages is set between the road and the Atlantic. Among them is Milton (Gearraidh Bhailteas), birthplace of the Jacobite heroine Flora MacDonald who helped Bonnie Prince Charlie in his escape after the Battle of Culloden. The **Kildonan School Museum** is also situated here and has historical exhibitions on display throughout the summer. Check the Tourist Information Centre for times, as they can vary.

Beyond the unremarkable village of Howmore (Tobha Mor) – which does have ruined chapels from the 12th and 13th centuries, as well as the **burial grounds** of the Clan Ranald Chiefs – is the National Nature Reserve and Bird Sanctuary of **Loch Druidibeg**, home of the largest British colony of greylag geese and the elusive corncrake. The western section of the reserve is moorland, rich in plant species. On the dunes which back the Atlantic coast the remains of a circular Pictish dwelling can be seen.

The island of **BENBECULA** is unique among the Outer Hebridean islands in that it has no ferry port, being connected to North and South Uist by causeways built across the sandbanks. It does have an airport, however, with regular BA flights to Glasgow, and Loganair flights to Stornoway and Barra. At the southern end of the island is the village of CREAGORRY (CREAG GHORAIDH), where a narrow road leads to **Peter's Port**, site of a pier which was never used because ships are unable to navigate the loch entrance. Following the B892 further north is **Sgoil Lionacleit (Linaclete Community School)**, which houses the local museum and library as well as sports facilities. Many ceilidhs and events in the summer are held in the village theatre. The **Dark Island Hotel** is situated here (Tel 0870 602412), offering rooms from £20 upwards, and is recommended by 'The Taste of Scotland'.

Along the west coast are the ruins of an ancient castle at Borve (Borgh) and of a nunnery at the hamlet of Nunton. Balivanich (Baile a Mhanaich) was once a monastic site, but is now a centre for the military personnel who work at the firing range on South Uist. Like so many of the Western Isles, Benbecula is awash with tales of Bonnie Prince Charlie, who set off from here to Skye. The **Creagorry Hotel** (Tel. 0870 602024) offers bed and breakfast from £25 and is open all year.

Across the causeway from Benbecula, the island of **NORTH UIST** is dominated by the 1,050-foot hill of Eaval. The island contains many lochs offering good fishing. At its centre, the land is a mixture of bog and heather moorland, while the west coast repeats the familiar pattern of crofting townships, sandy beaches and fertile machair.

At **CARINISH (CAIRINIS)** are the ruins of a former religious and educational establishment, **Teampull-na-Trionaid**, where the 13th-century historian and theologian Duns Scotus studied. A left turn at Claddach Baleshare (Cladach a Bhaile Shear) leads across a causeway to the sandy and peaceful island of Baleshare. From Clachan-na-Luib a minor road runs alongside the picturesque inlet of Loch Eport (Loch Euphoirt) to the hamlet of the same name. The road comes to a dead end after six miles.

Fine sandy beaches and white-painted crofts stretch along the west coast to the nature reserve at **BALRANALD (BAILE RAGHAILL)**. On the north coast, **SOLLAS (SOLAS)** was the scene of some of the most unpleasant fighting during the Highland Clearances, with crofters and police engaged in pitched battle. The north coast is sculpted into a pattern of islands and shallow bays which dry out at low tide. The B893 runs north through the machair to **NEWTON FERRY (PORT NAN LONG)**, where the ferry runs daily (twice on Saturdays) between Uist, Berneray and Harris. **LOCHMADDY (LOCH NAM MADADH)** is the capital of the island, but like Lochboisdale it owes its existence almost entirely to the car ferry which plies between here, Skye and Harris. **Uist Outdoor Centre** offers sub-aqua diving and other water sports, as well as walking, climbing, and wildlife and field studies (Tel. 08763 358). Dormitory accommodation is available. The

Lochmaddy Hotel (Tel. 08763 331) has spectacular views over the bay and across to Skye – dinner, bed and breakfast from £25.

The island of **BERNERAY** lies between North Uist and Harris, and its population of 300 people supports itself by crofting and fishing.

Strictly speaking, **HARRIS** and **LEWIS** constitute one island, but they are so well separated by an imposing range of hills, crossed by only one road, that the traditional division persists in the administrative boundaries. The ferry arrives at **TARBERT (AN TAIRBEART)** from Skye and Lochmaddy, twice a day except Sunday. The **Harris Hotel** (Tel. 0859 2154) provides good bed-and-breakfast accommodation from around £27, as well as teas and coffee throughout the day. South of Tarbert, the west coast is notable for its pleasant sandy beaches. On the south coast, the town of **RODEL (ROGHADAL)**, sitting above a picturesque harbour, has the attractive **Church of St Clement** which dates from the 16th century. The east coast has an extraordinary, almost lunar landscape, reminiscent of Iceland. Scotland's newest and most remote celebration of the arts is the **Isle of Harris Arts Festival**. It will run from the end of August into the first week of September, featuring various exhibitions of a local and international flavour.

North from Tarbert, the road leads to the North Harris Hills. The four peaks are all over 1,800 feet, with Clisham the highest, reaching 2,400 feet. Here you will find **Ardvourlie Castle**, a Victorian hunting lodge set on the shores of Loch Seaforth amidst the hills. Approved by the 'Taste of Scotland', it offers rooms from £40 upwards. **LEWIS** begins over the hills, beyond the bleak countryside which is home to red deer. Between the townships of Ardvourlie (Aird a Mhulaidh) and Arivruaich (Airidh a Bhruaich) is an area of recently planted forestry, one of the few areas of commercial woodland in the whole of the Outer Hebrides.

Beyond **GARYNAHINE (GEARRAIDH NA H-AIBHNE)** the B8011 enters a region rich in archaeological remains. The isle of **GREAT BERNERA (BEARNARAIGH)** is the site of standing stones and Iron Age remains. Twelfth-century ivory chessmen were recently discovered at **ARDROIL (EADAR DHA FHADHAIL)**.

(Copies of these make an attractive memento, and can be bought in the British Museum in London, the Scottish Museum of Antiquities in Edinburgh and the local Tourist Information Centre.) A series of stone circles can be seen on the main coastal road, the best known among them being the **Circle of Callanish** (CALANAIS). The stones have a burial cairn at their centre where cremated bones were found on excavation. The 48 stones were uncovered in 1857 and are an impressive sight second in importance only to Stonehenge. Standing stones and forts of similar age abound along the west coast. Among the best preserved is **Dun Carloway**, an Iron Age broch which stands 30 feet high.

The road passes through many west coast villages where Harris tweed is produced. SHAWBOST (SIABOST) has a tweed mill open to the public and a local history museum housed in the village school. In the nearby village of ARNOL, off the A858, you can see one of the typical dwellings in which some Highlanders and Islanders lived until the mid-20th century – a 'black house', so called because of its open hearth and the layout of the living quarters under one roof. STORNOWAY (STEORNABHAGH) is the main town and is the shopping and administrative centre of the Outer Hebrides. There is also a good 18-hole golf course, and Stornoway is a well-known sea-angling centre. On the south side of the harbour, **Lews Castle** is now a school and further education college, while a narrow neck of land at the near end of the Eye Peninsula is the site of **St Columba's Chapel**, burial place of the MacLeods of Lewis. The town has a number of very good three-star hotels offering comfortable accommodation from around £40: the **Caberfeidh** (Tel. 0851 702604) with 40 rooms has recently been refurbished and the **Seaforth** (Tel. 0851 702740) with nearly 60. The visitor to Stornoway could also try the **Royal Hotel**, Cromwell Street (Tel. 0851 702109), ideal for families, or the **Crown Hotel**, Castle Street (Tel. 0851 703181), which charges from £27 upwards.

Skye and South-west Ross

INTRODUCTION

Both Skye and South-west Ross are impressive mountainous regions, the former possessing the beautiful Cuillins, the steepest and most rugged range in Britain. Similar adjectives apply to its coastline, made uneven by many sea lochs, and the magnificent scenery throughout the island is what attracts its many visitors. Here is the archetypal 'romantic Highland Scotland'. The scenery is outstanding, the pace of life slow, and the potential for a wonderful touring holiday, huge. The capital of Skye is Portree, its only town, which like the rest of the island is socially quiet throughout the week, and especially on Sundays when strict observation of the Sabbath brings everything except the churches and the Kyle of Lochalsh ferry to a halt. Dunvegan Castle (Sundays from 1 p.m. to 5.30 p.m., Easter to the end of October) and the Clan Donald Centre (all day Sunday) also remain open.

Along with the importance of the Gaelic culture and language, much of the history of Skye, such as the impact of the early Christian missionaries and the Norse occupation, is common to the Hebrides in general. The island has also witnessed intense and chronic feuding between the local clans of the MacDonalds and MacLeods, but it is probably best known as the place of refuge for Charles Edward Stuart aided in his famous flight from Hanoverian pursuers by Flora MacDonald in the wake of the vicious Jacobite defeat at Culloden. Visitors can see Flora MacDonald's grave and monument in Kilmuir in the north-west of the island, while her house in Flodigarry, in the north-east, still stands. The Young Pretender's presence on the island has been recorded in place names such as Prince Charlie's Cave near Elgol, where he was treated to a banquet on his way to the mainland, and Prince Charlie's Point where he alighted in the north-west with Flora MacDonald.

The two roads in South-west Ross, the A87 from the east and the A890 from the north, both lead to Kyle of Lochalsh. The A890 is the latter section of the route from Inverness which runs through some of the finest countryside to be seen anywhere in Britain. This route is accompanied by Brtish Rail's 'Great Scenic Railway'. This terminates at Kyle of Lochalsh where each day throughout the year there is a 24-hour car ferry to Skye, the crossing taking only a few minutes. Other crossings can be made in similar time between Glenelg and Kylerhea (from mid-April to the end of September, Monday to Saturday. It's not suitable for caravans. Call 0599 81 302 for more details). The 30-minute journey between Mallaig and Armadale operates five times a day, from Monday to Saturday in summer, and with a passenger-only service in winter (for details contact Caledonian MacBrayne: Tel. 0687 2403). The island's bus service is infrequent, seasonal and, like everything else, inactive on Sundays, except for major routes.

WHERE TO GO FOR WHAT

The A87 coming from the south-east descends from the hills around Loch Cluanie through the Pass of Stachel and below the serried peaks of the Five Sisters five miles from **SHIEL BRIDGE** on the south-east corner of Loch Duich. **Tourist Information** is available here from Easter to October (Tel. 0599 81 264). The unclassified road west runs through some magnificent countryside and leads to **Glenelg Brochs**. At 25 and 33 feet high respectively, these are two of the most outstanding examples of this type of Iron Age defensive stone tower on the Scottish mainland and are remarkably well preserved.

Returning to the A87 and a short distance beyond Shiel Bridge, **Morvich Countryside Centre** (open from June to September) gives information on the National Trust's **Kintail Estate** and its many hillwalks, climbs and guided walks. The **Kintail Clan Maclennan Museum** depicts the history of the clan and makes an interesting visit.

 Eight miles further on, Scotland's most scenic castle, **Eilean Donan** (open Easter to September, daily, 10 a.m.–6 p.m.), stands at the end of a causeway in Loch Duich. It was built in 1220 for the purpose of repelling the Viking invasion and was blown apart in 1719 by a Hanoverian warship. The present structure was rebuilt some 200 years later and now houses items relating to the Jacobites, MacKenzies, and MacRaes. Four miles further on, the road passes **Lochalsh Woodland Garden and Coach House** containing a natural history display, from where it is three more miles to **KYLE OF LOCHALSH** whose **Tourist Information** office is open from Easter to September (Tel. 0599 4276).

A few hundred yards separate Kyle of Lochalsh from the island of **SKYE**. The 24-hour year-round daily ferry service here is supplemented in summer by another equally short crossing, not much further south, between Glenelg and Kylerhea (operating from April to the end of October, Monday to Saturday).

From Kyle of Lochalsh the ferry crosses the strait known as Kyle Akin, not to be confused with the village and docking point of **KYLEAKIN** on Skye. The ruin beside the water is **Castle Moil**, dating from the 12th century. Following the A850 to Harrapool is the **Skye Environmental Centre**, complete with museum and displays on the geological and natural history of Skye. There are also children's displays from around the island, and a gift shop (open Monday to Saturday, 10 a.m. to 5 p.m.). The centre is an important base for environmental, geological and biological studies, and is able to offer seashore study trails and wildlife holidays. There is even a comfortable guest house offering bed and breakfast accommodation on site. For more information Tel. 0471 822 487. About half-way between Kyleakin and Broadford a single-track road leads south-east to the **Kylerhea Otter Haven**, where a half-hour walk takes you to an observation hide where you can sit and watch the wildlife. A short distance before Broadford, the road from Kyleakin joins the A851 running south to Ardvasar and skirts the coast before coming to **ISLEORNSAY** opposite the island of Ornsay. The village offers a pleasant beach and good fishing. At Knock Bay there are the remains of **Knock Castle** which, like **Armadale Castle** further along the coast, was built by the MacDonalds. The latter was constructed in 1815–19 and now houses the award-winning **Clan Donald Centre**, featuring a museum and audio-visual programme. Forty-six acres of restored

19th-century woodland gardens, several miles of nature trails, a licensed restaurant and a programme of arts events means it is well worth spending the day. Luxury self-catering accommodation is available (Tel. 04714 305/227).

Returning by the A851 to **BROADFORD** where the **Tourist Information Centre** is available from Easter to October (Tel. 0471 822 463), the A881 south-west to Elgol makes for the most scenic route on the entire island, curving round the sea inlet of Loch Slapin and passing through the hamlet of **KILMARIE**, on the shore near which can be seen the remains of the ninth-century fort **Dun Ringill**. For serious hillwalkers there is a path running for three miles, from Kilmarie to Camasunary by Loch Scavaig, and from there a more arduous and occasionally hazardous path for another three miles to Loch Coruisk and then on to Sligachan in eight miles – this is not a walk for the inexperienced or the ill-equipped. About half-way along the latter stage, the **Bloody Stone** near the mouth of Harta Corrie is the site of the last clan battle between the MacDonalds and the MacLeods in 1601.

From the village of **ELGOL** there are fine views across Loch Scavaig to the **Cuillin Hills** which rise to a height well in excess of 3,000 feet and present an arduous challenge to experienced rock climbers and walkers. There are sailings across the loch from Elgol by arrangement with Donald MacKinnon (Tel. 047 16 244). South of the village, **Prince Charles's Cave** is where Charles Edward Stuart was received by the MacKinnons and treated to a banquet on his way to the mainland. From Elgol it is a short drive along a very narrow track to Glasnakille. Visit **Spar Cave** to see its stalagmites – check tides before going and take a torch – and it was from this beach that Bonnie Prince Charlie escaped to the mainland.

Returning again to Broadford, the A850 runs north by the shore, with views across the narrow strait, Caolas Scalpay, to the island of Scalpay. On reaching Loch Ainort, the road passes the **Old Skye Crofter's House** at Luib, where a display grants an insight into local life in the early 20th century. In **SCONSER** a high standard of accommodation is provided by the former Victorian shooting lodge, **Sconser Lodge Hotel** (Tel. 047852 333), where prices start at around £25 B&B. During the summer there are five 15-minute crossings each day, Monday to Saturday, from Sconser to the island of Raasay. Winter services are less frequent.

In order to cover as comprehensive a circuit as possible, leave the A850 for the A863 which runs across and up the west of Skye. Off the A863 just before Drynoch, is the B8009 which leads to the village of Carbost and **Talisker Whisky Distillery**, the only whisky made on Skye. Here, you can enjoy a guided tour, sample the unique single malt whisky and buy the product from the visitor centre shop (open Easter to October, Monday to Friday, 9.30 a.m. to 4.30 p.m. During the winter only the visitor centre is open, from 1.30 p.m. till 4.30 p.m.). Four miles beyond the mouth of Loch Harport the hill fort of **Dun Taimh** comes into view before the road reaches the village of **STRUAN**. Here you will find **Hillcroft Open Farm** at 6 Totarder (Tel. 047072 242) where visitors are allowed to see the farm animals and enjoy the bed and breakfast accommodation. **Sandford Trekking and Riding Centre** is also near Struan and is open from April to October (Tel. 047072 225). Near here to the north-west is the island's best preserved broch, **Dun Beag**.

The village of **DUNVEGAN** stands at the head of the loch of the same name and is notable for **Dunvegan Castle** (open from Easter to the end of October, Monday to Saturday, 10 a.m. to 5.30 p.m. and Sunday 1 p.m. to 5.30 p.m.; in the winter by arrangement only, Tel. 047 022 206). The seat of the chiefs of Clan MacLeod since the 12th century and the home of the present chief John MacLeod, the castle displays various architectural styles in vogue between the 15th and 19th centuries during which period it was built and frequently extended. The star attraction inside is the silken banner known as the Fairy Flag on display in the drawing room. Of Middle Eastern origin and dating from the fourth to seventh centuries, it is said to have been endowed with the magical property of saving the clan from danger on up to three occasions. Two of these have already been used up. Other items on display include the 10th-century Irish drinking vessel, the Dunvegan Cup, paintings by Ramsay and Raeburn, and letters from illustrious visitors such as Sir Walter Scott and Dr Johnson. From here frequent short boat trips can be taken from the castle jetty to the seal colony. There are also longer loch cruises aboard *MacLeod of MacLeod* to see the seabird colonies and spectacular views by Dunvegan Head and Lampa Island.

The peninsula west of Loch Dunvegan, known as Duirinish, saw some of the fiercest disturbances during the crofter riots of 1881–5, and this record is commemorated by a roadside memorial on the way to Milovaig. Before that, the B884 across the north of the peninsula passes through the village of **COLBOST**, home of the **Colbost Folk Museum**, and **GLENDALE** where visitors can see the **Skye Watermill**, restored and in operation, as well as the **Toy Museum** in Holmisdale House (open all year, Tel. 047 081 240). A little more to the north-east at Borreraig is the **Piping Centre**, showing the remarkable history of the Highland bagpipe and the family MacCrimmon, pipers to the chiefs of the Clan Macleod from 1500 to 1800 (open Easter to October, Monday to Saturday 10 a.m. to 6 p.m., Sunday 2 p.m. to 6 p.m., Tel. 047 081 352).

The A850 links Dunvegan with **PORTREE**, Skye's only town and its capital. The name, meaning 'port of the king', was coined after a visit by James V and succeeded 'Kiltaragleann', meaning 'church at the foot of the glen'. Although there is little to distinguish it, the town occupies a picturesque setting and the view from the hills surrounding the bay is quite spectacular. From Portree pier there are two cruises on board the *Tristar*, with commentary, around the scenic Sound of Raasay, home to many varieties of wildlife including eagles. Available from April to October (Tel. 047842 272). South of Portree on Broadford Road is the **Glen Varragill walk** which leads through woodland and extends to the forest road with spectacular views over Portree Bay. Less than a mile long, it has car park facilities and picnic areas. The **Aros Heritage Centre** at Portree is due to open in 1993, incorporating an exhibition on the Gaelic language and culture, and the history of the island with audio-visual displays and life-size models to recreate events. There is also a restaurant and shop.

The visitor to Skye will find a wide variety of accommodation. **Viewfield House Hotel** (Tel. 0478 2217) on the outskirts of the town is a family-run country house hotel standing in 20-acre grounds. Prices start at around £18. Also on the outskirts in attractive grounds is **Cuillin Hills Hotel** (Tel. 0478 2003), charging from between £25 and £51. At a similar price there are **Rosedale Hotel** (Tel. 0478 3131) and **Royal Hotel** (Tel. 0478 2525) in a central location overlooking the harbour. The room in which Bonnie Prince Charlie bade Flora MacDonald goodbye before leaving for Raasay has been preserved as it was in the Royal Hotel. One-crown commended bed and breakfast accommodation with good home-cooking is available two miles outside of Portree at the **Shielings Guest House**, Torvaig (Tel. 0478 3024) from between £11 and £13.50 per person. Slightly cheaper B & B accommodation can be found in Portree itself and the **Tourist Information** centre is able to assist with accommodation bookings for all price ranges (Tel. 0478 2137).

Seventeen miles north of Portree stands the **Kilt Rock**, columns of basalt which look distinctly like the national dress, and two miles further north, off the A8555, two miles west of Staffin, is the **Quirang**. This group of pillars and pinnacles is where cattle used to be driven for safety during raids. There is a track leading to '**the Needle**', a 120-foot-high obelisk, from which the views are outstanding. A little further south at Uig is '**Whitewave Canoeing**', a centre of instruction and fun sessions on and around the Isle of Skye (Tel. 047042 414).

The A856 runs along the east shore of Loch Snizort where there is evidence of its inhabitation since prehistoric times in the form of standing stones near **KENSALEYRE** and standing stones one mile north between the road and the loch. Across the River Hinnisdal stand the remains of **Caisteal Huisdean**, formerly the property of the 17th-century pirate Hugh Gillespie. A few miles north of Uig, Prince Charles's Point is where the Young Pretender and Flora MacDonald landed before heading south and taking up refuge in Kingsburgh and Portree in their famous escape to Skye following the Jacobite defeat in 1746. Flora died in 1790 and her grave, along with a monument to her, can be seen in the burial ground in **KILMUIR** which is also the location of the **Skye Museum of Island Life** (open from May to October, Tel. 047 052 213). As the road curves round the head of the peninsula, it passes the ruins of the 17th-century **Duntulm Castle**, and heading south it runs through **FLODIGARRY** where Flora MacDonald set up home with her husband Allan MacDonald from Kingsburgh, and bore her seven children in the house still standing next to the hotel. Beyond Staffin Bay, the remains of a broch can be seen standing on a promontory in Loch Mealt whose flow into the sea culminates in the 300-foot drop over the cliffs at **Mealt Falls**. Further south, the road reaches **The Storr**, a cliff over 2,000 feet high, and, at its foot, the 150 foot tapering column known as the **Old Man of Storr**.

Fort William and Lochaber

INTRODUCTION

In this sparsely populated region, it is the scenery which exerts the strongest attraction for visitors, whether it is the dramatic and rugged coastline in the west, the beautiful mountain backdrop of the 'Road to the Isles', between Fort William and Mallaig, or the forbidding Loch Morar, greater in depth than the North Sea.

Historically, the best-known episode in this part of Scotland is that of the Glencoe Massacre which took place during the early hours of 13 February 1692. After having enjoyed their confidence and hospitality for the preceding two weeks, members of the Clan Campbell acting in collusion with the ministers of King William, slaughtered 40 members of the Clan MacDonald, indiscriminately attacking women, children, the elderly, and the infirm. The pretext for the assault was the late receipt, from MacDonald of Glencoe, of submission to the regal authority of William and Mary in place of James VII. The punitive action carried out by Campbell of Glenlyon, at the behest of the Under-Secretary of State, Sir John Dalrymple, was a wanton show of strength by the Crown, aiming to frighten off any insurgent notions harboured by the Highlanders who opposed the replacement of the Catholic James II by his Protestant sister Mary and her husband the Dutch King William. The savagery of the deed, from its conception to its insidious execution, is manifest in the wording of the minister's instructions to Campbell: 'they must all be slaughtered, and the manner of execution must be sure, secret and effectual'. Three years later, the Scottish Parliament decided, after an inquiry, that the assault amounted to murder, but none of those responsible were brought to justice. Campbell escaped through being in service abroad, and the worst punishment meted out to Dalrymple was his removal from office. This part of the country is also notable for its involvement in the '45, for it was on the shore of Loch nan Uamh that Charles Edward Stuart, the Young Pretender, landed on the mainland in July 1745 to commence his campaign to gain the throne of Great Britain. He raised his standard along the road in Glenfinnan and in the following year the region's involvement in this episode in history came full circle when the Prince returned to the same loch to finally depart these shores following the failure of his campaign.

Good transport links converge on Fort William at the heart of the district of Lochaber. The A82 connects it with Inverness 66 miles to the north and also Glasgow 103 miles to the south. The car journey from London takes 9 to 10 hours. Fort William is on the InterCity line from London Euston via Glasgow and offers the option of an overnight sleeper service. The nearest airport is at Inverness which receives flights from Glasgow, Aberdeen, Stornoway, Orkney, Shetland, and London.

Lochaber's best-known feature is Ben Nevis to the east of Fort William where the tourist information office can provide climbers with advice on its ascent. Elsewhere the region's mountainous terrain makes for breathtaking scenery and one leisurely way of enjoying it is to make the journey, either by rail or road, from Fort William to Mallaig. Rail users have the added advantage of travelling by steam train (see below, in the section 'West from Fort William').

Fort William

The best way to cover the district of Lochaber is by way of a number of routes outward from **FORT WILLIAM** which lies approximately in the centre of the region on the eastern shore of Loch Linnhe. From the opposite shore there is the impressive sight of Britain's highest mountain, **Ben Nevis** (4,406 feet), immediately behind the town. Lacking a definite peak, the mountain's rounded bulk gives a diminished impression of its true height. This is one of Britain's most dangerous climbs and should not be tackled lightly. There is a tourist route which avoids the dangerous areas. Those keen to climb to the snow-clad summit should take the footpath beside the golf course (it is a 4½-hour ascent, 3-hour descent). Also here is the **Scottish Crafts and Ben**

Nevis Exhibition (open from Easter to November). Nearby in Cameron Square, the **West Highland Museum** contains material relating to natural and folk history. Scotland's newest ski area – the **Nevis Range** on Aonach Mor – is only four miles from Fort William. The cable car is open all year round and the view from the top at 2300 feet is magnificent. Just four miles outside Fort William is **Treasures of the Earth,** where visitors can go on a journey through a secret subterranean world of caves and mines to discover the natural wonders that lie beneath our feet.

Fort William's extensive choice of accommodation includes the centrally situated **Alexandra Hotel**, Fort Parade (Tel. 0397 702241), from around £39. For £25 or less there are the **Highland Hotel**, Union Road (Tel. 0397 702291); the **Croit Anna Hotel** on the shores of Loch Linnhe (Tel. 0397 702268); and the **Cruachan Hotel**, Achintore Road (Tel. 0397 702022) overlooking the Ardgour Hills. There are numerous bed and breakfasts available including the two-crown commended **Glen Lochy Guest House**, Nevis Bridge (Tel. 0397 702909), offering rooms from £13 upwards, and the **Loch View Guest House**, off Argyle Terrace (Tel. 0397 703147), also two-crown commended, and situated on a hillside with panoramic views over Loch Linnhe, charging from £16. Two miles up Glen Nevis is the **Glen Nevis Caravan Park** (Tel. 0397 702191), charging from £7.10 for touring caravans and £6.90 for motor caravans and tents. There are also caravans to let for two to six persons.

One of the best places to eat in Fort William is the **Crannog Seafood Restaurant,** Town Pier (Tel. 0397 705589), which uses only the freshest ingredients.

The **Tourist Information** centre in Cameron Square (Tel. 0397 703781) is open all year.

North from Fort William

Two miles north-east from the town centre is the ruin of the 13th-century **Old Inverlochy Castle,** and nearby is another structure which revived the name in the 19th century. This more recent

Inverlochy Castle (Tel. 0397 702177) is now one of Europe's finest country house hotels, providing exquisite dinner with wine, bed and breakfast at an equally exquisite price in the region of £230 per night for two. A few miles north-east of Fort William is **Snow-goose Holidays and Activities** situated at the Old Smiddy, Station Road, Corpach (Tel. 0393 772467), offering three-crown highly commended self-catering accommodation and activity training courses including various water and mountain sports. Family activity holidays are also catered for. Also at Corpach is a new visitor attraction, **Treasures of the Earth**, with remarkable displays of gem stones, crystals and fossils set in subterranean caverns and mine galleries. It also tells the story of the dinosaurs and the primeval forests (open all year 10 a.m. till late).

A few miles north the A82 passes the **Commando Memorial**, a sculpture in honour of the Second World War commandos who trained in the area, erected by Scott Sutherland in a spot with excellent panoramic views. Further north, and away from the road to the east, are the '**Parallel Roads**' in Glen Roy, terraces in the hillside left by the falling level of the lake formed in the glen during the Ice Age. Just south of the village of **INVERGARRY** are the ruins of **Invergarry Castle**, for long the ancestral home of the MacDonalds of Glengarry, while to the north, just off the A82 on the west shore of Loch Oich is the **Well of the Seven Heads**, an unusual monument, inscribed in English, Gaelic, French and Latin and bearing the graven image of seven male heads. It records the occasion when the severed heads of seven brothers were washed in the well following their execution for the murder of the two sons of a 17th-century chief of Keppoch.

South from Fort William

South from Fort William, the A82 runs through the village of **GLENCOE** where Jacobite relics and displays on the local agricultural and slate-quarrying industries are among the material contained in the **Glencoe and North Lorne Folk Museum**. The name 'Glencoe' is synonymous with the events outlined at the start of this chapter and the scene where the bloodshed took place is reached a few miles beyond the village. The circumstances and background of the 1692 massacre are described at the National Trust's **Glencoe Visitor Centre**, which also has information on the glen's magnificent scenery; challenges to the experienced mountaineer; and the variety of wildlife including red deer, golden eagles, and wildcats at home on the National Trust for Scotland's 14,000 acres of land here. Further on, near Kingshouse, the **Glencoe Chairlift** carries visitors to a height of 2,100 feet from where there are panoramic views over Glencoe and Rannoch Moor. The 40-bedroom **Isles of Glencoe Hotel** and leisure centre, is one of the first major hotels to be developed in the Highlands in a decade. Situated at the spectacular Pass of Glencoe, it offers the best in Highland accommodation and hospitality (Tel. 08552 606).

Backtracking the few miles along the A82 to where it meets the A828, there is a monument to 'James of the Glens', James Stewart, who had the charge foisted on him of murdering Colin Campbell of Glenure in 1752. Tried by a Campbell judge and jury, the verdict was inevitable and Stewart was hanged near Ballachulish. A monument by the road just north of Kentallen marks the site of the murder, and Stewart is buried further south in the churchyard at Keil. The village of KENTALLEN is the location of the highly recommended **Holly Tree Hotel** (Tel. 063174 292), where all 12 rooms have an excellent view across Loch Linnhe. Prices start from £20. Near Kentallen is a long and winding private road leading to **Ardsheal Country House Hotel** (Tel. 063174 227), where, in a secluded spot beside Loch Linnhe, one night's bed and breakfast combined with dinner for two will cost £100–150. By the shores of Loch Linnhe at Onich, a few miles north of Kentallen, is the **Alt-nan-Ros Hotel** (Tel. 08553 210), with spectacular views of the loch and the surrounding mountains. Prices start at £36. **Mrs Flavia MacArthur** offers bed and breakfast accommodation at **Ardsheal Home Farm** (tel. 063172 229), from only £12.

West from Fort William

For train passengers, the West Highland Railway from Fort William not only follows one of the most scenic routes in Britain, or, indeed Europe, but also offers the exceedingly rare opportunity to travel by steam train on selected days in summer. There is a supplement to the normal fare and details are available from any of the main stations in Scotland. The A830 runs parallel to the railway and, while road users are denied the nostalgia of the steam locomotive, they can travel through the same breathtaking countryside.

From Fort William the A830 curves sharply to run westward along the northern shore of Loch Eil beyond which is the village of **GLENFINNAN**. It was here on 19 August 1745 that Charles Edward Stuart raised his standard at the start of his campaign to regain the throne of Great Britain for the House of Stuart. The **Glenfinnan Monument** recording this historic event was erected in 1815. Climb to the top of the monument and experience the view down to Loch Shiel. The National Trust **Visitor Centre** presents the history of the Prince's campaign which saw him win territorial advances as far south as Derby but ended in the catastrophic defeat at Culloden in April 1746. Further west, the scenery becomes increasingly grand before reaching the shores of Loch nan Uamh where the **Prince's Cairn** beside the road marks the spot where the Young Pretender arrived on the Scottish mainland to begin his campaign and also where, as the point of his furtive departure from the country the following year, it ended. From the village of **ARISAIG** there are frequent day-cruises to the islands of Eigg, Muck, Rhum, Canna, Mull, Soay, and Skye operated by Bruce Watt Cruises (Tel. 0687 2320) and Arisaig Marine Centre (Tel. 0687 5224). From here the A830 brushes the western shore of the deepest stretch of freshwater in Britain, **Loch Morar**, whose depth exceeds 1,000 feet, before the road comes to an end at the coastal town of **MALLAIG**. There are boat trips from here as from Arisaig above and also a car ferry to Ardvasar on Skye (Caledonian MacBrayne: Tel. 0687 2403).

Mallaig's small selection of accommodation includes the commendable **Marine Hotel** (Tel. 0687 2217) from under £25, and the slightly more expensive **West Highland Hotel** (Tel. 0687 2210) overlooking the sea. From £12 upwards, the **Anchorage Guest House**, Gillies Park (Tel. 0687 2454), and the **Western Isles**

Guest House, East Bay (Tel. 0687 2320), provide good bed and breakfast accommodation. The **Tourist Information** centre is open from May to September (Tel. 0687 2170).

Backtracking for a few miles along the coastal stretch, the A830 meets the A861 at the village of Lochailort and goes south to Loch Moidart. On the northern shore, not far from Kinlochmoidart, stands the **Seven Men of Moidart**, a memorial to the men who accompanied the Young Pretender to Scotland from France. Nearby is the ruin of **Old Kinlochmoidart House** where the Prince spent his first week in Scotland while his Highland forces were raised. As a result of his stay the house was destroyed by government troops the following year. Five miles further on, a minor road branches north for two miles to the ruined **Castle Tioram**. Dating from the 13th or 14th century, this is the ancient seat of the MacDonalds of Clan Ranald, standing on an island in Loch Moidart which is accessible at low tide. Returning to the main road, the A861 joins the B8007 which runs along the scenic northern shore of Loch Sunart before veering inland round Beinn nan Losgann to reach the village of KILCHOAN. Near here is the ruin of the 13th-century stronghold **Mingarry Castle**. Standing on a promontory, it was the possession of the McLeans, a branch of the MacDonald Lords of the Isles, from where they guarded the entrance to Loch Sunart and the Sound of Mull. From Kilchoan in summer, there is a passenger ferry making the 35-minute crossing to Tobermory on Mull, operating from Monday to Saturday (contact Caledonian MacBrayne: Tel. 0688 2017). In five miles visitors will reach the western extremity of the British mainland at **Ardnamurchan Point**, and just north of here is a wonderful beach at Sanna Bay.

South-west from Fort William

For the route down the west shore of Loch Linnhe, either leave Fort William by the A830 as above, but branch off just west of Loch Eil on to the A861. Alternatively, take the A82 south from Fort William as far as **CORRAN** where there is a frequent car ferry (Tel. 0855 243) which takes about 10 minutes to cross the Corran

Narrows to **ARDGOUR**. From here the A861 runs south through the village of Inversanda just beyond which is an excellent viewpoint taking in the magnificent scenery of Loch Linnhe and its banks. At this point the A861 veers west to the head of Loch Sunart near which is the small town of **STRONTIAN**. The now idle leadmines to the north provided much of the lead for the bullets fired in the Napoleonic wars and the similarity between the town's name and an element in the periodic table stems from the discovery here in 1790 of Strontium. From Strontian it is worth taking a detour up Strontian Glen. The road, which is very rough, first reaches the five mines disused since the beginning of the century. There are some superb views especially of Beinn Resipol and Sgurr Dhomhnuill. The road climbs steeply then drops alarmingly to **Loch Doilet** and then merges with a Forestry Commission track which runs along the shores of Loch Shiel to Glenfinnan. Nearby **Ariundle Nature Reserve** is notable for its varieties of Atlantic mosses, liverworts, and lichens. The A884 heads south-east to **Kinlochaline Castle** standing at the head of Loch Aline and built in the 15th century for the chiefs of the Clan MacInnes. At the mouth of the loch a car ferry operates between the town of **LOCHALINE** and **FISHNISH** on Mull (contact Caledonian MacBrayne: Tel. 0475 33755).

The Small Isles

INTRODUCTION

If you really want to get away from it all, visit the Inner Hebrides, a group of islands which lie fragmented along the western coastline. All share the same timeless existence and rugged, individual beauty enjoyed only in the West Highlands of Scotland. This section will look at each of the 'Small Isles', namely Rhum, Eigg, Canna and Muck – ideal locations for the botanist, the ornithologist and the escapist.

COMMUNICATIONS

Access to the islands is not as frequent as to the larger more popular islands such as Skye; this, however, only adds to their exclusivity. Caledonian MacBrayne operate a ferry service from Mallaig four to five times a week throughout the year. The isles can also be reached from Skye and the peninsulas of Morar and Moidart. Ferries from Arisaig provide additional daily services during the summer months.

Rhum

Rhum is about eight miles square, making it the largest of these four islands. It is owned by Scottish Natural Heritage and managed as a **National Nature Reserve**, especially in the area of deer research. Diamond-shaped, it is an island of mountains and glens, particularly to the south with peaks of up to 2,500ft. The **Rhum Cuillins** to the south-west of the island provide the best ridge-walking in Britain. Four glens separate the mountains and provide excellent challenges for walkers, especially with the numerous nature trails also at hand: **Kinloch Glen**, next to Loch Scresort; **Kilmory Glen**, the main area for deer research so very often closed to visitors; and **Glen Harris** – a boggy area where you can spot the unique Rhum Ponies. The weather is often very wet and windy so bringing a pair of good boots is advisable.

Having been in the hands of so many owners, Rhum was eventually bought by John Bullough of Lancashire, a mill machinery manufacturer and inventor. In 1901 his son Sir George Bullough built one of Scotland's most outstanding properties, **Kinloch Castle**. A strange combination of Scots, Tudor and Italian architecture, it is now a 5-star hotel, providing the main accommodation on the island. The pink sandstone ramparts and piper's turret together provide a stunning exterior. Visitors to the hotel are welcome to visit its many rooms, all with their original Edwardian furnishings. Staying here promises to be a unique experience. Each bedroom has its own fireplace, and original eccentric sanitary fittings, and at a very large banquet table breakfast and dinner are served overlooking the bay. Hostel accommodation is also available in what were once the servants' quarters. For more information contact the Mallaig Tourist Board, or phone the hotel direct Tel. Mallaig 0687 2037.

Eigg

Eigg is the most developed of the small isles and has a population of 80, many of whom are involved in crofting and, to some extent, tourism. Accommodation – mainly self-catering – is therefore not quite so limited as on the other islands. The island's two hills, **Ben Buie** and **The Sgurr**, dominate the landscape. Elsewhere the land is green, with woods on the east side of the island at **Galmisdale**. The climate is mild but wet, with sub-tropical species growing in sheltered areas – such as the amazing Eucalyptus trees near the pier. On the west of the island is Laig Bay, a wonderful stretch of untouched beach, and a mile north are the famous Singing Sands, so called because the quartz sand seems to whisper underfoot. South of the island is the site of many caves including the **Macdonalds' Cave** where four hundred members of the clan suffocated whilst taking refuge in 1577 from the raiding Macleods of Skye. The remains were removed only in the last century and taken to the island's 15th-century chapel, now in ruins and marked by a contemporary carved cross in the graveyard.

Canna

With a population of only 30, Canna is five miles long and is owned by the National Trust for Scotland. It is a very green and fertile island with a strangely mild climate. Daffodils are known to flower here in January, and lambs and the potato crop are unusually early. Known also for its amazing cliffs, arches and stacks, it is a prime spot for botanists and bird-watchers with a wide variety of plant, bird life and butterflies. The stack **An Coroghan** is the site of a ruined tower, where it is said a Macdonald chieftain imprisoned his unfaithful wife who starved to death there. The **Cross of St Columba** is also an interesting sight, once part of a 7th-century chapel dedicated to him by the monks of Iona. They remained on the island until the Reformation, but the island has remained Catholic in spite of the efforts of the Church of Scotland. Accommodation is extremely limited but you can always try the National Trust for Scotland self-catering cottages by contacting 5 Charlotte Square, Edinburgh Tel. 031 226 5922.

Muck

Two miles long, Muck is easily the smallest of the isles. Its name, translated from Gaelic, means 'sea pig', referring to the porpoises which play in **Gallanach Bay**. It is also the site of a beautiful shell beach fed by the Atlantic drift where West Indian beans are often washed ashore. Killer whales, dolphins and grey seals can also be sighted off-shore. The most fertile of all the isles, it has a vast tree plantation of native and exotic species. Again, there is very little accommodation.

Argyll and the Inner Hebrides

INTRODUCTION

Argyll and the Isles is an area endowed with considerable and varied natural beauty embracing magnificent woodland, mountain and coastal scenery, while the warming effect of the Gulf Stream encourages many excellent floral displays in public gardens throughout the region. There is also a rich historical legacy for visitors to discover in the form of numerous castles, ancient monuments and prehistoric sites.

HISTORY

The large number of burial cairns and ritual stones, clustered in an area just north of Lochgilphead, were erected by a group of Gaelic-speaking Celts who crossed the water from Ireland in the early Dark Ages. They are said to have brought the Stone of Destiny with them (see chapter on 'Perth') and by the end of the fifth century they had established the Kingdom of Dalriada covering much of present-day Lorne and Arygll. By the mid-sixth century the influx of missionaries from Ireland, including St Columba, had turned Argyll and the Isles into a burgeoning centre of Christianity with Iona at its heart. In the ninth century the Norsemen descended upon Scotland, but nowhere apart from Orkney and Shetland did they ensconce themselves as firmly as they did in the Western Isles and the west coast of the mainland. Their control of the islands in the west, all the way down to Bute, lasted until the defeat of King Haakon of Norway at the Battle of Largs in 1263. It is from the Nordic leaders that the powerful chiefs of the clans of MacDonald and Campbell are descended. From the 12th century Argyll was the scene of their fierce struggles for power and land, for they rarely paid any heed to the authority of the Crown. Their most infamous clash took place in the Glencoe massacre of February 1692, when the Campbells conspired with the officers of William and Mary in a vile and treacherous assault on the MacDonalds, contrived by the Crown in an effort to make an example of how it would deal with recalcitrant Highlanders who continued to refuse unconditional submission to its authority.

COMMUNICATIONS

Oban is within easy reach of Glasgow either by car or by train. From here there are ferry services to the islands of Mull, Iona, Coll, Tiree, and Colonsay. Further south at the head of the Kintyre peninsula there are sailings from Tarbert to Islay and Jura. The service to Rothesay on the Isle of Bute sails from Wemyss Bay, while departures to Arran are from Ardrossan to Brodick and from Claonaig to Lochranza. Details of the services can be obtained from the Head Office of Caledonian MacBrayne, The Ferry Terminal, Gourock (Tel. 0475 33755) or from local offices listed throughout the chapter where appropriate.

WHERE TO GO FOR WHAT

For those who want to get away from the clamour of the city, any of the islands off the west coast will offer something close to perfect tranquillity, particularly Jura, Islay, Coll, Tiree, and Colonsay. These islands are also notable for their wildlife and there are special wildlife day excursions on Mull. There are few places in the region which will fail to please the fisherman, although the salmon and trout in Loch Awe are especially recommended. The traditional seaside resort of Rothesay has much to commend it in the way of family holidays.

Starting in Oban, this chapter continues to Mull, Colonsay, Coll and Tiree; Lorne; Mid Argyll; Kintyre; Islay and Jura; and Arran and Bute.

Oban

OBAN is the principal town of the region, situated in the scenic district of Lorne, and it is the departure point for sailings to many of the islands. Its fine sandy beaches, good sea angling and amenities such as golf and pony-trekking make it a popular family holiday resort. In the town centre **Oban Distillery**, best known for its 'Oban 12 year old' malt, admits visitors to see the various stages of the production process (advance booking compulsory. Tel. 0631 64262) as does **Oban Glass Works** on Lochavullin Estate. **World in Miniature** on North Pier has displays of miniature furniture and dioramas. What looks like a Roman Amphitheatre in the hillside above the harbour is **McCaig's Tower**, an unfinished 'folly' started in 1897, providing excellent views across the water to the Inner Hebrides. The **Highland Theatre** George Street, offers a Highland Exhibition and audio-visual presentation, with its theatre and cinema open for shows and the very latest films. Two miles north of the town is **Ganavan**, site of a safe, sandy bathing beach. Sailing from Gallanach, two miles south of Oban, there is a frequent ferry service for passengers only to **KERRERA**, the closest island to Oban where the principal attraction is the ruined 16th-century **Gylen Castle** on the southern shore. The **Sealife Centre**, ten miles north of Oban at Barcaldine, is an enjoyable way for all the family to spend a day. You can see a wealth of marine life, especially Oban's famous seals. The new Sealab provides a hi-tec audio-visual display for an even better insight into sea creatures. On the A816, seven miles south of Oban at Kilvener, is the **Highland Salmon Centre**, yet another attraction for all the family. It presents the fascinating story of the Atlantic salmon from its birth in the burns to its migratory journey to the Arctic, and its amazing return journey back to the waters of Scotland. There is a walk-on salmon farm and live exhibitions. The centre also has a restaurant with views over Loch Feochan, a gift shop and a special counter selling smoked salmon and shellfish, which can even be sent to family and friends by way of vacuum-packed post. **Hebridean Pursuits Ltd** are based by Oban (Tel. 063171 317) and deal in walking, sailing and painting holidays to the Outer Hebrides and Island of St Kilda on board a converted fishing vessel.

Visitors to Oban have a generous choice of fine accommodation. The **Alexandra Hotel** (Tel. 0631 62381) on Corran Esplanade is in an attractive position overlooking the harbour and charges upward of £29. The **Columba Hotel** (Tel. 0631 62183) on the Esplanade has a similar seascape view and charges from around £25. Prices at the **Caledonian Hotel**, Station Square (Tel. 0631 63133), start around £30. Two-crown commended bed and breakfast accommodation is available from **Mrs A. Edwards**, Drummore Road (Tel. 0631 63544), who charges from £15, and **Mrs Harold**, Longsdale Road (Tel. 0631 64974), whose rooms cost £16.50 upwards. Two caravan parks convenient for Oban are, the **Ganavan Sands Caravan Park** (Tel. 0631 62179) and the **Oban Caravan Park**, Gallanchmore Farm, Gallanch Road (Tel. 0631 62425), with room for tents as well as touring caravans and motors. Caravans can also be let. **Tourist Information** is available all year in Argyll Square (Tel. 0631 63122).

Islands of Lismore; Mull, and Iona; Colonsay, Coll and Tiree

Caledonian MacBrayne operate ferry services to all of the above islands. For details contact Caledonian MacBrayne Ltd, Ferry Terminal, Railway Pier (Tel. 0631 62285). The name of the island of **LISMORE** means 'Great Garden' and hints at the verdant countryside and abundance of flowers to be seen here, along with a variety of fauna and the ruined 13th-century castles of **Achadun** in the south-east and **Coeffin** in the north-east. Near the latter is the **Broch of Tirrefour**. **COLONSAY** benefits from the Gulf Stream which contributes in no small measure to its 500 different types of flora, many of which can be seen in **Kiloran Gardens**. Angling in the island's lochs is free. The smaller island of **ORONSAY** to the south, reached over a beach at low tide, contains the 14th-century ruins of **Oronsay Priory** on the site of an earlier foundation by St Columba. Within its 300 miles of coastline, **MULL**, the third largest of the Hebridean islands, has tremendously varied scenery: from fine sandy beaches and trout-filled lochs to volcanic cliffs and wooded hills. The ferry from Oban takes only 45 minutes and docks at **CRAIGNURE**. **Shieling Holidays** offer the unusual idea of carpeted cottage tents with real beds. A Shieling holiday will include facilities for a variety of activities including watersports, fishing and painting. Prices are from £30 per person. For more information Tel. 06802 496. From here visitors can travel with the **Mull and West Highland Narrow Gauge Railway Company** which runs a scheduled service on its 10¼-inch gauge railway to **Torosay Castle and Gardens**. The Victorian castle is open in part to the public from May to September, daily from 10.30 a.m. to 5.30 p.m. The 11 acres of garden are open all year during daylight hours. The journey from Craignure of just over one mile takes 20 minutes and includes some splendid mountain and woodland scenery. Torosay can also be reached direct from Oban by motor-boat as can the nearby home of the Chief of Clan MacLean, **Duart Castle**, built in 1250, restored in 1912 (open from May to September, daily from 10.30 a.m. to 6 p.m.). **TOBERMORY** in the north-east is the capital of Mull. A colourful and quiet town in an attractive location overlooking the bay, it is noted for its sea angling and has in Main Street the **Mull and Iona Museum**. The **Isle of Mull Wildlife Expedition** (Tel. 0688 2044) departing from Ulva House Hotel is an all-day Land Rover excursion in search of eagles, otters, red deer and other wildlife.

Accommodation is available from under £25 at the **Tobermory Hotel**, Main Street (Tel. 0688 2091), pleasantly situated on the waterfront, and the **Western Isles Hotel** (Tel. 0688 2012) in its position high above the bay has an excellent view across the Sound of Mull. Prices start at around £28. Less expensive are **Mishnish Hotel** (Tel. 0688 2009), **Ulva House Hotel** (Tel. 0688 2044), and **Ach Na Craoibh** (Tel. 0688 2301). **Tourist Information** is available at 48 Main Street (Tel. 0688 2182) from April to October (also from November to April, Monday to Friday, 9 a.m. to 11 a.m.).

South-west of Tobermory, the village of **DERVAIG** was credited by the *Guinness Book of Records* as once having the smallest theatre in the world in the 43-seat **Mull Little Theatre**. It also has **The Old Byre Heritage Centre**, with an audio-visual show, gift shop and licensed tea room (open from Easter to October). The **MV Alpha Beta** (Tel. 06884 223) sails from Quinnish Estate to take in the wildlife around the islands of Staffa, Coll, and Treshnish Isles and offers whale/dolphin-watching trips.

Calgary Bay has splendid sandy beaches and at its southern end the fine gardens of the **House of Treshnish**, whose owner took the name of the bay and nearby town over to Canada when he founded the city of Calgary. Three miles south of Ballygown is **ULVA FERRY** where there are regular sailings on the **MV Forss** (contact BJ & JD Burgess: Tel. 06885 239) to the **Treshnish Isles**, with their spectacular wildlife, and the uninhabited island of **Staffa**, famous for its spectacular rock formations and caves, the best known of which is **Fingal's Cave**, made famous by Mendelssohn in his Hebridean overture. **Adrioch Farm Guest House** at Dervaig (Tel. 06884 264) offers multi-activity holidays including sailing and bird-watching, as well as comfortable farm house accommodation, and is recommended by 'Taste of Scotland'. Prices are from £270 per week. The A849 runs along the northern shore of the peninsula in the south-west known as the Ross of Mull, terminating at **FIONNPHORT** from where Caledonian MacBrayne (Tel. 0631 62285) operate a ferry service making the short crossing to **IONA**. This island is famous as the 'Cradle of Christianity' in Scotland as a result of the arrival of St Columba and 12 followers in the mid-sixth century and their foundation of a monastery. Frequently attacked by Norse raiders, the original monastery was replaced at the start of the 13th century, and although this fell into decay, significant restoration work has taken place since the early 20th century and today it is the home of the Iona Community. Although the National Trust owns the island, the Iona Cathedral Trust owns and protects the religious buildings, the oldest of which is the restored **St Oran's Chapel** dating from the 11th century. The main sites are open to the public and within walking distance of each other. A singularly beautiful and spiritual place, Iona offers something different and special to the visitor. Take your time to discover the island if you should visit it. To learn more about the island, the **Iona Heritage Centre** at the Heritage Trust, The Manse (Tel. 06817 364), is worth a visit. **The Argyll Hotel** (Tel. 06817 334) is a small, friendly hotel by the sea shore with dinner, bed and breakfast from £36; vegetarians are catered for especially well. For slightly cheaper accommodation, **Mrs Manson** (Tel. 06817 523), and **Mrs Black** (Tel. 06817 323) offer dinner, bed and breakfast from £20.

The adjacent islands of Coll and Tiree, like Colonsay further south, are ideal holiday venues for anyone wishing to 'get away from it all', particularly if in addition they are fond of fine sandy beaches and wildlife. All three islands can be reached by ferry from Oban (details from Caledonian MacBrayne, the Ferry Terminal, Oban. Tel. 0631 62285; or Oban Tourist Information centre. Tel. 0631 63122). The journey to Coll takes three and a half hours, to Tiree four and a half hours, and to Colonsay two and a half hours. There are also flights from Glasgow to Tiree, from Monday to Saturday (contact Loganair, Glasgow. Tel. 041-889 3181).

The most populous of the three islands, with 800 inhabitants, **TIREE**'s excellent surfing conditions have earned it the nickname of the 'Hawaii of the North', and, along with Coll, it is rich in historic sites, the most notable of which is the Iron Age tower (broch) **Dun Mor Vaul** in the north-east of the island. There are also the remains of such structures near many of the lochs on **COLL** in addition to **Breacachadh Castle**, a restored 15th-century tower house near **Totronald** in the south-west (open occasionally. Tel. 08793 444).

Lorne

Four miles north of Oban, just off the A85, are the ruins of the 13th-century **Dunstaffnage Castle and Chapel** where Flora MacDonald was held prisoner, for helping Bonnie Prince Charlie in 1746 (open April to end of September, Monday to Saturday, 9.30 a.m. to 7 p.m., Sunday, 2 p.m. to 7 p.m.). At Connel Bridge one can, dependent on tide, view the **Falls of Lora** before crossing and continuing on the A828 through some of Lorne's magnificent countryside. Near **LEDAIG** on the A828 is the sumptuous country house hotel **Isle of Eriska** (Tel. 0631 72371), standing on a 300-acre private island in Loch Linnhe, linked to the mainland by a bridge. Dinner with wine, and bed and breakfast for two will cost in excess of £220 per night. **Benderloch** ('the hill between two lochs') offers some excellent hillwalking, while a less strenuous walk can be enjoyed in the grounds of **Ardchattan Priory and Gardens** (open from April to November) east of the main road on the northern side of Lower Loch Etive. **BARCALDINE** on the southern shore of Loch Creran has a fascinating display of seals, lobster, octopuses and other local marine life at the **Sea Life Centre**. From the quiet coastal village of **PORT APPIN** there is a frequent passenger-ferry service to the island of Lismore (see above) and luxury accommodation from March to November in the **Airds Country House Hotel** (Tel. 063173 236). Meals are prepared by Scotland's only female Chef Laureate of the British Academy of Gastronomes in conjunction with Graeme Allen the son of the owners. Last year they were awarded a Michelin Star. North of Port Appin, **Castle Stalker**, built around the turn of the 15th century and recently restored, stands on an island in Loch Laich. Not much further north is Appin Home Farm, location of **Appin Wildlife Museum** and its examples of local wildlife, and beyond that, **Dalnashean**, a three-acre garden lined with beech and spruce trees protecting its collection of delicate shrubs.

Mid Argyll

Running diagonally south-west/north-east **LOCH AWE** for 30 miles forms a natural border separating Argyll from Lorne and has an excellent reputation for trout and salmon fishing. Water from Loch Awe is pumped to a reservoir 1,200 feet up Ben Cruachan, for inside this mountain is a 400,000KW pumped storage power station. A visitor centre here explains hydro-electricity, and guided tours are available. Open from Easter to October off the A85, 18 miles east of Oban. From the shore at the northern end of the loch, visitors can see the ruins of the 15th-century **Kilchurn Castle** (not open to the public) standing on an island. From here the A819 runs south through the village of **Cladich** where there is a monument in memory of the writer Neil Munro, best known as the author of *Para Handy* and a native of **INVERARAY**, which lies nine miles south of here by the shore of Loch Fyne. Much of this picturesque town was reconstructed in elegant style in the 18th century after being largely destroyed in 1644 by the Marquess of Montrose in his attack on the Duke of Argyll.

The Duke of Argyll is the chief of the Campbells of Argyll, and Inveraray Castle has long been the family seat. What remained of the 15th-century original castle was demolished and rebuilt, along with much of the town, under the supervision of the 3rd Duke at the start of the 18th century. William and John Adam – father and son, respectively – along with Roger Morris contributed to this majestic edifice, with John Adam responsible for much of the interior decoration and mantelpieces. This was added to by Robert Mylne under the auspices of the 5th Duke and the fine decor, along with portraits by Gainsborough, Ramsay, and Raeburn can be admired by the public (open from April to June, and then September to mid-October, Monday to Thursday and Saturday, from 10 a.m. to 12.30 p.m. and 2 p.m. to 5.30 p.m., and during July and August, Monday to Saturday, 10 a.m. to 5.30 p.m., Sunday 1 p.m. to 5.30 p.m.). The bell tower of **All Saints Episcopal Church** houses Scotland's heaviest ring of 10 bells (and the third heaviest in the world). **Inveraray Jail** houses 'living' exhibitions of this 19th-century prison with sounds, smells and trials in progress to help bring the past to life, as well as a macabre collection of items from the Scottish Prison Service. It was recently awarded the 'Scottish Tourist Board Attraction of the Decade' award (open all year, 9.30 a.m. till 6.00 p.m.). **Argyll Wildlife Park** can be found two miles from Inveraray, with Europe's largest collection of wildfowl and a strong emphasis on Scottish wildlife.

Overlooking lochs Shira and Fyne, the **Great Inn** (Tel. 0499 2466) has 25 rooms with prices starting at around £23. For a similar price there is the **George Hotel** (Tel. 0499 2111); **Fern Point Hotel** (Tel. 0499 2170); and **Loch Fyne Hotel** (Tel. 0499 2148). For bed and breakfast accommodation, there are the two-crown commended **Mrs MacClaren**, Old Rectory (Tel. 0499 2280) and **Mrs MacLugast** Creag Dhubh (Tel. 0499 2430), charging from £11 upwards.

The **Tourist Information** centre (Tel. 0499 2063) is open from April to September.

Two miles along the A83 from Inveraray, **Argyll Wildlife Park** has over 50 acres of woodland and waterways, providing a home for over 100 species of wildfowl. **Auchindrain Old West Highland**

Township and Museum of Country Life is a fascinating recon-struction of an 18–19th-century Highland village with period furnishings and displays on a bygone way of life. A few miles away is **Crarae Quarry Fish Farm** with its informative visitor centre and nearby **Crarae Gardens** with their fine collection of azaleas and rhododendrons and three-colour-coded walks through the glen and in to some beautiful coutryside. The road curves sharply to skirt the shores of Loch Gilp, at the head of which is **LOCHGILPHEAD** (**Tourist Information** available from April to September, Tel. 0546 602344).

Kintyre

TARBERT is situated on an isthmus, south of which extends the longest peninsula in Scotland, Kintyre. The town is a prosperous fishing village and yachting centre with good sea angling in Loch Fyne. It is overlooked by the ruined 15th-century **Tarbert Castle** which stands on the site of an earlier one built by Robert the Bruce in 1325. **Tourist Information** is available from April to September (Tel. 0880 820429). **Stonefield Castle Hotel** (Tel. 0880 820836), two miles north on the A83, is an elegant baronial house designed in 1837 by the renowned architect Sir William Playfair. Guests can stay here in considerable comfort from around £41 for dinner, bed and breakfast, but admission for visitors to its splendid 50 acres of garden – containing Himalayan rhododendrons and rare trees and shrubs from South Africa and New Zealand – is free.

From Tarbert the A83 runs down the western shore of the peninsula, passing through the small town of Tayinloan from where there are day cruises making the short journey across the Sound of Gigha to the island of that name. Once on **Gigha**, visit **Achamore House Gardens** to see the many species of subtropical plants which flourish in the mild climate here. Just to the south of Ardminish are the ruins of 13th-century **Kilchattan Church**. The road crosses back to the east coast of Kintyre further south and comes to an end at **CAMPBELTOWN**, a popular tourist centre with good fishing. There are boat trips to the small island of **Davaar** where, on the wall of a cave on the opposite side of the island to the lighthouse, the artist Archibald MacKinnon painted a lifesize Crucifixion scene in 1887. **Campbeltown Library and Museum**, Hall Street, boasts a display of archaeological remains. Campbeltown's **Tourist Information** centre is on the Pier (Tel. 0586 552056) and is open year round.

Opposite the north end of Kintyre, and across Loch Fyne, lies the **Cowal Peninsula** and the town of **DUNOON**. This 19th-century coastal holiday resort makes for an interesting day or two. Among the attractions on offer is the opportunity to take one of the steamers on the Clyde around the Cowal Peninsula. Fine walking country lies all around you, and the four-mile promenade and traditional seaside entertainments make it a popular family day's outing from Glasgow. The highlight of the season comes with the **Cowal Highland Gathering**, held on the last Friday and Saturday in August. Over one hundred pipebands can be heard, and traditional dancing and Highland sports can be seen.

In town, the remains of the 13th-century **Dunoon Castle** are a fascinating sight, but for livelier times, make for the social hub of Cowal – the **Royal Clyde Yacht Club**, just outside the town at Hunter's Quay. There's hardly a weekend during the summer without some regatta or race on, and the atmosphere is always lively and sociable. The **Cowal Golf Course** is also in Dunoon, on Ardenslate Road, charging £13 daily Monday to Friday, and £17 on Saturday and Sunday. Golfing holiday packages are very popular in this area and are booked through the various golf hotels.

Dunoon is the gateway to some of Scotland's magnificent west Highland scenery, and the ferry to Gourock is a popular approach for those travelling up from the south. **Tourist Information**, 7 Alexandra Parade (Tel. 0369 3785) is open all year. There are plenty of good hotels in the area, as this is a popular Scottish holiday resort; amongst the best are the **Esplanade Hotel**, West Bay Promenade (Tel. 0369 4070), family-run with 57 bedrooms and under £30 a night; and the **Ardfillayne Hotel**, West Bay, Dunoon (Tel. 0369 2267). This 150-year-old mansion, set in seven acres of woodland, has an elegant Victorian restaurant where 'Taste of Scotland' dishes are served, with prices starting from £29 to £55 per night.

Accommodation in Dunoon will only be a problem when a major regatta is on, or in the 'Glasgow Fair Holidays', when the tradesmen of Glasgow take their annual two weeks in mid-July. Except during these times, the large supply of hotels and bed and breakfast accommodation should be sufficient.

Another attraction in this area is the **Younger Botanic Garden** at Benmore, seven miles north of the town, off the A815. Open during the months from 15 March to October (from 10 a.m. to 6 p.m.), this is an important collection of trees and shrubs, with unusual species. Equally popular is the **Argyll Forest Park** further north, with its many nature walks and trails, some of which leave from the Younger Botanic Garden. The Tourist Information Centre can assist ramblers with a series of hill and forest walk maps, along with a hill walker's guide and information on all the routes.

Islay and Jura

The beautiful and romantic island of **ISLAY** is reached by car ferry from Kennacraig near Tarbert in 2¼ hours. Caledonian Mac-Brayne operate a service three or four times a day to Port Ellen in the south-east of the island. (Caledonian MacBrayne, Ferry Terminal, Kennacraig. Tel. 088973 253; or Port Ellen: Tel. 0496 2209). The island has many attractions for the visitor. Its unspoilt scenery forms the ideal backdrop for holidaymakers seeking a restful time away from it all. The angler is well catered for with good trout and salmon fishing in the rivers, and there is plenty of wildlife for those prepared to seek it out. The **Museum of Islay Life** is at Port Charlotte, and has a display of artefacts telling the story of the people of Islay. Alongside is the **Ellister Bird Sanctuary** with approximately 30 species of swans, geese and ducks in a scenic environment. The **Trekking and Riding Centre** at Rockside Farm, Bruichladdich (Tel. 0496 85231), offers horses to suit all aptitudes as well as farm rides for children. The island is most famous for its whisky production and at **PORT ELLEN** visitors can enjoy a tour round the world-renowed **Laphroaig Distillery** (advance booking compulsory. Tel. 0496 2418/2393).

North on the A846, the village of **BOWMORE** is home of the oldest distillery still in full-time production, **Bowmore Distillery**, and also **Bowmore Round Church**, built thus to deny the devil corners to hide in.

From here the road runs north-east to **PORT ASKAIG** where the frequent car ferry crosses the narrow Sound of Islay to **FEOLIN FERRY** on the island of **JURA**. Caledonian MacBrayne (as above) also operate a service to Feolin Ferry from Kennacraig. There is only one road which runs up the east coast of this mountainous island through a number of small communities, the largest of which is the village of **Craighouse**. Although the population of the island in the east is sparse, it still exceeds that of the west, where there are some magnificent beaches and caves, but no people. The **Paps of Jura** at 2500 feet attract climbers and birdwatchers. This is the Scotland of postcards – desolate, spectacular and untouched by man. Interestingly, George Orwell wrote much of his famous novel *1984* whilst staying on the island.

Arran and Bute

The island of **ARRAN**, off the west coast of Ayrshire, is a popular holiday destination. Caledonian MacBrayne (Ferry Terminal, Gourock. Tel. 0475 33755; Brodick: Tel. 0770 2166; Ardrossan: Tel. 0294 63470) run ferry services from Ardrossan on the mainland to Brodick, and from Claonaig in Kintyre to Lochranza. The north of Arran is a beautiful mountainous region, and from the highest peak – **Goatfell** at 2,866 feet – one is in the rare position of being in sight of three countries: Scotland, Ireland, and England (four if one includes the Isle of Man). Goatfell is quite easily reached from **BRODICK**, one of the island's largest villages, situated in a bay half-way down the east coast. The hire of boats and wind-surfing equipment is available from **Brodick Boat Hire** on the beach (Tel. 0770 2388). Mountain bikes and 3-speed cycles to tour the island can be hired from **Brodick Cycles**, Roselynn (Tel. 0770 2460). Dating from the 13th century, **Brodick Castle**, to the north, is the ancient seat of the dukes of Hamilton and houses many fine paintings, and silver and porcelain items (open during April and October, on Monday, Wednesday and Saturday; and May to September daily, 1 p.m. to 5 p.m.). In 1980 the castle's gardens became a country park, and contain a pleasant woodland trail and a fine collection of rhododendrons (open all year, daily, 9.30 a.m. to sunset). The **Isle of Arran Heritage Museum**, on the edge of town, occupies an 18th-century croft and has an exhibition on the history of the island up to the 1920s.

Brodick has a good selection of accommodation. **Auchrannie Country House Hotel** (Tel. 0770 2234/5) charges from around £22.50. From around £21 or less there are Douglas Hotel (Tel. 0770 2155); and the Glenartney Hotel (Tel. 0770 2220). For bed and breakfast accommodation costing £12 upwards, try **Mrs Sutherland**, West Mayish (Tel. 0770 2364) or **Mrs S. MacMillan**, Glenard (Tel. 0770 2318). The two-crown commended **Glendoy Farm House** (Tel. 0770 2351), offers rooms and with good home cooking in a peaceful setting in a century-old sandstone house. Prices start at £16. **Carraig Mhor** (Tel. 0770 6453) is a first-class restaurant in Lamlash serving *haute cuisine* using local produce. The **Tourist Information** centre on the Pier (Tel. 0770 2140) is open all year. **Brodick Highland Games** are worth noting, held around the beginning of August each year. Check the Tourist Information Centre for details.

The island's main road runs in a complete circuit all around Arran's coast passing through many picturesque villages and taking in some splendid seaside scenery. In the west, just north of Blackwaterfoot, there is a series of caves including **King's Cave**, rumoured to have been the site where Robert the Bruce had his famous encounter with a spider. According to legend, Bruce took refuge here and was contemplating abandoning the struggle to secure Scotland's independence when the sight of a spider, persevering against numerous setbacks to spin its web, inspired Bruce to likewise reapply himself and persevere with the fight. Further north and east the standing stones of **Machrie Moor** are fascinating to visit. Relics from the Neolithic and Bronze Ages have been found here also. In **LOCHRANZA** in the north are the ruins of **Lochranza Castle**, once a popular hunting seat of Scotland's kings.

The island of **BUTE** is a popular choice for family holidays, particularly the busy resort of **ROTHESAY** on its east coast (car ferry from Wemyss Bay on the mainland. Caledonian MacBrayne, Tel. 0475 520521). This town has for long been a popular destination for holidaymakers from Glasgow, attracted by its picturesque appearance, fine beaches and sporting amenities such as golf, bowls, and tennis. The phrase going 'doon the water' became synonymous with holidays to Rothesay. **Rothesay Castle** was built at the turn of the 11th century, since when it has changed its structure and ownership many times. What remains of the castle today is an outstanding example of a high-walled 13th-century fortification with a unique circular courtyard.

The **Winter Garden Pavilion** on the town promenade dates from the late 19th century. Recently restored to its former glory, complete with bandstand, it now forms part of a 90-seat cinema and houses a Heritage Centre highlighting the history of the town. A Promenade Bistro and souvenir shop complete this thoroughly 1990s restoration. **Bute Museum**, on Stuart Street, exhibits local and natural history as well as the archaeology of the island (open daily in summer 10.30 a.m. to 4.30 p.m, reduced hours in winter).

Rothesay has a large choice of accommodation in keeping with its popularity. In six acres of garden, **Glenburn Hotel**, Glenburn Road (Tel. 0700 502500), charges from around £26. From under £20 there is a very good standard of accommodation available at the **Royal Hotel**, Albert Place (Tel. 0700 503044); **Guildford Court**, Watergate (Tel. 0700 503770); and **Ardyne Hotel**, Mountstuart Road (Tel. 0700 502052). For good bed and breakfast accommodation, there is **Mr and Mrs Clegg**, Glenarch (Tel. 0700 502033), charging from £11.50, and **Agnes Patrick Guest House** (Tel. 0700 505271), charging from £16. **Roseland Chalet Park**, Canada Hill (Tel. 0700 504027), offers pitches for touring and motor caravans as well as tents from £4 to £5 per night. There are also holiday caravans to let.

The **Tourist Information** centre is at 15 Victoria Street (Tel. 0700 502151) is open all year.

Stirling, Loch Lomond and the Trossachs

INTRODUCTION

The area covered in this chapter is one chiefly characterized by countryside of outstanding natural beauty. Stirling in the south–east is dominated by its ancient castle and is closely linked with Scottish history and the battles for Scottish independence in the 13th and 14th centuries. Further west, in the centre of this region are the breathtaking hills and lochs of the Trossachs district, praised in prose by, among others, Sir Walter Scott, Dorothy and William Wordsworth and Queen Victoria. It is also Clan Gregor country and its association is particularly strong with the most infamous clansman of them all, Rob Roy Macgregor. The town of Callander, east of the Trossachs, is known as the 'gateway to the Trossachs', while Stirling is 'gateway to the Highlands'. In the west, Loch Lomond is the largest, and arguably most attractive, inland stretch of water in Britain, with its picturesque towns and villages, such as Luss, the 'Take the High Road' TV village, and to the south-west the villages are set against the magnificent scenery of the banks of the Clyde and Gare Loch.

HISTORY

In the south-east of the region, Stirling occupies a prominent place in the history of Scotland, for it was at Stirling Bridge in 1297, and nearby Bannockburn in 1314, that William Wallace and Robert the Bruce, respectively, won decisive battles which repelled the English threat to Scotland's independence. Under the Stuarts, Stirling developed into a favourite royal residence. James III was born here in 1451 and James V spent much time in Stirling, often moving among his subjects in disguise in order to learn more about them. It was here that Mary Queen of Scots was crowned at the age of nine months and her son James VI of Scotland and I of England spent his childhood. The hereditary office of Keeper of Stirling Castle was restored to the Earl of Mar and Kellie in 1923 after having been forfeited by his ancestor in 1715. Before then the office had been held by the Erskine family from 1370. The town's history prior to the 12th century is largely unknown, although there is evidence that the site had been developed by the Romans and by the ancient Britons before them. In the west, Dumbarton was the capital of the former Kingdom of Strathclyde and is believed to have been the birthplace of St Patrick late in the fourth century.

COMMUNICATIONS

Stirling has good road and rail links to all parts of the country, including the Trossachs and the southern shores of Loch Lomond, while the motorway puts it within quick and easy reach of Glasgow and Edinburgh (30 and 40 minutes away, respectively). In the west, the A82 runs all the way along the west bank of Loch Lomond, making it easily accessible in a 30-minute drive from the centre of Glasgow.

WHERE TO GO FOR WHAT

In a region characterized by its outstanding countryside, it is hard to isolate the beauty spots, but for wide vistas, forests, lochs and spectacular Highland mountain scenery the **Trossachs** is particularly recommended. **Loch Lomond**, in addition to its scenery, has much to offer those interested in boating, from yachts to pleasure cruises. In the north-east, **Lochearnhead** is Scotland's premier watersports centre, while **Killin** is notable for its salmon and trout fishing in the rivers Lochay, Dochart, and Loch Tay. The sightseer with a sense of history will find much to enjoy in and around Stirling.

This chapter begins with Stirling in the south-east of the region before going north-west to the Trossachs, north to Killin, and then south-west via Crianlarich to Loch Lomond and the Clyde.

STIRLING is one of the most important towns in Scotland's history, having featured prominently in the campaigns of Sir William Wallace and Robert the Bruce to secure the country's independence in the 13th and 14th centuries. In later years it was a popular royal residence of the Stuarts. Nowadays it is of strategic importance to the tourist, lying, as it does, within easy reach of Glasgow and Edinburgh, and connected by good road and rail links to all parts of Scotland.

The town's most imposing feature is **Stirling Castle** (open from April to September, Monday to Saturday, 9.30 a.m. to 5.15 p.m., and 10.30 a.m. to 4.25 p.m. on Sunday; and from October to March, Monday to Saturday, 9.30 a.m. to 4.20 p.m., and on Sunday, 12.30 p.m. to 3.35 p.m.). Most of its present buildings date from the 15th and 16th centuries, but it is believed that the castle rock may have been occupied by the Romans and subsequently, according to legend, by King Arthur. At the castle entrance, on the esplanade, is a statue of the victorious Bruce – the hero of the battle of nearby Bannockburn in 1314 – and a visitor centre with an audio-visual display. Most of the buildings inside the castle are open to the public and include the **Argyll and Sutherland Highlanders' Museum** (open all year). There are also displays of artwork, and, at Queen Victoria's Look-out at the north-west corner of the ramparts, panoramic views of the surrounding countryside.

Down from the castle esplanade, in Castle Wynd, is **Argyll's Ludging**, an admirable example of an old town residence, dating from 1632. Further on, at the corner of St John Street, is **The Church of the Holy Rude**, which dates from 1414, and is the only functioning Scottish church to have witnessed a coronation: James VI, aged 13 months in 1567, and before that, Mary Queen of Scots in 1543, aged nine months. Also in St John Street is **The Guildhall** or **Cowane's Hospital**, built between 1634 and 1649 as an almshouse. Continuing in the same direction and along Spittal Street, one arrives at the **Old Burgh Buildings** and nearby, on Corn Exchange Road, the **Municipal Buildings**, in whose stained glass one can trace the history of Stirling. Part of the **Old Town Wall** can be seen opposite the Albert Halls. Further west on Dumbarton Road is the **Smith Art Gallery and Museum**. At the north end of town is the **Old Bridge** across the River Forth, dating from around 1400 and situated near the site of **Wallace's** famous victory over the English at the Battle of Stirling Bridge in 1297. His memorial, the **Wallace Monument**, is one and a half miles north-east, off the A997. It is a 220-foot tower on top of Abbey Craig, built between 1861 and 1869, with a statue of the man above the doors. Inside, Wallace's struggles and victories are retold in imaginative ways. Visitors can talk tactics in the battle tent, see Wallace's mighty two-handed sword, and enjoy some of Scotland's most striking views. The circumstances of Scotland's most famous victory are explained at the **Bannockburn Memorial and Information Centre**, two miles south on the A80. One mile east of the town are the ruins of **Cambuskenneth Abbey**, founded in 1147 (closed in winter). A short distance north on the road to Bridge of Allan is the University of Stirling, on whose modern campus is the **MacRobert Art Centre**, which is the venue for film shows, theatre, opera, and art exhibitions. Phone the box office for programme details (Tel. 0786 461081/473171, ext. 2543). During the summer there is an explosion of events with the award-winning **Royal Stirling Summer Programme**. It includes traditional Scottish entertainment such as ceilidhs, pipe bands, fiddlers and a two-week tartan festival. History also comes alive around this time in the form of street plays, medieval markets and banquets, heritage trails and ghost walks. Carnival is celebrated around the second Sunday in June, and the Beating of the Retreat with fireworks provides a spectacular finale to it all.

Stirling is the base for the company **C'n Do Scotland Ltd**, Howlands Cottage, Sauchieburn (Tel. 0786 812355), who offer Scottish walking holidays at all levels in the Trossachs and elsewhere in Scotland.

As a busy town with much to offer its many visitors, Stirling and its environs have a wide choice of accommodation. The **Park Lodge Hotel**, 32 Park Terrace (Tel. 0786 474862), overlooks the park and castle and prides itself on its *haute cuisine* and wine cellar. Prices start from around £37.50. A little more expensive is the four-bedroom **Heritage Hotel**, 16 Allan Park (Tel. 0786 473660), with its fine restaurant. The **Golden Lion Hotel**, 8 King Street (Tel. 0786 475351), has 70 bedrooms from just under £28. At a more modest price is **Garfield Hotel**, 12 Victoria Square (Tel. 0786 473730), which has seven rooms from over £24. From less than £16 there are: **Dalglennan House**, 4 Allan Park (Tel. 0786 473432); **Firgrove Guest House**, 13 Clifford Road (Tel. 0786 475805), which is only open from April to October; and **Forth Guest House**, 23 Forth Place (Tel. 0786 471020). Outside Stirling, the **King Robert Hotel** (Tel. 0786 811666) overlooks the site of the Battle of Bannockburn, and has 22 bedrooms from around £23. In the beautiful Ochil countryside, **Blairlogie House Hotel** (Tel. 0259 761441) stands in 11 acres of private gardens, and has seven bedrooms from around £27. Slightly further away, in Alloa to the north-east of Stirling, is **The Gean House** (Tel. 0259 219275), a magnificent country house hotel with a growing reputation for excellent cuisine and comfort. It is unashamedly at the luxury end of the market, with dinner costing £29 a head and the cheapest double room £120 a night. A new flagship hostel has opened in Stirling in the very centre of the old town built to the highest European standards and providing small dormitories and self-catering facilities. Contact the Scottish Youth Hostel Association, 7 Glebe Street, Stirling (Tel. 0786 451181). Two restaurants offering good value in the centre of town are **Littlejohns**, Port Street (Tel. 0786 463222), and **The Arches**, 35/37 Upper Craigs (Tel. 0786 470972).

The **Tourist Information** office at 41 Dumbarton Road (Tel. 0786 475019) is open all year, and at 16 Broad Street (Tel. 0786 479901) from April to September.

The A91 east from Stirling runs through **MENSTRIE** and the 16th-century **Menstrie Castle**, home of Sir William Alexander who founded Nova Scotia. It houses a Nova Scotia Exhibition Room and is open by arrangement with the National Trust for Scotland's office in Perth (Tel. 0738 31296). The road continues through the old weaving town of Alva to **TILLICOULTRY**, where the **Clock Mill Centre** in Upper Mill Street has displays on the weaving industry. The **Mill Glen** is a beautiful glen in the Ochil Hills, worth the walk to the upper glen where there are eight waterfalls close together.

Further on is the beautiful town of **DOLLAR**, one mile south of **Castle Campbell** which was built in the late 15th century by the Earl of Argyll and burned in 1654 by Cromwell's troops. It is an impressive sight, lying on a steep slope beneath the Ochil Hills, amid the attractive woodland of Dollar Glen (open from April to September, Monday to Saturday, 9.30 a.m. to 6 p.m., and on Sunday 2 p.m. to 6 p.m.; and October to March, Monday to Saturday, 9.30 a.m. to 4 p.m. and on Sunday, 2 p.m. to 4 p.m. Closed Thursday afternoon and Friday, October to March). **Dollar Glen** has many interesting walks to Castle Campbell and hillwalkers can continue across the Ochil Hills to Glendevon.

Head north-west from Stirling, off the A84, and you come to the safari park **Blair Drummond**, the first of its kind in Scotland. (Phone 0786 841456 for opening hours). North of here is **DOUNE**, notable for **Doune Castle** (open to the public). It was built around the turn of the 14th century and is one of the best preserved and restored examples of medieval architecture in Scotland. The cars in **Doune Motor Museum** (open from April to October) belong to the Earl of Moray and include the world's second oldest Rolls Royce.

From Doune, head west towards the Trossachs and what is arguably the most spectacular scenery anywhere in Britain. It can be approached via either Callander in the east or Aberfoyle in the south. The road from Doune to the latter passes the **Lake of Menteith** (the only lake in Scotland) and the island on the lake which houses the ruins of the 13th-century **Inchmahome Priory**. Access is by **PORT OF MENTEITH**, a popular spot with anglers.

ABERFOYLE is a good base from which to explore the splendour of the countryside, a worthwhile introduction to which is provided by the Forestry Commission's excellent **Queen Elizabeth Forest Park Visitor Centre** (open March to October – Tel. 08772 258), one mile north of Aberfoyle, off the A821. Here the visitor will find valuable information on the extensive activities available in the park, including fishing, mountain paths, and cycle ways in an area of outstanding natural beauty. Alternatively, the beauty of the countryside can be enjoyed in more leisurely fashion by following Forest Enterprise's **Loch Achray Forest Drive** north of Aberfoyle, leading to picnic places, walks, cycle-ways and spectacular views of the Trossachs. **Dounan's Outdoor Centre** (Tel. 08772 291) is an ideal place for youth groups with cedar wood cabin accommodation and sports equipment for hire. Prices per night for those between the ages of 8 and 16 are £14; for those over 16 it is £16.10. Contact the centre for details of full board and self-catering charges.

There is a reasonable choice of accommodation in and around Aberfoyle. From £19 there is the **Forth Inn**, Main Street (Tel. 08772 372). **Inverard Hotel**, Loch Ard Road (Tel. 08772 229), is a large country house, commanding fine views from its hillside location and offering free fishing to residents. Prices start at around £25. Accommodation at the **Bailie Nicol Jarvie Hotel** (Tel. 08772 202) is available from £25; the attractive **Covenanters Inn** (Tel. 08772 347) is a little more expensive. For bed and breakfast accommodation, **Mrs Coe**, Manse Road (Tel. 08772 427), overlooking the Trossachs, charges from £14 per person. For camping and caravan facilities, there are two sites: the **Cobleland Campsite**, Forest Enterprise, two miles south of Aberfoyle (Tel. 08772 392), charging between £4.50 and £5 for motors, tourers and tents; and the **Trossachs Holiday Park**, three miles south of Aberfoyle (Tel. 08772 2614), charging between £6 and £8. Ten holiday caravans for up to six persons are also available to let. A restaurant of note in Aberfoyle, with national awards and an excellent reputation, is the **Braeval Mill**, just outside the village, by the golf course on the Stirling road (Tel. 08772 711).

Aberfoyle has a new major attraction in the **Scottish Wool Centre**, which demonstrates sheep-shearing and has exhibitions on the importance of wool in Scotland's history. There is also a large shop and tearoom. Located near the car park in the centre of the village, it is popular with all the family, and an example of the new, more upmarket type of tourist attraction being developed in both Aberfoyle and Callander, where tatty souvenir shops are being replaced by craft shops and tearooms offering home baking.

The north-eastern shores of Loch Lomond can be reached by the scenic road to Inversnaid. From Aberfoyle the B829 runs along the wooded shores of Loch Ard and Loch Chon, then north through

Loch Ard Forest before joining the road connecting Stronachlachar on the banks of Loch Katrine and **INVERSNAID**. For most of its four miles, the road skirts the northern shore of Loch Arklet. Accommodation is available at this tranquil spot on the banks of Loch Lomond at the **Inversnaid Hotel** (Tel. 087786 223), which stands in grounds of 65 acres and offers guests private fishing, moorings, and boat trips from its own harbour. It is open from February to November, and prices start at around £20. A footpath north along the shore (actually part of the 'West Highland Way') leads to **Rob Roy's Cave** one mile away.

STRONACHLACHAR is a departure point for the *SS Sir Walter Scott* (Tel. 041–355 5333), which cruises the loch regularly, and it is three miles by foot or bicycle – there is no public access road, the land around Loch Katrine being the property of the Strathclyde Water Board – along the shore to **GLENGYLE**, the birthplace of Rob Roy.

Returning to Aberfoyle and heading north for seven miles through Achray Forest and the Duke's Pass, one reaches the **TROSSACHS**. The name may mean 'bristly country' and refers to the narrow wooded gorge running between Loch Achray and Loch Katrine and flanked by Ben A'an in the north and Ben Venue in the south-west. Loch Katrine is in the midst of an area of outstanding natural beauty which has been widely celebrated in literature, most notably by Sir Walter Scott, who used Ellen's Isle, in Loch Katrine, as the setting of his poem. 'The Lady in the Lake'. It also fired the imaginations of William and Dorothy Wordsworth, and was witness to Rob Roy Macgregor's exploits in the 18th century. The scenic beauty of the loch can be enjoyed on the SS *Sir Walter Scott*, which cruises the loch daily in summer. **Ellen's Isle** is situated near the shore at the east end of the loch and is named after Ellen Douglas. On a less salubrious note, it was used by the Macgregors to store their stolen livestock. In Callander's old St Kessogs Church in the Main Street is a visitor centre devoted to Rob Roy and the Trossachs, with a multi-vision theatre and a talking-head life and time exhibition.

From the Trossachs, the A821 runs east for nine miles along the banks of lochs Achray and Venachar to join the A892 and on to **CALLANDER**. The town is an excellent location from which to see the splendid scenery of the Trossachs, and was the setting, under the fictitious name of 'Tannochbrae', for the television series 'Dr Finlay's Casebook'. On the road in from Doune is the **Heather Centre** at Keltie Bridge, which has, in addition to heather, extensive collections of trees, shrubs, house plants, and a miniature railway to transport visitors around the grounds (open all year, 10 a.m. to 6 p.m.). A short distance to the east and west of town, respectively, are the **Bracklinn Falls** and the **Falls of Leny**, notable beauty spots in an area of outstanding scenery in general.

As it is a popular place with tourists, Callander has a wide choice of accommodation. **Arden House Guest House**, Bracklinn Road (Tel. 0877 30235), has magnificent views and the distinction of being the 'home' of Dr Finlay in the television series. It is open from March to October and prices start below £16. The cost is similar at **Brook Linn Country House** (Tel. 0877 30103) which stands in two acres of gardens amid splendid countryside. **Gart House** (Tel. 0877 31055) is a 19th-century baronial mansion standing in 12 acres verging on the River Teith. It offers private salmon and trout fishing and a snooker room. Prices are from £24–30. The 17th-century **Roman Camp Hotel** (Tel. 0877 30003) is of luxury standard, standing in 20 acres of garden beside the River Teith. It too offers guests the opportunity of private fishing. Open all year, prices start at around £35. The restaurant of this country house hotel is the town's best and booking is advisable. The highly commended **Arran Lodge Hotel**, Leny Road (Tel. 0877 30976), offers bed and breakfast accommodation from £17. The Knowe, Ancaster Road (Tel. 08777 30076), is family-run with good home-cooking. Prices start at £15. Camping and caravan facilities are available from the following: **Callander Holiday Park**, Invertrossachs Road (Tel. 0877 30265), and **Gart Caravan Park** (Tel. 0877 30002), charging from £8 for tourers and motor caravans; **Cambusmore Estate, Auchenlaich Caravan Park** (Tel. 0877 30811), charging from £5.50 for tourers and £4.50 for motor caravans and tents.

The **Tourist Information** office is at the Rob Roy and Trossachs Visitor Centre, Ancaster Square (Tel. 0877 30342), open from March to December.

From Callander the visitor has the choice of either going west to the Trossachs or following the A84 north through the Pass of Leny towards Killin near the south-western extremity of Loch Tay. On its way the road runs through spartan moorland, woodland, and along the entire eastern shore of Loch Lubnaig before coming to **STRATHYRE**, celebrated in the song 'Bonnie Strathyre'. The village, in the shadow of Ben Sithean, is a popular hillwalking centre, and to the south is Strathyre Forest with Forest Enterprise's **Strathyre Forest Information Centre** which has displays on all aspects of sylvan life, as well as picnic areas and walks (open May to September).

There is a modest selection of small hotels and guest houses in the town. **Ben Sheann Hotel** (Tel. 08774 609); the 17th-century farmhouse **Creagan House** (Tel. 08774 638); and **The Inn** (Tel. 08774 224) all offer accommodation from under £20.

Stoneslaney Farmhouse (Tel. 08774 676), offers bed and breakfast accommodation in a restored 18th-century building, with trout fishing available. **Mr and Mrs Reid** (Tel. 08774 288) are in the centre of the village and charge from £12. On the southern outskirts of Strathyre, **Immervoulin Caravan and Camping Park** (Tel. 08774 285) charges £5.50 for motor caravans and tents and from £6 for tourers.

The A84 goes north through Strathyre Forest to Kingshouse where there is a road branching west to **BALQUHIDDER** on the shore of Loch Voil. The churchyard contains **Rob Roy's Grave**, which, along with those of his wife Helen and two of his sons, Coll and Robin Oig, are marked by three flat gravestones enclosed by railings. **Balquhidder Glen** is one of Scotland's most beautiful glens with views from the Braes of Balquhidder across Loch Voil and Loch Doine. Balquhidder is also the location of the luxurious **Stronvar Country House Hotel** (Tel. 08774 688), a former laird's mansion with fine views of the mountainous countryside and Loch Voil. Prices start at around £40.

Situated on the western shores of Loch Earn, **LOCHEARNHEAD** claims to have Scotland's leading centre of its kind in **Lochearnhead Watersports Centre** (Tel. 05673 330/245), offering instruction in water-skiing, dinghy sailing, and windsurfing. Equipment is also available for hire without tuition. Further north, **KILLIN** is reached by bridge over the spectacular **Falls of Dochart**. It is surrounded by splendid mountainous countryside, and is an excellent base for the angler to enjoy the salmon and trout fishing in Loch Tay, and the rivers Dochart and Lochay. **Killin Church** was founded in 1744 and contains a ninth-century font. Half a mile north are the remains of **Finlarig Castle**, and its macabre beheading pit. **Ardeonaig Outdoor Centre**, by Killin (Tel. 0567 820523), has trained staff, accommodation and expert instruction in outdoor pursuits. Family holidays are also available. Bed and breakfast prices start at around £10.60 per person.

The wide choice of accommodation in the town reflects the appeal Killin has for its many visitors. **Morenish Lodge Hotel** (Tel. 0567 820258) is a former shooting lodge on the banks of Loch Tay, offering guests private fishing rights. Prices including dinner start at just under £35, and it is open from April to October. Special provision for fishing is also offered by **Dall Lodge Hotel** (Tel. 0567 820217), a room costing from £22, and **Clachaig Hotel** (Tel. 0567 820270), near the Falls of Dochart, with rooms from around £18.

The **Tourist Information** centre is on the Main Street (Tel. 0567 820254), open from April to October.

The A85 runs south-west through Glen Dochart to **CRIANLARICH**, from where the A82 heads north to the magnificent scenery around **TYNDRUM** and the Highlands beyond, and south through the villages on the west bank of Loch Lomond, through Dumbarton by the River Clyde, and then on to the centre of Glasgow. The **West Highland Visitor Centre** is just south of the junction of A82/485 at Tyndrum for information about the wildlife of Scotland and the West Highland Way; outdoor swimming pool, restaurant, caravan and camping park are also available.

At **TARBET** (on Loch Lomond, not to be confused with Tarbert, Loch Fyne) in 1263 the men of King Haakon of Norway relaunched their boats in Loch Lomond after sailing up Loch Long and hauling them two miles overland from **ARROCHAR**. Both towns are popular with climbers heading north-west to some of the most impressive mountains in Argyll. Tarbet has a good choice of accommodation. On the edge of the loch is the Scottish baronial-style **Tarbet Hotel** with 91 rooms (Tel. 03012 228) which costs from £15 per person and is open all year round. **Loch Long Hotel**

(Tel. 03012 434) in Arrochar is a lochside hotel and has 81 bedrooms from under £25 (open February to December.).

Tourist Information is available from April to October on the main street. (Tel. 03012 260).

At 24 miles long, and five miles across at its widest, **LOCH LOMOND** is the largest inland stretch of water in Britain. More importantly for the visitor, it is also one of the most attractive. The wide southern half contains almost all of the loch's 30 islands. The largest is **Inchmurrin** which contains the ruins of **Lennox Castle** and, along with **Inchlonaig**, was used as a place to isolate the drunk and insane. The islands of **Clairinch, Torrinch**, and **Inchcailloch** are nature reserves. The latter, which incidentally means 'Island of the Old Women', was formerly the burial ground of the MacGregors.

The best way to appreciate the beauty of the loch and its islands is by boat, either on a scheduled cruise or by hiring your own. **Loch Lomond Sailings**, Balloch Marina (Tel. 0389 51481), run cruises all the year round. **Sweeney's Cruises**, Riverside, Balloch (Tel. 0389 52376, evening: 51610), operate all the year round and also let fishing and rowing boats. **MacFarlane & Son**, The Boatyard, Balmaha (Tel. 036087 214), operate a year-round service to the islands and also have fishing boats for hire. **Cullins Yacht Charters**, in Ardlui (Tel. 03014 244), have a variety of boats for hire, from dayboats to two- and three-berth yachts.

Of the towns and villages around the banks of Loch Lomond, **BALLOCH** in the south is a popular resort and departure point for cruises on the loch, quickly reached by car or train from Glasgow. **Balloch Castle and Country Park**, dating from the early 19th century, stands in 200 acres of its own country park and is open to the public from Easter to September. Park open daily, sunrise to sunset.

A new de luxe hotel has recently opened at **Alexandria**. The **Cameron House Hotel** (Tel. 0389 55565) is in the country club mould, complete with time-share accommodation complementing the country house hotel. Standards are impressive and for a few days relaxation after Glasgow, it is well worth considering with bed and breakfast from £64 per person. Only a 30-minute drive from

Glasgow International Airport the hotel stands on its own 108-acre estate, including one mile of private lochside. The 68 luxury bedrooms have superb views over the loch. Leisure facilities are extensive: 225-boat marina, nine-hole golf course, tennis, croquet, squash, badminton, two swimming pools, gymnasium and health and beauty facilities. Dining in one of three restaurants offers an excellent choice of the finest Scottish cuisine. As a convenient base from which to enjoy the attractions of Loch Lomond and its banks, Balloch offers a generous choice of reasonably priced accommodation. **Balloch Hotel** (Tel. 0389 52579), to the south-east of Loch Lomond, has rooms from £29. **Anchorage Guest House**, Balloch Road (0389 53336), provides accommodation from just over £15. Information on the many bed-and-breakfast and guest houses can be obtained from the **Tourist Information** centre in the refurbished Balloch Station building (Tel. 0389 53533), March to November.

BALMAHA, at the end of the B837 on the east shore, is a popular spot for fishing and boating, and the point at which the **West Highland Way**, the footpath running 95 miles from the outskirts of Glasgow to Fort William, joins the shore of the loch. There is a boat service from here to **Inchcailloch Island**, which forms part of the **Loch Lomond Nature Reserve**. Further up the shore, the road comes to an end at **ROWARDENNAN**, from where there is a well-trodden path to the top of **Ben Lomond**. The time taken for the upward journey averages about three and a half hours, and about two hours for the return.

South of Loch Lomond the coastal road from Dumbarton on the banks of the Clyde and Gare Loch passes through some picturesque seaside towns and spectacular scenery. **DUMBARTON**, 14 miles from the centre of Glasgow, was important in the ancient Kingdom of Strathclyde, and is reckoned to have been the birthplace of St Patrick in the late fourth century. It was here he was captured, and from here he sailed as a prisoner to Ireland. The attraction for the visitor today is the historic **Dumbarton Castle** at the summit of the 240-foot-high Dumbarton Rock, views from the top of which are superb. Further on is **CARDROSS**, where Robert the Bruce died in 1329, and **HELENSBURGH**, birthplace in 1888 of John Logie Baird, the inventor of television. On Upper

Colquhoun Street, visitors can admire the work of the architect and designer Charles Rennie Mackintosh in the form of the **Hill House** and its furniture. It was built between 1902 and 1903 and is open daily throughout the year from 1 p.m. to 5 p.m. The **Hieland-man's Road** is a footpath one mile west of the town on the A814, leading to a viewpoint giving outstanding views across the Clyde to Kintyre. The **MV Kenilworth** sails from Helensburgh for cruises around the scenic **Holy Loch** from May to September (Tel. 0475 21281). **Tourist Information** is at the Clock Tower (Tel. 0436 72642), from April to October.

Glasgow

INTRODUCTION

Glasgow, over the years, has acquired a reputation for many things, some of them good, some of them bad, some of them true. The early 1980s saw an extended PR campaign by the city fathers to change the negative image that had for a long time been circulating in the outside world. It was true that the city in its modern form was built on the backs of an undervalued workforce, and that on the other side of the grand Victorian architecture were slum conditions arising from desperate overcrowding and inadequate pay. But conditions in Glasgow were essentially no different from any other industrial centre; they just existed on a larger scale, and the extremes of poverty on one side of the city were matched by extremes of grandeur on the other. It is the latter, rather than the former, which is now being emphasized for the benefit of the outside world. Glaswegians were already appreciative of the fact that Glasgow had some of the finest Victorian architecture in Britain, and some of the era's grandest townplanning to be seen anywhere in Europe; that it had more acres of parkland than any other city in Europe, and so on. But for many, the recent redemption of the city has come too late. The now gleaming sandstone buildings were cleaned up and returned to something like pristine condition, only after half of the city had been demolished. Glasgow suffered particularly badly from the craze for what was euphemistically known as 'urban redevelopment' which afflicted Britain's town planners and architects in the three decades after the war. Witness the outlying estates – rows and rows of shapeless, characterless houses which sprang up to accommodate people whose city-centre tenement homes were demolished; and districts like Springburn, once a vital part of the city and home to the huge workforce of its world-renowned locomotive works, but now reduced to a wasteland. With all this the excitement over the 1990 'Cultural Capital of Europe' accolade could be interpreted as an inversion of priorities. The 'Glasgow's miles better' campaign

GLASGOW

1 Provand's Lordship
2 Glasgow Cross, Mercat Cross, Tron Steeple, Tolbooth Steeple
3 People's Palace and Templeton's Carpet Factory
4 Kelvingrove Art Gallery
5 Glasgow School of Art
6 The Tenement House

7 Third Eye Centre
8 Museum of the Royal Highland Fusiliers
9 Mitchell Library
10 Museum of Transport
11 Hunterian Museum and Art Gallery including Mackintosh House
12 Glasgow Botanic Gardens including Kibble Palace
13 Haggs Castle
14 Museum of Education
15 Calderpark Zoo
16 Burrell Collection
17 Pollok House
18 Springburn Museum
19 Glasgow Royal Concert Hall
20 McLellan Galleries

has been replaced by a new slogan, 'Glasgow's Alive', which continues to enhance Glasgow's status as one of the great cities of Europe. The unpalatable facts about the past should not deter the visitor. It is an indication of how grand Glasgow once was that there is still plenty to admire, even though the city has changed so much that many former citizens no longer recognize it.

The main reason to visit Glasgow is not to admire the perfectly restored Victorian architecture, nor to indulge in the culture, nor take part in some of Europe's hottest nightspots now on offer, but to meet, listen to and befriend the city's greatest asset – the Glaswegians. A more warm-hearted, humorous, pithy, thoroughly likeable bunch of people would be difficult to find (and this is written by a lass from Edinburgh – the traditional rival). To appreciate some of their repartee get hold of a copy of *The Patter* by Michael Munro – a compendium of Glasgow sayings which is guaranteed to enrich your stay in the city.

HISTORY

Glasgow's history can be traced back to the sixth century, when its patron saint, St Mungo, founded a church on the site of the present Glasgow Cathedral. The cluster of houses which grew around it went under the name of Gles Ghu, meaning 'green place', and which later underwent the slight transformation to 'Glasgow'. Significant expansion took place from the 12th century onward, as a result of the increased importance of the cathedral, and, unlike towns in the east, Glasgow's development continued unimpeded as the city remained untouched by the civil conflict arising from the Stuart succession and the squabbles of the nobles. Even the Reformation, which made an indelible mark on important ecclesiastical towns such as Perth, St Andrews and Elgin, impinged on Glasgow only to the extent that Catholic icons were removed from the cathedral, the structure itself remaining undamaged to the present day. In the 16th and 17th centuries Glasgow was winning the admiration of many visitors from England and abroad, among whom Daniel Defoe was moved to declare its architecture the finest in Britain outside London.

Towards the end of the 17th century, Glasgow began to import tobacco, sugar, and cotton from America, business which expanded considerably when the Act of Union gave Scotland's traders access to England's colonies. By the time this trade was foreclosed by the American War of Independence, Glasgow had been reshaped by the profits of the 'tobacco lords', wealthy merchants who brought tobacco from across the Atlantic and re-exported it to the rest of Europe. Although this trade disappeared almost as soon as the first shot was fired in the American campaign for independence, the economy did not falter, for the export of tobacco was replaced by the weaving of cotton and the export of cloth to the same European markets.

The most significant phase in the city's economic and social history came in the 19th century, with the development of steam power and heavy industry. The River Clyde was enlarged to accommodate steam ships, and the dockyards which built them – along with the engineering works and other heavy industry – earned Glasgow a world-wide reputation as the 'Second City of the Empire', and, until recently, served as the mainstay of the local, and indeed, national, economy. The Victorian period left an enduring mark on the city, not just in its architecture, but in its population. Glasgow took on a cosmopolitan character as people from all over Scotland and Ireland migrated here in search of work. But the laissez-faire capitalism which brought wealth to the city also brought dire poverty and slum housing; facts about Glasgow which somehow managed to travel further abroad than any other, spreading a distorted image of the city, which has only been redressed in the last decade.

Glasgow, today, is in the early stages of revival, emerging from the bleak postwar period in which the solution to overcrowding was deemed to be the wholesale demolition of parts of the city, the construction of concrete tower blocks, and the resettlement of the urban population in outlying, barren estates. This absurd thinking only changed when the money ran out in the late 1970s, and the authorities were forced into devising a cheaper strategy; and so it was that the Victorian buildings, which give the city so much of its essential character, were cleaned and restored to such good effect that the authorities now bend over backwards to preserve an original façade where, only a few years ago, they were intent on destroying it. It is to be hoped that this new respect for past achievements is not to be subject to the vagaries of municipal fashion. One need not stray too far from George Square, however, to realize that in many places, the damage has been irrevocable.

COMMUNICATIONS

Glasgow has an excellent road system. From the city centre, both Edinburgh and the bonny banks of Loch Lomond are accessible in under an hour. There are two railway stations. Central Station is for trains serving western Scotland, London Euston, the west of England, and Wales; Queen Street Station serves eastern Scotland, the West Highlands and has a half-hourly service to Edinburgh.

Within the city, there is an efficient, but limited, underground railway, which runs on one circular line covering the centre and the west of Glasgow. There is a more extensive overground railway network, which, like the underground and buses, is operated by Strathclyde Transport, whose information office is in St Enoch Square (Tel. 041–226 4826).

There is a bus service from the city centre to Glasgow International Airport (Tel. 041–887 1111) at Abbotsinch, seven miles to the west, receiving flights from numerous UK airports, including Aberdeen, Belfast, Leeds, Manchester, Newcastle, Birmingham and London, as well as a number of direct flights from Europe. Also transatlantic flights, direct from the USA and Canada, were introduced in 1990. A useful service for visitors is provided at the airport by Airparks (Tel. 041–887 3321), Linwood, who run a security car-parking service. Daily rates are around £2.60, or £20 for a week, £30 for a fortnight – which are well below NCP prices.

TOURIST INFORMATION

The Greater Glasgow Tourist Board and Convention Bureau has offices in the city centre at 35 St Vincent Place (Tel. 041 204 4400) at Glasgow International Airport (Tel. 041–848 4440) and at Paisley Town Hall (Tel. 041-889 0711). Another office, at Gourock Pierhead (Tel. 0475 39467), is open during the summer months only.

ACCOMMODATION

Glasgow has a long list of hotels and guest houses offering a wide choice of accommodation to suit all pockets and tastes.

FIRST CLASS
In the luxury bracket, in addition to the new Hilton, there are several four-star AA hotels and the five-star Moat House International. The **Moat House International** (Tel. 041–204 0733), Congress Road, is a grand addition to this vibrant city: a glass-panelled skyscraper on the River Clyde, the facilities match anything you will find in Hong Kong or New York. Its position next to the Scottish Exhibition Centre assures that it has a large clientele, so book ahead. The **Copthorne Hotel** (Tel. 041–332 6711), George Square, in an ideal central location, offers excellent service and comfort in each of its 141 rooms. So too do the **Glasgow Marriott** (Tel. 041–226 5577) in Argyle Street, the magnificent **Stakis Glasgow Grosvenor** (Tel. 041–339 8811) in Grosvenor Terrace, and the **Forte Crest Glasgow** (Tel. 041–248 2656) in Bothwell Street. An alternative is the **White House**, 11–13 Cleveden Crescent (Tel. 041–339 9375). An Adam-style town house offering self-catering flats and mews cottages. **One Devonshire Gardens** (Tel. 041–339 2001) offers 27 *en-suite* antique-strewn bedrooms, an excellent dining room, and country house service. At 5 Devonshire Gardens is the **Devonshire Hotel** (Tel. 041 339 7878), a splendid Victorian town house which comes highly commended and offers 16 rooms with *en-suite* facilites. The **Town House Hotel** in West George Street (Tel. 041 332 3320) and **Cathedral House** in Cathedral Square (Tel. 041 552 3519) offer excellent central accommodation. The new **Glasgow Hilton**, in William Street (Tel. 041 204 5555), has top-class accommodation in its 320 bedrooms. It is Glasgow's first five-star hotel and Scotland's first Hilton International.

BUSINESS CLASS
Carrick Hotel (Tel. 041-248 2355) in Argyle Street offers a high standard of accommodation. Equally commendable is the **Buchanan Hotel** (Tel. 041-332 7284) in Buchanan Street, and the **Marie Stuart Hotel** (Tel. 041-424 3939) in Queen Mary Avenue. An out-of-town suggestion is the **Black Bull Thistle Hotel**, in Main Street, Milngavie (Tel. 041-956 2291). Just north of Glasgow, this is an ideal choice for those continuing on to the Trossachs.

ECONOMY
Glasgow has a high proportion of inexpensive hotels and guest houses, such as the **Ewington Hotel** (Tel. 041-423 1152) in Queen's Drive on Glasgow's southside. The **Adamson** (Tel. 041-882 3047) in Crookston Drive offers comfortable accommodation in a central location. The **Burnbank** (Tel. 041-332 4400) on West Princes Street has a distinctive Victorian-style interior, and offers guests a high standard of accommodation. Hostel accommodation is available at *Jordanhill College* to the west of the city at 76 Southbrae Drive (Tel. 041 950 3320). Prices are from £16.70. Sports facilities are freely available on campus. Glasgow's most recent youth hostel at 7/8 Park Terrace (Tel. 041 332 3004) was formerly the well-known Beacons Hotel. Catering for 170 visitors, it still promises the same high standard of service and has *en-suite* facilities. Prices are from £7.25 per person.

EATING OUT AND NIGHTLIFE

It was no fluke that Glasgow became Britain's choice as Cultural Capital of Europe 1990. Its resources in the visual arts are matched in the performing arts; the city being home to the BBC Scottish Symphony Orchestra, Royal Scottish Orchestra, Scottish Opera, Scottish Ballet, and many theatres. The **Glasgow Royal Concert Hall**, 2 Sauchiehall Street (Tel. 041 332 6633), is the city's prestigious new venue for an exciting variety of events, and the home of the Royal Scottish Orchestra. The **Theatre Royal** (Tel. 041-331 1234), Hope Street, is the city's

premier theatre and regular host to the excellent Scottish Opera
and Scottish Ballet. The **Kings Theatre** (Tel. 041–227 5511) in
Bath Street is a major venue for a variety of top national and
international acts, while the **Pavilion Theatre** (Tel. 041–332 1846)
in Renfield Street is a regular venue for variety shows and rock and
pop concerts. The **Citizens' Theatre** (Tel. 041–429 0022/8177) in
Gorbals Street always has an interesting programme, as does the
Mitchell Theatre (Tel. 041–552 5961) in Granville Street and the
Tron Theatre (Tel. 041–552 3748) in Parnie Street.

Glasgow has a large selection of excellent restaurants which
cover just about every price range. Below is a selection of one or
two of the best eating places listed in three price brackets.

FIRST CLASS
Rogano (Tel. 041–248 4055), 11 Exchange Place: has an art deco
style, exceptional food (especially the fish) and an impressive wine
list – remember to book ahead.

Café Gandolfi (Tel. 041–552 6813), 64 Albion Street: has a
continental ambience, excellent smoked salmon dishes, and good
value with its daily specials.

One Devonshire Gardens, (Tel. 041 339 2001) offers beautiful
cuisine matching the fine quality of the house.

The Buttery (Tel. 041–221 8188), 652 Argyle Street: an
excellent restaurant, decorated to resemble a Victorian hunting
lodge, serving Scottish *nouvelle cuisine*.

BUSINESS CLASS
Forte Crest Glasgow (Tel. 041–248 2656), in Bothwell Street:
Glasgow's most sumptuous hotel has a superb carvery restaurant
offering tremendous value.

The Belfry (Tel. 041–221 0630), 652 Argyle Street: with its
interior design modelled on an English church, complete with
pews and pulpit, this is in the basement of the more classy Buttery.
The menu is particularly good on fish dishes.

The Ubiquitous Chip (Tel. 041–334 5007) in Ashton Lane, just
off Byres Road: menu equal in originality to its name, backed by
one of the most extensive, and impressive, wine lists in Scotland.

ECONOMY

Baby Grand (Tel. 041–248 4942), Elmbank Gardens, Charing Cross: specializes in fish dishes.

Turban Indian Restaurant (Tel. 041–638 0069), 2 Station Road, Giffnock: specializes in Glasgow's favourite culinary delight – excellent Indian food (open from 5 p.m. to midnight).

The **Fire Station** (Tel. 041–552 2929), 33 Ingram Street: offers lots of pasta with original sauces (open on Sundays and bank holidays).

SIGHTS

GEORGE SQUARE is situated at the very heart of Glasgow. Famous figures represented among the statuary here include James Watt, Robert Burns, William Gladstone, Robert Peel, and Sir Walter Scott. The likeness of the latter surmounts an 80-foot column intended for that of George III, after whom the square was named. However, in consequence of the monarch's insanity towards the end of his reign, Glasgow's authorities decided to give the premier spot to Scotland's foremost writer. The most striking aspect of the square is the **City Chambers**, dominating the whole of the east side, and built between 1883 and 1888 in Italian Renaissance style by William Young, and extended by John Watson in 1923. The external grandeur of the building is matched by the interior, which can be admired under the auspices of free guided tours, conducted Monday, Tuesday, Wednesday and Friday, at 10.30 a.m. and 2.30 p.m.

At the east end of Cathedral Street, **Glasgow Cathedral** stands on the site of the sixth-century original, around which the city developed. The present building, an imposing Gothic edifice, has been significantly enlarged since its construction in the late 12th and early 13th centuries. Although none of his bones survived the Reformation, **St Mungo's tomb** is in the cathedral's crypt, and a light burns permanently in the saint's honour. The choir and lower church date from the 13th century and are two of the most interesting parts of the building. There is free public admission to the cathedral, open daily throughout the year. The **St Mungo Museum of Religious Life and Art**, due to open in April 1993, will show the way religion in its many forms has influenced Glasgow. Divided into three main areas, there is also a gallery focusing on the great art inspired by religion.

Many of Glasgow's famous sons lie in the elegant and elaborate tombstones in the **Necropolis**, east of the cathedral, including the 19th-century Glaswegian merchant, William Miller, whose claim to fame is as author of the 'Wee Willie Winkie' nursery rhyme.

Just opposite the cathedral, in Castle Street, **Provand's Lordship** is the oldest house in Glasgow, and the only surviving late-medieval domestic building in the city. Originally built in 1471 as a priest's house, it now houses a small museum, incorporating much of the original timbers and furniture (open daily 10 a.m. till 5 p.m., Sunday 12 noon to 6 p.m. – no admission charge). It is thought that Mary Queen of Scots stayed in this house when she came to Glasgow in 1567 to visit her ailing husband Lord Darnley, who, incidentally, after making a quick recovery, returned to Edinburgh and was promptly murdered.

South of here, Castle Street and High Street lead to **Glasgow Cross** which, until the 19th century, constituted the city centre. The site is occupied by two of Glasgow's oldest landmarks: the **Mercat Cross**, a replica (1929) of the medieval original which was removed in 1659, and the **Tolbooth Steeple**, which is all that remains of the building of 1626. Around the corner in Trongate, the **Tron Steeple**, completed in 1637, is all that remains of the Church of St Mary, which was partially destroyed by fire in 1793.

South-east of the Cross, at the centre of **Glasgow Green**, is the **People's Palace** which houses a fascinating exhibition illustrating the social history of Glasgow. The material on display ranges from the writing desk of John McLean – the famous political activist whose work and courage brought him to the attention of Lenin – to the banana boots designed by the Paisley artist and playwright, John Byrne, and worn on stage by Billy Connolly. Other displays feature exhibits connected with the electoral reform movement of the last century, housing and working conditions over the years, and much more. The Winter Gardens, at the back of the building, house a variety of tropical plants and birds. From the entrance to the People's Palace, the visitor's gaze is inevitably drawn to the extravagant building on the right, which is a good example of the city's Victorian architecture. This is **Templeton's Carpet Factory** though it looks like the opulent residence of royalty. It was built in the late 18th century, and as its name implies, for nothing more luxurious than the manufacture of carpets. Its resemblance to the Doge's Palace in Venice is wholly intentional. Today it houses assorted offices.

West of **GEORGE SQUARE,** the stretch of Buchanan Street between Argyle Street and St Vincent Street contains a number of fine shops behind elegant façades, and also the recently opened Princes Square, an up-market shopping precinct full of designer labels. **St Enoch Centre** on Argyle Street offers high street shopping in a glass-covered mall. There is also a vast food court and an ice rink to amuse the shoppers and the non-shoppers alike. At the north end of Buchanan Street, Sauchiehall Street, running west, was once the premier thoroughfare in Glasgow, if not Scotland, but the years of 'urban redevelopment' have taken their toll and left scars, like the Sauchiehall Centre. Sauchiehall Street runs for two miles to Kelvingrove Park and Kelvingrove Art Gallery and Museum, passing a number of notable sights on the way, such as the **Glasgow School of Art** on the corner of Scott Street and Renfrew Street, designed by the city's outstanding architect, Charles Rennie Mackintosh. Escorted tours of the art school are available throughout the summer. North-west of here at 145 Buccleuch Street, the **Tenement House** is a relic of early 20th-century domestic life, built in 1892, and occupied by Miss Agnes Toward from 1892 until 1975. Miss Toward's concessions to changes in fashion in interior design were minimal, such as replacing her gas lighting with electricity in 1959. The flat is now owned by the National Trust who have restored the gas lighting and preserved the flat as an example of a bygone era (open from April to October, Monday to Sunday, 12 noon to 5 p.m., and from November to March on Saturday and Sunday, 2 p.m. to 4 p.m.).

Back on Sauchiehall Street, the **Centre for Contemporary Arts** at number 305 is a multi-purpose art centre, hosting frequently changing exhibitions during the day and occassional performances in the evening. **The Willow Tea Room** at Number 217 is housed in an original Mackintosh building. The 'Room de luxe', is once again a tea room restored to the original lilac and silver decor designed by Mackintosh in 1903 for Miss Katie Cranston. '**Glimpses of Mackintosh**' architecture tours are provided by the Charles Rennie Mackintosh Society in association with Strathclyde Buses. Departures are from St Enoch Square (Tel. 041 226 4876). At 270 Sauchiehall Street is the **McLellan Galleries**, an important venue for major touring and temporary art exhibitions. At number 518 is the **Museum of the Royal Highland Fusiliers**. On nearby Kent Road stands the **Mitchell Library**, the largest public reference library in Europe.

At the west end of Sauchiehall Street, where it joins Argyle Street, the area around Kelvingrove Park has enough places of interest to occupy the visitor for a day or more. **Kelvingrove Art Gallery and Museum** contains Britain's finest civic collection of European art. Particularly commendable are the displays of Impressionist and Scottish Colourist paintings and one of Salvador Dali's most famous works, *Christ of St John of the Cross*. The museum includes material on natural history, archaeology, Scottish history and ethnology, and collections of silver, pottery, porcelain, arms and armour. Across the road, the **Museum of Transport** was founded in 1964 but transferred to its present premises in 1988. It houses all forms of transport through the ages, from bicycles to railway engines. Its salient features include the reproduction of a 1938 Glasgow street scene, an extensive collection of trams, a reconstructed underground station, and a shipping display. Admission is free and it is open Mondays to Saturdays 10 a.m. to 5 p.m., and Sundays 12 noon to 6 p.m.

On the other side of the attractive **Kelvingrove Park** is Glasgow University, whose **Hunterian Museum and Art Gallery** are open to the public free of charge (open from Monday to Friday, 9.30 a.m. to 5 p.m. and on Saturday, 9.30 a.m. to 5 p.m.). The museum's founding in 1807 makes it the oldest in Scotland, which contrasts with the art gallery which was opened as recently as 1980. The latter has received much acclaim for its collection, which includes a number of works by Whistler and 19th- and 20th-century Scottish artists. An important feature of the gallery, for which there is no admission charge, is the **Mackintosh House**, occuping three floors and containing an interior reconstruction, including original furniture, of the architect's former Glasgow home.

Clyde Helicopters at the City Heliport on the same side of the river as the Scottish Exhibition and Conference Centre (Tel. 041 226 4261), offers a truly unique way of seeing Glasgow, with its daily scheduled helicopter tours. There is the City tour, concentrating on the city centre and the famous football stadiums for around £30, the City of Culture Tour which takes in the wider parameter of Glasgow's galleries, the University and Hogganfield Loch for around £40. The Spirit of Scotland Tour visits the Campsie Hills and Glengoyne Distillery, while another tour goes to Loch Lomond.

Beyond the City Centre

Two miles north-west of the city centre, the frequently changed floral displays at the **Botanic Gardens**, on Great Western Road, occupy over 40 acres, and include an impressive orchid collection inside the **Kibble Palace**. The gardens are open 7 a.m. till dusk, the palace 10 a.m. till 4.45 p.m. and the main glass houses open at 1 p.m. (noon on Sundays) and close at 4.45 p.m. (4.15 p.m. in winter). **Greenbank Garden** in Clarkston has 16 acres of public garden woodland in the care of the National Trust for Scotland and is open, for a small admission charge, all year from 9.30 a.m. till dusk.

At 100 St Andrew's Drive, three miles south-west of the centre of Glasgow, the 16th-century **Haggs Castle** is a museum designed primarily for children and featuring a reconstructed kitchen and Victorian nursery (open Monday to Saturday 10 a.m. to 5 p.m., Sunday 12 p.m. to 6 p.m.). The nearby **Museum of Education** in Scotland Street School contains an exhibition of furniture, equipment and material from Glasgow schools over a period of 80 years (open Monday to Friday from 10 a.m. till 5 p.m. and on Sunday 2 p.m. to 5 p.m.). **Rouken Glen** is one of Glasgow's most attractive parks with shaded walks, a waterfall and a butterfly house.

Glasgow Zoo, six miles south-east of the city centre, is open daily, 10 a.m. to 5 p.m.

When it opened in 1983, the **Burrell Collection**, three miles south of the city centre in Pollok Country Park, received a huge amount of publicity and visitors. The building, constructed specifically to accommodate the private collection amassed by the millionaire Sir William Burrell and gifted to the city in 1944, has received considerable critical acclaim for its design and is probably as interesting as some of its exhibits. The 8,000 artefacts from the ancient world, plus many later examples of oriental art and a few paintings from Europe, may resemble a rich man's bric-à-brac but it makes for a fascinating visit and there is no admission charge. Also in Pollok Country Park, **Pollok House** was the family home of the Maxwells from 1750 until gifted to the city in 1966 by Mrs Anne Macdonald. In addition to some ornate plasterwork and period furnishings, the house includes one of the finest collections of Spanish paintings in the UK.

Important aspects of the more recent, and relevant, past are preserved at **Springburn Museum**, Ayr Street (near Springburn railway station, a mile and a half north-east of George Square). The museum mounts long-running temporary exhibitions concerned with the social history of the area, famous for its railway works which formed one of the cornerstones of Glasgow's industrial success. Once a vital part of the city, Springburn was flattened in the 1970s and a decade later it consisted of little more than a motorway through wasteland. Happily now there has been some major building redevelopment with new flats, shops and the museum. The latter is strongly recommended to visitors wanting to get behind the 'City of Culture' cant for a more authentic view of Glasgow (open Monday to Friday from 10.30 a.m. to 5 p.m., Saturday 10 a.m. to 4.30 p.m. and on Sunday 2 p.m. to 5 p.m.).

East of Glasgow is the **Monklands district**, once called the 'workshop of the world'. Its spirit lives on in the award-winning **Summerlee Heritage Park** on West Canal Street, Coatbridge, with Victorian workshops and social history displays as well as the reconstructed historic buildings which house the tearoom and museum shop. There is also a working electric tramway and restored canal. The **Monklands Time Capsule** is nearby at Buchanan Street. Half-ice, half-water, this new attraction invites you to take a journey through time, with a health suite inside a

tropical volcano, prehistoric ice caves and ice discos, and it's
rubber ring and tidal wave machine along with a fully supervised
kiddies' play area.

Eight miles south-east of Glasgow at Blantyre, is the **David
Livingston Centre**, birthplace, memorial and now museum to
Scotland's celebrated explorer and missionary (open Monday to
Saturday 10 a.m. to 6 p.m., Sundays 2 p.m. to 6 p.m., tearoom
open April to September).

Still in the Strathclyde region, nestling in the Clyde valley less
than one hour either from Edinburgh or Glasgow, is the award-
winning **New Lanark Village and Visitor Centre**. This two-
hundred-year-old cotton-spinning village, is the finest example in
Scotland of an industrial township. Ideally situated next to a nature
reserve, there is an adventure playground, craft shops and a
Scottish wildlife centre. Both the village and the visitor centre are
open all year round 11 a.m. to 5 p.m.

The Firth of Clyde: 'doon the watter' to Largs

Following the Clyde for 30 miles or so from Glasgow, you can take
in several interesting towns and seaside resorts. This area was once
world renowned as part of the great Clyde shipbuilding industry.

Halfway between Glasgow and Greenock is a country house
hotel worth noting: **Gleddoch House**, Langbank (Tel. 0475
54711), which was built as a private house for the famous
shipbuilder, James Lithgow, and is now a de luxe hotel with 33
bedrooms, a fine dining room and a golf club. A stop-off is well
worth while to sample some of Scotland's finest fare.

Two interesting towns in this area are **Greenock** and **Gourock**.
The former was once home of the world's finest shipbuilding yards
but is now revamping in much the same way as Glasgow. It has a
number of fashionable new eating-places such as **C. C. Brown's** at
210 Dalrymple Street (Tel. 0475 888369) which serves good food in
a relaxed atmosphere. The seaside town of **Gourock**, from where
ferries leave for Dunoon and over to Argyll, joins on to the smart
West End of Greenock. It is an important centre for yachtsmen and
offers good views out over the Firth of Clyde. The **Cloch**

Lighthouse, a late 18th-century example, is still used to guide shipping through the water here, though these days it's more likely to be the yachts of wealthy Glaswegians than the great liners of 20 years ago. Watch out for the new Gourock Tourist Information centre which now incorporates Inverclyde's famous yellow kettle, one of the most popular attractions at the 1988 Glasgow Garden Festival (Tel. 0475 39467).

The medieval **Castle Levan** ruins are worth a look, and if you want to break your journey before crossing the water, **Castle Levan Hotel**, Cloch Road (Tel. 0475 31047), is a pleasant place to do it.

Largs is perhaps the most attractive of the coastal resorts, and is 10 miles up the coast from the Ayrshire town of Ardrossan. Looking across to Great Cumbrae Island and Bute, with their respective resorts of Millport and Rothesay, it is a town of guest houses, traditional seaside entertainments, and a plethora of retirement homes boasting invigorating sea air! Treat yourself to afternoon tea or an ice-cream in **Nardini's**, a famous waterfront café in art deco style. **Largs Yacht Haven** (Tel. 0475 675333) is an ultra modern marina complex, providing a water sports centre with excellent facilities. **Kelburn Country Centre, Fairlie** (Tel. 0475 568685) is set in the beautiful grounds of Kelburn Castle. Woodland walks, gardens and pony-trekking are just a few of the many facilities available open Easter to Mid-October, daily 10 a.m.-6 p.m. **Teddy Bear picnics** are also held here around the beginning of May. The **Elderslie Hotel** (Tel. 0475 686460), John Street, is situated on the seafront with superb views of Cumbrae, Bute and Arran. Prices from £30 per person. Don't miss **Viking Festival** at Largs in September, when the whole town commemorates the famous victory in 1263 when the Scots held off the Norwegian attack, their only defeat on mainland Scotland. An influx of Scandinavian entertainers descend upon the town.

Ayrshire and Burns Country

INTRODUCTION

This region is inextricably associated with Robert Burns, and has many place names familiar to his readers as the setting for his verse, particularly in **Ayr, Alloway,** where he was born, and **Mauchline** where he married. Less well known is the fact that another national hero was born in the region, namely Robert the Bruce, at **Turnberry** (although it must be added that there is a rival claim from another town further round the coast for this same distinction).

Most of Ayshire's places of interest are situated along its 60 miles of coastline, where visitors will find sandy beaches, resorts, castles, and a bountiful selection of golf courses. The golfer will immediately recognize the names of **Troon** and **Turnberry** as hosts of the British Open, though less well known is **Prestwick,** which until 1990 was the location of Scotland's only transatlantic airport before Glasgow was also granted 'gateway' status, and the venue of the first ever Open in 1860. These, however, are but a small selection of the courses in the area which are said to number almost 20 in as many miles. For family holidays, **Ayr** is recommended for its amenities and beach, while **Troon** and **Girvan** are also popular, but quieter, coastal resorts. Robert Adam's magnificent 18th-century **Culzean Castle and Country Park** is managed by the National Trust for Scotland, for those who appreciate history, architecture, and gardens.

The region is easily reached by road from north and south, and, being one of the major holiday resorts for Glasgow, the connections south from this city to the area are particularly comprehensive.

WHERE TO GO FOR WHAT

The ideal place from which to commence a tour of Ayrshire and
There is a plentiful choice of accommodation to suit all pockets

Burns Country is from the region's principal town and bustling holiday resort. **AYR** has an abundance of facilities for a family holiday, while being at the same time close to the tranquility of the countryside and the haunts where Robert Burns found the inspiration for his poetry. It is also an ancient town, having a Royal Charter from the very early 13th century, although few of its early buildings have survived. One exception is the **Auld Brig,** which features in Burns's dialogue, 'The Brigs of Ayr'. All that remains of the 13th-century church of St John the Baptist is **St John's Tower**, which may have been a late addition to the original structure. It is open to the public by arrangement, and from the top there is an excellent view of the town and its bay. Dating from 1654, the **Auld Kirk**, just off the High Street, is where Burns was baptized and attended the occasional service. The grand merchant's house in the town centre, **Loudoun Hall,** was built at the turn of the 15th century and is one of the oldest surviving examples of burgh architecture in Scotland.

Ayr has three 18-hole golf courses open to visitors, although it is specified that parties first apply in writing: **Belleisle,** Belleisle Park (Tel. 0292 41258); **Dalmilling,** Westwood Crescent (Tel. 0292 263893); **Seafield,** Belleisle Park (Tel. 0292 41258). Special golf holiday packages are provided by **Golf Enterprises,** PO Box 54, Ayr KA6 6HP (Tel. 0292 570067), including accommodation, green fees, and transport to and from the courses. Prices vary widely according to the type of accommodation required, ranging from top hotels to self-catering cottages. Similar packages with Ayrshire's Golfing Holidays can be arranged through the Ayrshire Tourist Board at Prestwick Airport, Suite 1005 (Tel. 0292 79000). **Ayr Golf Week** is held throughout Ayr around the beginning of June. Scotland's foremost course for both Flat and National Hunt racing is **Ayr Racecourse** (Tel. 0292 264179). Phone for fixtures and prices. Those who would rather be in the saddle than the grandstand can receive tuition and hire horses for trekking and jumping at the **Ayrshire Equitation Centre,** Castlehill Stables, Hillfoot Road (Tel. 0292 266267). For football fanatics there is the **International Youth Football Tournament** which is held in Rozelle Park at the end of May. Scotland's biggest flower show is also held here later, in August.

and tastes. At the top end of the range with prices starting from
between £30 and £45 are the **Savoy Park Hotel,** 16 Racecourse
Road (Tel. 0292 266112); the **Pickwick Hotel,** 19 Racecourse Road
(Tel. 0292 26011); the **Chestnuts Hotel,** 52 Racecourse Road (Tel.
0292 264393); **Stakis Station Hotel,** Burns Statue Square (Tel.
0292 263268); and the **Caledonian Hotel,** Dalblair Road (Tel.
0292 269331). From around £15 to £20 and less there are **Beach
Crest Hotel,** 9 Queens Terrace (Tel. 0292 264172); and **Arrandale
Hotel** (Tel. 0292 289959). Bed and breakfast accommodation is
plentiful in Ayr and costs from around £13 upwards per person.
For camping and caravan facilities, there are the following sites:
Croft Head Caravan Park (Tel. 0292 263516), charging £6 for
tourers and tents and £5 for motor caravans; **Heads of Ayr
Caravan Park,** Dunure Road (Tel. 0292 442269), charges from £7
for tourers and £6.50 for motor caravans and tents; and the
Sundrum Castle Holiday Park, Coylton, four miles east of Ayr,
(Tel. 0292 570057), charges from £8.50 for tourers, motor caravans
and tents. There are 193 holiday caravans to let.

For eating out, **Fausto's Restaurant,** 16 Cathcart Street (Tel.
0292 268204), offers a traditional Italian menu, while **Fouter's
Bistro,** 2A Academy Street (Tel. 0292 261391), has a menu with a
French flavour.

The **Tourist Information** centre at 39 Sandgate (Tel. 0292
284196), has a 24-hour answering service, open all year.

To the north of Ayr is **PRESTWICK,** Scotland's
oldest baronial burgh, known to have been a centre of
population since the 10th century. The town is famous in golfing
circles, having staged the world's first Open in 1860. The new
Ayrshire Tourist Board at Prestwick Airport has only recently
opened. For more information on the area, contact Administration
Centre, Suite 1005 (Tel. 0292 79000). Not far north is the quiet
seaside town and popular holiday resort of **TROON,** whose **Royal
Troon Golf Club** has, between 1923 and 1989, staged the British
Open on six occasions. Visitors are allowed to play here and on the
town's other three courses. **Troon Marina and Sailing Club** at
North Beach attracts yachting enthusiasts and visitors are very

welcome. Away from the centre of town the beautiful woodlands and gardens of **Fullerton Estate** offer a variety of walks and picnic areas. For a small town, Troon has some excellent hotels. **Marine Highland Hotel** (Tel. 0292 314444) overlooks the 18th fairway of Royal Troon Golf Course. It has 72 bedrooms and a superb leisure club with swimming pool and squash courts. Across the road is the small, friendly **Piersland House Hotel** (Tel. 0292 314747). The hotel was built for Sir Alexander Walker, founder of the famous whisky brand bearing his name, and is set in four acres of grounds including a Japanese garden. Prices are from around £42.50 for bed and breakfast per person. **Highgrove House** (Tel. 0292 312511), and **Lochgreen House** (Tel. 0292 313343), are sister hotels in Troon run by prize-winning chefs. For bed and breakfast accommodation around £13 **Mrs M. Gibson**, 16 Harling Drive (Tel. 0292 312555); **Mrs Hamilton**, 30a South Beach (Tel. 0292 313270) and **Mrs Irene Sharpe**, 7 Kilkerran Drive (Tel. 0292 312417).

Tourist Information is available at Municipal Buildings, South Beach (Tel. 0292 317696), from April to September.

On the southern outskirts of Ayr is **ALLOWAY**, made famous as the birthplace in 1759 of Robert Burns. The house where the poet was born has been turned into the **Burns Cottage and Museum** and there is an extensive collection of manuscripts and letters among the memorabilia on display. His association with the part of south-west Scotland that has become known as 'Burns Country' is explained at the **Land o'Burns** visitor centre by way of audio-visual display and exhibition. **Alloway Kirk** is the resting place of the poet's father, William, and, along with the 13th-century **Brig o'Doon**, features in the tale of 'Tam o'Shanter'. Near the bridge is the **Burns Monument** of 1820.

In 1777 the family moved to Lochlea Farm, and nearby **TARBOLTON**, several miles north-east of Ayr, was the centre of Burns's social life between the ages of 18 and 24. Here the visitor can see the 17th-century house known as the **Bachelors' Club**, taking its name after that of the literary and debating society set up here by Burns and his friends in 1780. It was also on these premises that he attended dancing lessons and was initiated as a freemason. The house is open from April to October and contains period furnishings and memorabilia.

The family moved further east to Mossgiel Farm, near **MAUCHLINE**, 11 miles along the A758 from Ayr, on the death of William Burnes in 1784 (around this time the 'e' was dropped from the family name). It was while ploughing the land here that Burns received the inspiration for the poem 'To a Mouse', from which the lines are frequently (and incompletely) taken: *'The best-laid schemes o' mice an' men/Gang aft a-gley/An' lea'e us nought but grief an' pain/ For promis'd joy!'* The **National Burns Memorial Tower** near Mossgiel Farm opened first in 1896 though it has been recently refurbished and now houses the Tourist Information centre, an interpretation centre and a viewing area on the roof of the tower. Back in Mauchline, where Robert met and married Jean Armour, the **Burns House Museum** (open Easter-September 1993) occupies the house where the couple leased a room in 1788. Four of their nine children are buried in the local churchyard along with many of the people characterized in the poet's work, while nearby is **Poosie Nansie's**, the inn which featured in the poem 'The Jolly Beggars'.

The **Tourist Information** centre is open all year (Tel. 0290 51916).

Nine miles south of Ayr on the A77, **MAYBOLE** is a busy town whose **Tolbooth** retains its 17th-century clock tower. The restored **Maybole Castle** (private) is a good example of Scottish baronial architecture, while the ruined **Collegiate Church** dates from the 15th century. Two miles further on are the substantial and extensive ruins of **Crossraguel Abbey**, founded in 1244 for Cluniac monks from Paisley. It remained in occupation until 1592, which is more recent than any other abbey in Scotland. Robert Burns attended school in the village of **KIRKOSWALD**, where visitors can see **Souter Johnnie's Cottage** (open from April to October). Souter (cobbler) Johnnie was a character in Burns's poem, 'Tam o'Shanter', based on real life cobbler, John Davidson, while Tam was modelled on Douglas Graham of nearby Shanter Farm. On display inside is period furniture, items connected with Burns, and cobbler's tools, while in the garden there are life-size figures depicting Souter Johnnie, Tam, the innkeeper, and his wife.

The A77 continues towards the coast and the internationally renowned golfing centre of **TURNBERRY**. The sumptuous **Turnberry Hotel** (Tel. 0655 31000) overlooks the Ailsa and the Arran courses, both of which are private, although visitors are admitted if a booking is made in writing. Little remains of **Turnberry Castle** which shares with Lochmaben, near Dumfries, the claim to be the birthplace of Robert the Bruce in 1274. This link led to its decline and the castle's destruction in 1307. The coastal road back to Ayr passes **Culzean Castle and Country Park**, a magnificent building constructed between 1777 and 1792 by Robert Adam, standing in 560 acres of woodland, deerpark, and gardens. Notable features of the castle are the Round Drawing Room, the fine plaster ceilings, and the majestic oval staircase. The Eisenhower Presentation explains the castle's connection with the United States General – later to become President – who was gifted an apartment within the castle. In the grounds, Adam's farm buildings of 1777 have been converted to accommodate the Visitor Centre which, along with the castle and **Tourist Information** centre (Tel. 06556 293), is open from April to October. The park is open all year.

Five miles south of Turnberry is **GIRVAN**, whose sandy beach helps make it the leading coastal resort in south-west Scotland. The town grew up around its picturesque harbour which today is a busy dock for the fishing boats. It is situated below **Knockcushan Hill**, marked at the summit by a stone indicating the site where Robert the Bruce held his court. There are boat trips to the granite rock 10 miles off the coast, **Ailsa Craig**, two miles round and 1,114 feet high. Now a bird sanctuary, the rock was used as a refuge by Catholics during the Reformation and was famed as the source of the best curling stones in Scotland. Event-wise, Girvan has a **folk festival** at the beginning of May, a **Civic Week** around 21–28 June and a **jazz festival** at the end of September.

There is a moderate selection of accommodation in Girvan, with the **Kings Arms Hotel**, Dalrymple Street (Tel. 0465 3322), at the top of the range, from between £23 and £35. From £15 there are **Auchendolly Hotel**, 30 Louisa Drive (Tel. 0465 4289), and **Royal Hotel**, 36 Montgomerie Street (Tel. 0465 4203). The **Glendrissaig Guest House**, Newton Stewart Road (Tel. 0465 4631), offers commended bed and breakfast accommodation from £15 upwards, and caters very well for vegetarians.

Tourist Information is at Bridge Street, Girvan (Tel. 0465 4950), from April to October.

The road south passes the ruins of **Carleton Castle** half-way to **BALLANTRAE**, and although R. L. Stevenson made a record of his visit here, it is not the setting for 'The Master of Ballantrae' (that distinction belongs to the town of Borgue, south-west of here near Kirkcudbright). The ruined **Ardstinchar Castle** which stands above the village was host to Mary Queen of Scots in 1566.

The South-west

INTRODUCTION

The most interesting scenery in the south-west of Scotland is along the Solway coast where rolling pasture and woodland is dotted with pleasant towns, whose character has remained essentially unchanged for 200 years and more. The shoreline contains many quiet and unspoilt corners and the sandy beaches are excellent for bathing. Apart from the magnificent Galloway Forest Park, covering 200 square miles and encompassing peaks in excess of 2,000 feet, the inland region consists of undulating moorland and heath.

The creation of the region of Dumfries and Galloway came out of the local government reorganization in 1974, and revived the ancient name of Galloway which up until the late 12th century had been known as the 'extensive area spreading south of Ayr and west of Nithsdale'. The name comes from 'Gallwyddel' meaning 'stranger Gaels'. The people of this region were so called because of their behaviour which set them apart from the rest of Scotland: they mixed with the Norsemen who settled towards the end of the ninth century, for example, and failed to declare allegiance to any Scots crown until the time of Malcolm Canmore in the middle of the 11th century. Even then, Galloway preserved a sense of independence, overseen by its lords until the death of the last in 1234, and subsequently governed by powerful local families such as the Balliols and the Comyns.

Galloway is also the seat of Scottish Christianity. St Ninian built the country's first church in Whithorn at the end of the fourth century, and there are many ancient Christian memorial stones revealing how the religion spread through the land.

The region is well served by good road links, only a couple of hours' drive from Edinburgh and Glasgow or three hours on the M6 from Manchester. InterCity trains from London Euston call at Carlisle which connects to Dumfries. From Glasgow, there is a local service to Stranraer. A ferry service operates from Larne in

Northern Ireland to Stranraer and nearby Cairnryan and there is the new Seacat service which takes 90 minutes from Belfast to Stranraer. Further up the coast, Prestwick Airport, near Ayr, receives flights from across the Atlantic though how long this will continue, with Glasgow's rise as Scotland's gateway airport, is debatable.

WHERE TO GO FOR WHAT

Going through the region in a westward direction, this chapter begins right on the border with England in the town of Gretna, not far north of which is **GRETNA GREEN**, long famous as the site of wedding ceremonies for eloping English couples. The attraction for southerners was that the marriage law in Scotland was more lax than that in England. In the latter, a statute of 1573 required that advance public notice be given of the intention to marry, and that a wedding be accompanied by a licence and church ceremony. The public announcement, known as the banns, was usually made on three successive Sundays in the parishes of both partners, so that marriage was not only a time-consuming affair, but one which it was impossible to keep secret – should that be the wish for whatever reason. In Scotland, on the other hand, the only legal requirement until 1856 was that betrothal be validated by two witnesses, and so couples hastening across the border could be united in holy matrimony by the blacksmith, tollgate keeper, or anyone else amenable and on the spot. One of the only surviving original venues was the **Old Blacksmith's Shop** which now houses a museum and preserves the anvil marriage room and coach house. After 1856 the law was tightened up and a residential qualification for one of the partners put an end to immediate marriage by declaration before legislation in 1940 outlawed this type of wedding altogether. Although greatly diminished, the expedience of a Scottish marriage still attracts some couples over the border where they can marry at 16 without parental consent – two years earlier than in England. However, most of the three thousand or so weddings that take place each year are ordinary couples attracted by Gretna Green's romance. There is a new Registrar's Office in

Gretna, where couples can have an ordinary civil wedding followed by a mock 'anvil wedding' in one of the blacksmiths shops, the form of ceremony when traditonally the village blacksmith officiated at the proceedings. There is a Tourist Information centre in the old Blacksmith's shop (Tel. 0461 37834).

East of Gretna, the A7 runs north passing **Scots Dyke**, the remains of a wall made of earth and stones which used to mark part of the border between Scotland and England and located a short distance from the road, about seven miles south of **LANGHOLM**. This is the birthplace of one of Scotland's most eminent citizens of this century, the redoutable poet Hugh McDiarmid. At White Hill Yett, two miles east on the road to Newcastleton, McDiarmid is commemorated by a steel and bronze sculpture depicting some of the words written by him. Eskdalemuir, high in the hills behind Langholm, is the unusual setting for the largest Buddhist Temple in Western Europe, **Samye Ling**.

A more leisurely alternative to the A75 from Gretna to Dumfries is the B725, part of the **Solway Coast Heritage Trail** from Stranraer to Annan, which follows the coast and passes sights of some interest. **RUTHWELL**, for example, is the location of the **Savings Bank Museum**, which functioned as the very first British Savings Bank, founded by Duncan in 1810, while the local church houses **Ruthwell Cross**, dating from the seventh century. **Caerlaverock Castle** is an impressive structure with an unusual triangular plan and a striking contrast between its stout late 13th- to 15th-century defensive exterior and its ornate Renaissance interior, remodelled in 1634. (Open from April to 30 September, Monday to Saturday, 9.30 a.m. to 6.30 p.m. and Sunday 2 p.m. to 6.30 p.m., and 1 October to 31 March, Monday to Saturday 9.30 a.m. to 4.30 p.m., and Sunday, 2 p.m. to 4.30 p.m.)

The beautiful **Caerlaverock Wildfowl and Wetlands Trust**, covering 13,594 acres and extending for six miles along the Solway Firth and Nith estuary, is noted for its winter wildfowl, particularly barnacle geese. It is also a great place to walk in summer.

DUMFRIES shares with most other towns lying close to the border an eventful and often violent past. It suffered frequent depredation by the English, but the most significant event in its history was the murder of Comyn in 1306 by Robert the Bruce and Roger Kirkpatrick. Comyn was a supporter of John Balliol whom Edward I in England, having been asked to arbitrate on the matter, had declared to have the strongest claim to the Scottish crown. Edward's choice was, of course, not impartial and was intended to install a tractable ruler who would co-operate in turning Scotland into a satellite state. Bruce was the rival claimant to the throne and his killing of an influential English sympathizer set the tone of what was to come. A plaque in Church Crescent marks the site of the friary where the deed took place. In the same street, the site of the castle is now occupied by Greyfriars Church, in front of which is a statue of Robert Burns with whom the town has a strong association. He arrived in 1791 to take up a post as an excise officer and spent the last six years of his life here, writing over 100 poems in that time. He had come previously in 1788, and lived at **Ellisland Farm**, which can still be visited just six miles to the north, where he wrote 'Auld Lang Syne' and 'Tam o' Shanter'. The **Robert Burns Centre** in Mill Road on the River Nith has an exhibition on Burn's life in Dumfries and an audio-visual presentation in an auditorium which doubles as a public film theatre in the evenings. He was a regular customer at the **Globe Inn**, off the High Street, where his chair and inscribed window pane can be seen, among other relics. **Burns House**, in what has been renamed Burns Street since the poet's death here in 1796, has been completely refurbished and displays many mementoes. 'Rabbie' was buried in nearby St Michael's Churchyard and his remains were transferred to the present elaborate mausoleum in 1815. **The Burns Heritage Trail** leads from Dumfries into Ayrshire by following the A76 northwards. Other attractions in the town include **Dumfries Museum and Camera Obscura**, the 15th-century **Lincluden Collegiate Church**, and **Devorguilla's Bridge** on which stands the **Old Bridge House** of 1660 with its period furnishings, now a museum. There is also the Dumfries and Galloway **Aviation Museum** where you can sit in a jet fighter.

Accommodation in the town centre is available from £36 at the excellent **Station Hotel**, 49 Lovers Walk (Tel. 0387 54316), and from around £25 at the three-star **Cairndale Hotel** at English

Street (Tel. 0387 54111). It now includes the **Barracuda Club**, a super new leisure centre with pool, sauna, spa bath, gymnasium and beauty salon. Just outside the town, **Hetland Hall Hotel**, Carrutherstown, Dumfries (Tel. 0387 84201), is a country house hotel halfway between Dumfries and Annan. It has 29 rooms and has recently been refurbished. From under £25 there are the **Fulwood Private Hotel**, Lovers Walk (Tel. 0387 52262) and **Edenbank Hotel**, Laurieknowe (Tel. 0387 52759). The **Tourist Information** office at Whitesands (Tel. 0387 53862) is open all year, offering a wonderful selection of bed and breakfast accommodation including: **Mrs G. M. Henderson** 67 Rotchell Road (Tel. 0387 53932), and **Mrs A. Prentice**, 3 North Laurieknowe Place (Tel. 0387 54136), both of whom offer commended rooms from around £13. The Station and Cairndale hotels both offer attractive restaurants with fine cuisine, and entertainments are often laid on in season.

South from Dumfries the A710 reaches the village of **NEW ABBEY**, notable for **Shambellie House Museum of Costume** displaying a changing collection of European fashionable dress from the collection of Charles Stewart. Also here is an operational 18th-century **corn mill**, and the ruins of **Sweetheart Abbey** which was founded in 1273 by Devorguilla Balliol in memory of her husband John. Near **KIRKBEAN** are the woodlands and gardens of **Arbigland** while further round the coast at Rockcliffe is the delightful de luxe **Baron's Craig Country House Hotel**, a stout Victorian building standing high above the Solway coast, charging around £150 a night for bed, breakfast and dinner with wine for two (Tel. 055663 225). The nearby **Motte of Mark** is an ancient hill fort overlooking the bird sanctuary on Rough Island in the Urr estuary, and just off the B794 is the form of the **Motte of Urr** which dates from the 12th century.

From Dalbeattie, the coastal route continues by means of the A711, soon approaching the rare and attractive circular tower house from the 15th century, **Orchardton Tower**. The B736 north of here leads to the town of **CASTLE DOUGLAS** one of whose principal attractions is the ruined 14th-century **Threave Castle**, a tower stronghold standing on an island in the River Dee three miles west of town. One mile south of Castle Douglas are the 60 acres of **Threave Gardens** – containing upward of 200 varieties of daffodil – which is beautiful all year round, while nearby **Threave Wildfowl Refuge** attracts many species of wild geese and ducks.

Ten miles south–west of Castle Douglas is the town of **KIRKCUDBRIGHT** (pronounced kir-koobray) which, with its open waterfront, quay and broad 18th-century streets, enjoys the reputation of being one of the most attractive of the Solway towns and has for long been a place popular with artists. The **Harbour Cottage Gallery** beside the river (open March to December) exhibits paintings and occasional craft works, while **Broughton House** in the High Street exhibits work by the landscape painter E. A. Hornel principally known for his portraits of children, in the home he bequeathed along with its contents to the town on his death in 1933. In addition to Hornel's paintings visitors can also see the work of other artists, fine furniture, and a Japanese garden. (Open from Easter to October, Wednesday to Monday 11 a.m. to 1 p.m. and 2 p.m. to 5 p.m., closed Tuesday.) **Kirkcudbright Painting Holidays** can give you the chance to develop your artistic talent in small informal groups with expert tuition. For more information Tel. 0557 30274. Just off the High Street overlooking the harbour is **MacLellan's Castle**, a fine castellated mansion when it was built in 1577, but a ruin since 1752. The Market Cross of 1610 stands beside the 16th- to 17th-century Tolbooth which once held Paul Jones prisoner. Among the local material in the **Stewartry Museum** in St Mary Street (open Easter to October) is information on the colourful life and career of this mariner, born in Kirkbean in 1747, who was variously a Father of the American navy, an admiral in the Russian navy of Catherine the Great, and a marauder of English ships in European waters. Seven miles south-east on the A711 are the ruins of **Dundrennan Abbey**, dating from 1142, where Mary Queen of Scots spent her last night in Scotland on 15 May 1568. Left to dilapidate after coming into the possession of the Earl of Annandale in 1606, the abbey was subsequently used as a quarry and the village of Dundrennan is partly built of its stones.

Kirkcudbright's good selection of accommodation includes the highly commended **Selkirk Arms Hotel** (Tel. 0557 30402), from between £34 and £40, and the **Gordon House Hotel** (Tel. 0557 30670) and **Commercial Hotel** (Tel. 0557 30407), both of which have prices from under £20. Bed and breakfast accommodation is available from £14 at the highly commended **Anchorlee Guest House**, 95 St Mary's Street (Tel. 0557 30793). Slightly cheaper accommodation from £12 is available from **Mrs Elizabeth Duncan**, 25a Carlyle Road (Tel. 0592 200733). The **Tourist Information** centre in Harbour Square (Tel. 0557 30494) is open from Easter to October.

Signposted from the A75, **Cally Palace** near the town of **GATEHOUSE OF FLEET** is an elegant country house hotel in fabulous private grounds where bed, breakfast and dinner with wine for two costs £100–150. (Open from March to January, Tel. 0557 814341). It also has extensive leisure facilities, including an indoor swimming pool. At Gatehouse of Fleet you will find an important new Visitor Centre, the **Mill on the Fleet**. This centre, housed in a mill building, uses audio-visual displays and exhibitions to interpret the industrial, cultural and environmental heritage of Gatehouse and the surrounding areas. Beyond the town, the A75 passes the ruined **Cardoness Castle**, a four-storey tower house from the 15th century. Running beside the shore, the road comes to Ravenshall Point where there are several caves, the largest of which is **Hatteraick's Cave**, and a few miles further on is another ruined tower house, the 16th-century **Carsluith Castle**. The granite with which Liverpool docks were built came from **CREETOWN** where the **Gem Rock Museum** and **Crystal Cave** has a large display of gems, rocks, and minerals from all around the world. Two miles further on near **PALMURE** is **Kirroughtree Forest Garden** and visitor centre which is home to over 60 species of trees, and various colour-coded cycling routes.

NEWTON STEWART has a **Tourist Information** centre in Dashwood Square, open from Easter to October (Tel. 0671 2431). **The Newton Stewart Museum**, formerly St John's Church, York Street, has interesting displays depicting the local and regional life of the area. The town's greatest asset is its proximity to **Galloway Forest Park** which embraces 150,000 acres of varied and spectacular scenery and has mountains in excess of 2,000 feet, including the south of Scotland's highest peak, Merrick, at 2,764 feet. The wildlife at home here includes deer, feral goats, and golden eagles. The best of the park is only accessible to walkers and cyclists following the Forestry Commission's extensive trails, but there are two areas open to the motorist from Newton Stewart. The A714 runs through some magnificent countryside, leading to the heart of the forest and Loch Trool, on the north side of which **Bruce's Stone** commemorates the victory won by Robert the Bruce over the English here in 1306. The A712, the Queen's Way, runs north-east from Newton Stewart to beyond Clatteringshaws Loch, site of the **Clatteringshaws Forest Wildlife Centre**, a centre which has information on deer, feral goats, trout, botany and mineralogy. There are various cycling routes open to the public leading into the heart of the forest park. Near here another **Bruce's Stone** marks the site where Robert the Bruce triumphed over the English in the Battle of Rapploch Moss in March 1307.

Seventeen miles south of Newton Stewart, the town of **WHITHORN** is where Christianity was first introduced to Scotland by St Ninian, a local man who had studied in Rome. The town's name derives from the Anglo-Saxon 'huit aern' meaning white house and coined in reference to the small stone church covered in white plaster which St Ninian is said to have built here. The existence of just such a structure was confirmed by excavations in 1895 and 1948–63, the findings of which can be seen at the **Whithorn Dig and visitor centre** in George Street, while in Main Street there is the 12th-century **Whithorn Priory and Museum**. You will find more details at the visitor centre in Main Street.

Fifteen miles from Newton Stewart, the road to Stranraer runs through **GLENLUCE**, notable for the substantial ruins of **Glenluce Abbey**, founded in 1190. Six miles further on, **Castle Kennedy Gardens** actually belong to Lochinch Castle (closed to the public) and attract visitors to see their displays of rhododendrons, azaleas, magnolias, embothriums and the avenue lined with Chilean pine (monkey puzzle) trees. (Open daily Easter to September, 10 a.m. to 5 p.m.) Beyond the town of Stranraer is the double peninsula known as the Rhinns of Galloway, and keen hillwalkers will be interested to know that **PORTPATRICK** on the west coast is the starting point for the **Southern Upland Way** which runs diagonally 212 miles across the entire breadth of the country. It is also excellent countryside for cycling. The Tourist Office has details of a great number of outlets offering cycle hire, tours and holidays. Portpatrick is home to the **'Little Wheels' Toy Transport Display and Model Railway** featuring toys, dolls, miniature transport and model railways. **Knockinaam Lodge** was recently named 'Country House of the Year', having won a Michelin Star before that. Situated in a tranquil setting with fine views of the sea, it also boasts first class French cuisine. Rooms start from £67 per person.

Whilst in this area, a drive 14 miles south of Stranraer will bring you to **Logan Botanic Garden**. Open from March to October, this outpost of Edinburgh's Royal Botanic Garden has a collection of plants from sub-tropical regions which flourish here in some of Scotland's mildest weather conditions.

Index